In 1957, Kerala became the first region in Asia to elect a communist government through parliamentary procedure. Dilip Menon's book traces the social history of communism in Malabar, the bastion of the movement, and looks at how the ideology was transformed into a doctrine of caste equality, as national strategies were reshaped by local circumstance and tinged by pragmatism. Earlier, lower caste reform movements had projected the idea of a community of lower castes standing apart from society. Nationalists, led by members of upper caste, landowning households, attempted only to construct a limited 'Hindu' community based on the equality of all castes. Communism was characterised by a radical pragmatism which successfully challenged subordination and notions of deference, while not significantly altering the structures of power.

This is the first study to consider the social history of communism anywhere in India. While existing literature concentrates on the intricacies of party policy, Dilip Menon explores the diversity of political practice within a particular region. He particularly analyses the relationship between landowners and cultivators, demonstrating their economic and cultural interdependence. Inequality and difference were tempered by a perception of shared symbols and values. As the author points out, the success of communism in Kerala lies in its recognition of this fact.

T0371456

Cambridge South Asian Studies

Caste, nationalism and communism in south India

Cambridge South Asian Studies

Editorial Board

C.A. Bayly, G.P. Hawthorn, Gordon Johnson, S.J. Tambiah

A list of the books in the series will be found at the end of the volume

Caste, nationalism and communism in south India

Malabar, 1900–1948

Dilip M. Menon

University of Cambridge

CAMBRIDGE
UNIVERSITY PRESS

CAMBRIDGE
UNIVERSITY PRESS

University Printing House, Cambridge CB2 8BS, United Kingdom

One Liberty Plaza, 20th Floor, New York, NY 10006, USA

477 Williamstown Road, Port Melbourne, VIC 3207, Australia

4843/24, 2nd Floor, Ansari Road, Daryaganj, Delhi - 110002, India

79 Anson Road, #06-04/06, Singapore 079906

Cambridge University Press is part of the University of Cambridge.

It furthers the University's mission by disseminating knowledge in the pursuit of education, learning and research at the highest international levels of excellence.

www.cambridge.org
Information on this title: www.cambridge.org/9780521051958

© Cambridge University Press 1994

This publication is in copyright. Subject to statutory exception and to the provisions of relevant collective licensing agreements, no reproduction of any part may take place without the written permission of Cambridge University Press.

First published 1994
First paperback edition 2017

A catalogue record for this publication is available from the British Library

Library of Congress Cataloging in Publication data
Menon, Dilip M.
Caste, nationalism and communism in south India: Malabar, 1900–1948/Dilip M. Menon
   p. cm. - (Cambridge South Asian Studies: 55)
ISBN 0 521 41879 8
1. Kerala (India) – Politics and government. 2. Caste – India – Kerala.
3. Nationalism – India - Kerala. 4. Communism – India – Kerala.
5. Malabar Coast (India) – Politics and government.
I. Title. II. Series.
DS485, K48M46 1994
954 83 – dc20   93–6609 CIP

ISBN 978-0-521-41879-9 Hardback
ISBN 978-0-521-05195-8 Paperback

Cambridge University Press has no responsibility for the persistence or accuracy of URLs for external or third-party internet websites referred to in this publication, and does not guarantee that any content on such websites is, or will remain, accurate or appropriate.

Contents

Preface

This book began as a slim idea about 'popular culture' in Malabar, grew into a corpulent ambition to encompass the social and intellectual origins of communism in Kerala, and has now hopefully acquired the svelte shape of an enquiry into the historical origins of communism in Malabar with comparative excursions into other regions of India. Communism in Kerala was far more than just a political movement organising the proletariat and peasantry into militant entities pressing for exigent economic concessions. Euphoric visions of a new order and a rampant rejection of past hierarchies found expression in popular songs, literature and films. Malayalam literature, which had been peopled by gods, kings and the genteel, suddenly broke out in a rash of characters who were poor, indigent or criminal. Their heroism lay in the fact that they were rebels who were cynical of a society where caste, birth and privilege determined the status of a person. Between 1900 and 1950 a new aesthetic emerged, the story of which will have to be deferred for another book.

There is a reason. Very little work has been done on the contemporary history of what became the state of Kerala in 1956, cobbled together as it was from the princely states of Travancore and Cochin as well as the erstwhile district of the Madras Presidency, Malabar. The few studies that exist have been content to marvel at Malabar's unique features – matriliny, Marxism and the militant Mappila Muslims – and to try and establish a causal connection between these. Apart from the fascination of alliteration, the reluctance to accommodate variation from theoretical models constructed for the rest of the Presidency has been the major stumbling block. There is another consideration. The records of the Malabar Collectorate, held at the Kozhikode Regional Archives, were precisely catalogued only as late as 1986. This archival material allows the historian to begin to construct a social and economic profile of Malabar in the nineteenth and twentieth century – an image that thus far could be seen only as through a glass darkly. And it is as an initial enterprise that this work is intended. Malabar had its peculiarities and the trajectory of its politics may have been different at times; but on the whole the similarities that surface when compared with the historiography of other regions do not warrant its treatment as an anomaly.

The INLAKS Foundation granted me the initial scholarship to come to England, and were liberally accommodating of my idiosyncrasies; no one could wish for a more generous patron. I would like to thank Trinity College for awarding me an External Research Studentship in 1986 which enabled me to start work on my dissertation. The Edward Boyle Memorial Fund provided additional funds for research and other expenses. Both the Smuts Memorial Fund and the Prince Consort and Thirlwall Fund have helped with finances towards conducting archival research and fieldwork in India. Finally, I am indebted to the Master and Fellows of Magdalene College for electing me to a Research Fellowship in 1989, and providing me with the means and convivial surroundings to complete my book.

I am also grateful to the staff of the various archives and libraries where most of the research for this dissertation was done: the University Library and the Centre of South Asian Studies, Cambridge; the India Office Library and Records, London; the National Archives of India and the Nehru Memorial Museum and Library, New Delhi; the University Library, the Kerala Secretariat Archives and the CPI State Council Library, Trivandrum; the Appan Thampuran Library, Trichur; the Kozhikode Regional Archives, Calicut; the Tellicherry Courts Record Room, Tellicherry; the Tamil Nadu Archives and the Theosophical Society Library, Madras. In particular, I would like to thank: Dr Lionel Carter, a mine of information about library resources; K. Ravindran, Archivist, Kozhikode Regional Archives and his helpers, Verghese and Majeed who furnished friendly assistance while heroically cataloguing the mass of files and papers of the Malabar Collectorate; and Raghavan Nair at the Trivandrum Secretariat Cellar who was unstinting in his assistance.

Among the individuals who read through earlier drafts and offered criticism, both temperate as well as trenchant, I am grateful to: Chris Bayly, Raj Chandavarkar, Javed Majeed, Polly O'Hanlon, Sumit Sarkar and Tanika Sarkar. Dr Anil Seal's enthusiasm and support for the work in its early stages was a great source of encouragement. Above all, I would like to thank Anu, with whom this work has been debated every step of the way; if the book has any clarity, it is due to her.

Keraleeyan, K. Madhavan, T.C. Narayanan Nambiar, P.T. Bhaskara Panikkar and Sarmaji gave unselfishly of their time and knowledge, and provided me with much of the background of the communist movement in Kerala. Professor K.K.N. Kurup, Professor M.G.S. Narayanan and Dr Raghava Variar of the University of Calicut were a source of constant intellectual stimulation and encouragement. Murkkoth Kunhappa generously provided me with the unfinished manuscript of his father's autobiography.

The work has been discussed with many friends over a period of time: in particular, Hari and Tapati, Neel and Chitra, Uday, Nandini, and Riccardo. Finally, I would like to mention those who contributed in intangible but important ways: my parents, who brought Kerala alive for me in a way I cannot hope to match; N. Gopinathan Nair, who acted as the inspiration behind this dissertation; and Amin Saheb, in whose classes I learnt the pleasures of history.

Abbreviations

AICC	All India Congress Committee
ARDMP	Administration of the Registration Department of the Madras Presidency
ARMP	*Report on the Administration of the Madras Presidency*
CWMG	*Collected Works of Mahatma Gandhi*
FR	*Fortnightly Reports*
IOL	India Office Library and Records
KCP	Kerala Communist Party
KCSP	Kerala Congress Socialist Party
KPCC	Kerala Pradesh Congress Committee
KRA	Kozhikode Regional Archives
KS	Kerala Secretariat
MCTI	Malabar Compensation for Tenants' Improvements Act
MLTR	*Malabar Land Tenures Report*
MPBEC	*Madras Provincial Banking Enquiry Commission*
MPIR	*Report on Public Instruction in the Madras Presidency*
MSLRR	*Report on the Settlement of Land Revenue in the Madras Presidency*
MSP	Malabar Special Police
MTA	Malabar Tenancy Act
MTCR, 1927	*Malabar Tenancy Committee Report, 1927*
MTCR, 1940	*Malabar Tenancy Committee Report, 1940*
NAI	National Archives of India
NMML	Nehru Memorial Museum and Library
P and J	Public and Judicial
RAPMP	*Report on the Administration of Police in the Madras Presidency*
RARMP	*Report on Administration of the Abkari Revenue of the Madras Presidency*
RCLI	*Royal Commission on Labour in India*

RDAMP	*Report of the Operations of the Department of Agriculture of the Madras Presidency*
RDIMP	*Report of the Department for Industries of the Madras Presidency*
RSTMP	*Review of seaborne trade of the Madras Presidency*
SCRMP	*Season and Crop Report of the Madras Presidency*
SNDP	Sri Narayana Dharma Paripalana Yogam
TCRR	Tellicherry Court Record Room
TNA	Tamil Nadu Archives

Glossary

adhikari	village headman
amsam	revenue division, an aggregate of *desams*
cherikallu	branches of prominent households in outlying areas which negotiated terms of cultivation with tribal groups
desam	the smallest revenue paying division
janmi	landowner
jatha	political procession
kanakkaran	cultivating leaseholder or mortgagee
karanavan	an elder, head of the household
karshaka sangham	peasant union
kavu	shrine
kshetram	temple
kuzhikanakkaran	tenants on improvement leases
marumakkathayam	matriliny
melkoyma	right of suzerainty of kings/chieftains over religious institutions
modan	hill paddy
mundu	waistcloth
muthalali	term of deference, used while addressing landlords
paramba	garden lands
punam	shifting cultivation
tavazhi	branch of household
teyyattam	ritual dance at shrines
tharavadu	matrilineal household
uralan	manager of shrines/temples
verumpattakaran	cultivator, usually on wetlands

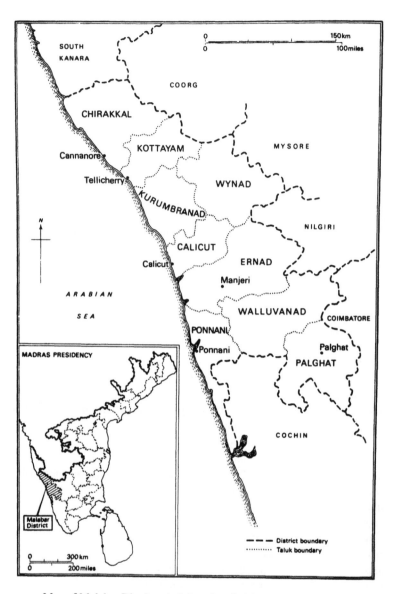

Map of Malabar District administrative divisions

Introduction

Ideologies, like poetry, lose a lot in translation: nuances evanesce, meanings merge and unintended ironies surface. Communism has inspired revolution, authoritarian rule and gerontocracy in different parts of the world, and as yet genuine socialism seems to have remained beyond reach. In Kerala, irony is the dominant motif of the metamorphosis of communist ideology. A movement perceived as a revolutionary threat both by the colonial government and the nascent Indian state came to power in 1957 through parliamentary means. Kerala became the first state in the world, apart from the minuscule Italian principality of San Marino, to form a democratically elected communist government. An egalitarian crusade against caste inequality was nevertheless led by caste elites. The adherents of a supposedly atheistic, or at best agnostic, creed were responsible for shoring up religion in the countryside. And last, but not least, when in 1970 Kerala became the first state in India to abolish landlordism, those who benefited were neither unambiguously tillers or even primarily engaged in agriculture. Despite this plethora of intriguing paradoxes, the history of the origins of communism in Kerala has not yet been written.[1] This may be said to be true of the history of communism in India as well. Most writings have tended to concentrate less on regional specificities and more on the unravelling of the theoretical tangles of the Party line and its ostensible transcriptions in local contexts.[2]

[1] There is a substantial literature on the Communist ministries and their achievements, of which T.J. Nossiter, *Communism in Kerala: a study in political adaptation* (London, 1982) is the most incisive. See also V.M. Fic, *Kerala: the Yenan of India* (Bombay, 1970); R.J. Herring, *Land to the tiller: the political economy of agrarian reform in south Asia* (New Haven, CN, 1983); G.K. Lieten, *The first communist ministry in Kerala, 1957–59* (Calcutta, 1982). The official party history of the movement is E.M.S. Nambudiripad, *Kammyunistu party keralathil (The Communist Party in Kerala)*, 3 volumes (Trivandrum, 1984–88). For a general account see R. Jeffrey, *Politics, women and well being: how Kerala became a 'model'* (Basingstoke, 1992).

[2] J. H. Kautsky, *Moscow and the CPI: a study in the post war evolution of international communist strategy* (New York, 1956); G.D. Overstreet and M. Windmiller, *Communism in India* (Berkeley, CA, 1959); B. Sengupta, *Communism in Indian politics* (New York, 1972); B. Josh, *The communist movement in Punjab, 1926–47* (Delhi, 1979) and *Struggle for hegemony in India, 1920–1947: the colonial state, the Left and the national movement*, vol. 2 (New Delhi, 1993). A good preliminary reader is P. Brass and M.F. Franda eds., *Radical politics in south Asia* (Cambridge, MA, 1973); S. Joshi, *Struggle for hegemony in India, 1920–1947: the colonial state, the Left and the national movement*, vol. 1 (New Delhi, 1992).

1

This book focuses on the erstwhile region of Malabar, the northern part of Kerala, which was the bastion of the communist movement and which continues to succour the party in its election forays. The major reason why the communists came to power in Malabar, while in the rest of India the Congress was basking in the afterglow of Independence, was the reshaping of communism into a doctrine of caste equality. This is part of a wider and as yet neglected question. While most historians writing on twentieth-century India have concentrated on the story of nationalism, South India seems to pose other issues. It witnessed few fervid demonstrations of nationalist activity. Rather, in the Madras Presidency, caste and its resolution seem to have informed political activity far more than nationalism. It has been argued that it was not until the last days of the British Raj that 'Dravidian ideology confront[ed] the question of colonialism as a central problematic of politics or perceive[d] British rule as the cause of social oppression'.[3]

In Malabar, as in the rest of the Presidency, political activity at different points addressed itself almost wholly to the issue of caste differences. This was not surprising, because there were refinements within its caste 'system', not found elsewhere in India. An extreme form of hierarchy meant that not only were there untouchable castes, there were 'unseeable' ones as well. What was different, and significant, in political activity in Malabar was the fact that the notion of community surfaced constantly and became a major source of contention within political discourse. This was not surprising in a region where inequality was evident; an imagining of community could mediate between differences. In a sense, we argue a paradoxical case. While the presence of inequality and differences acted as the spur to a desire for community, these very factors hindered its eventual realisation. The intimations of equality offered by caste movements, nationalism and communism were thwarted by the fractures within society – of caste, kinship, religion and locality. Nationalism tried to project a community of Indians, but its expansive sweep, eager to paper over cracks in society, found little purchase in Malabar. For a brief moment in 1921, Congress, Khilafat and local concerns of agrarian inequities came together. The Congress became wary of involving Malabar in the national struggle after the Mappila rebellion of 1921 had broken the fragile unity of the alliance of the Congress with the Khilafat movement. This fact has dominated most of the works published on Malabar, which have concentrated

---

[3] See D.A. Washbrook, 'Caste, class and dominance in modern Tamil Nadu: non Brahmanism, Dravidianism and Tamil nationalism' in F. Frankel and M.S.A. Rao eds., *Dominance and state power in modern India: decline of a social order* (Delhi, 1989), I, 211; also M.R. Barnett, *The politics of cultural nationalism in south India* (Princeton, NJ, 1976); E.F. Irschick, *Politics and social conflict in India: the non-Brahman movement and Tamil separatism, 1916-29* (Berkeley, CA, 1969).

mainly on the relations between Hindus and Mappilas in south Malabar, and
the origins of the Mappila rebellion of 1921.[4]

In the delineation of categories which aggregate the activities of individuals
in society, the notion of community has gained credence, of late, in the
historiography of modern south Asia. Community has been defined in diverse
and often contradictory ways. Some historians perceive it as a notion essential
to the reproduction of the existing social order. Others see the creation of a
sense of community as underlying the expression of opposition to entrenched
structures of power. Common to both positions is the assumption that there is
a coherence within these communities – of interests, actions and values – which
binds together the actions of individuals and engenders fixed identities. The
writings of the 'subaltern' group of historians suggests an *a priori* sense of
community among subordinate groups, which is born out of the experience of
oppression. It is a collectivity defined negatively, and in terms of resistance to
the existing, unequal social order.[5] While there is an element of staticity and
essentialism in the 'subaltern' approach, Sandria Freitag's recent work on
northern India tries to historicise notions of community. Communities are
studied in the process of formation. Nevertheless, in her work too, there is an
assumption that individual identities can be subsumed in collective action,
which then creates a 'coherent, consistent [realm] of symbolic behaviour'.[6]
There seems to be a misplaced concreteness in the idea that collectivities are
'created' in any real sense or for all time. While caste, occupation and language,
may act as 'fundamental community identities' which glue individuals together, these very factors could well create fissures and segmentation within
putative unities.[7]

Recent south Indian historiography has taken up the idea of religious
community, not in the context of the creation of oppositional entities, but in the
reproduction of social order. Common worship and festivals at temples are
seen as performing an integrative role by mediating between castes and

[4] S.F. Dale, *Islamic society on the south Asian frontier: the Mappilas of Malabar, 1498-1922* (Oxford, 1980); K.N. Panikkar, *Against lord and state: religion and peasant uprisings in Malabar, 1836-1921* (Delhi, 1989); C. Wood, *The Moplah rebellion and its genesis* (Delhi, 1987).
[5] This sense of an oppositional 'subaltern' community runs through the diverse pieces assembled in the six volumes of *Subaltern studies* published so far. For explicit theoretical statements, see R. Guha, *Elementary aspects of peasant insurgency in colonial India (Delhi, 1983);* A. Sen, 'Subaltern studies: capital, class and community' in R. Guha ed., *Subaltern studies: writings on south Asian history and society* (Delhi, 1987), V, 203-55; P. Chatterjee, 'Caste and subaltern consciousness' in Guha ed., *Subaltern studies*, VI (Delhi, 1989), 169-209.
[6] S.B. Freitag, *Collective action and community: public arenas and the emergence of commu-nalism in north India* (Berkeley, CA, 1989), 6. There is an implicit teleology in the 'emergence' of hardened Hindu and Muslim identities, from activities fostering a perception of 'commu-nity' among hitherto inchoate groups.
[7] Freitag, *Collective action*, 42. See R.S. Chandavarkar, 'Worker's politics in Bombay between the wars', *Modern Asian Studies*, 15, 3 (1981), 603-47, for an argument about how caste and occupation serve to fragment the labour force in the mills of Bombay.

creating a space for the redistribution of ritual resources.[8] Such an analysis is more holistic in that it tries to explain not only the behaviour of certain social groups but the working of society itself. However, there is little sense of fractures, of the initiatives of individual actors and of the continuing disparities between the constituents of the community which entails, surely, that unity must be fragile and transitory. Moreover, there is a tendency to treat ritual spaces as the microcosm of the social world – a substitution of the part for the whole – even though the participants at these festivals are nearly always only Hindus.

It will be argued here that the idea of community represents an aspiration and not an achieved entity; it is always in the process of formation without reaching realisation. While projections of community seek to be all-inclusive, disparities within society entail considerable fluctuations in the constituency appealed to, and therefore a constant redefinition. Competing notions of community seek to include more groups within it, and underlying its protean character, is the endeavour of negating difference. Moreover, there can only be *conjunctural* creations of community when a temporary balance is achieved between diverse individual initiatives and subjective perceptions of disparities. We shall be looking at several negotiations of community, all of which tried to mediate between differences in rural society: of caste and of access to agricultural resources. At brief moments in time, local attempts to construct community became enmeshed in the wider conceptions of nationalism, and communism but, inevitably, wider imaginings of community gave way to local resolutions.

The first theme is a *community of subsistence* which was negotiated between dominant landowners and cultivators. In north Malabar, settlement tended to be centred on the matrilineal households of the Nayars (tharavadus) which controlled wastelands and forests, and had a near monopoly over wetlands. These tharavadus were granted rights over non-navigable rivers as well, making their control over agricultural resources more complete than elsewhere in the Presidency. This seemingly absolute power was mitigated by several factors which prevented an unconditional exercise of authority. In the years before the Depression, the availability of land and the high prices of cash crops like pepper and coconut provided opportunities to small cultivators producing for export. The profits from exports, the availability of credit from diverse sources and, ultimately, the fact that tharavadus needed to secure cultivators, gave the latter a degree of independence. Moreover, in a period of land availability, when titles to far-flung plots of land were still disputed, politic

---

[8] A. Appadurai and C.A. Breckenbridge, 'The south Indian temple: authority, honour and redistribution', *Contributions to Indian Sociology* (NS), 10, 2 (1976), 190; A. Appadurai, *Worship and conflict under colonial rule: a south Indian case* (Cambridge, 1981), 225-6; N.B. Dirks, *The hollow crown: the ethnohistory of an Indian kingdom* (Cambridge, 1987), 211-12.

tenants and cultivators could play off landowners against each other. The ability of the tharavadus, with their wetlands and granaries, to provide subsistence, in a region deficient in food, arbitrated between the independence of cultivators and the authority of a tharavadu. This *community of subsistence* was attenuated by the Depression, when there was a slump in the exports of cash crops and a crisis of food which disturbed the balance that had been maintained so far. The first chapter deals with the negotiation of this community of subsistence.

Tharavadus, cultivators, and dependent labourers were involved in a *community of worship* around shrines where all worshipped together regardless of caste. This is the major theme of the second chapter. The pantheon of gods was flexible and all inclusive: Nayar ancestors, tribal gods, local heroes and heroines and brahminical deities jostled one another. Worship involved the use of alcohol and the sacrifice of animals though, occasionally, rituals enjoined vegetarianism and 'purer' forms. There were three kinds of shrine festivals, each of which envisaged a different notion of community. The first kind involved different castes at separate stages in the rituals, emphasising the interdependence of tharavadu, shrine and worshippers and indirectly, the status of each caste. In a sense, the community of subsistence was reproduced, since devotees made offerings of grain to the shrine and received grain in return. Secondly, both upper and lower castes went on pilgrimages together to shrines, and the bacchanalian rituals emphasised the possibility of subsuming differences. While one form of community emphasised disparity and interdependence, the other envisaged the concerted behaviour of equals. The third kind of shrine festival emphasised both community as well as the relations of power within rural society. Most of the deities worshipped were lower castes who had suffered injustice at the hands of their superiors. Festivals were marked by the performance of a ritual dance called the *teyyattam* which retold the circumstances of the outrage to an audience of lower and upper castes. People were involved in several forms of worship, each emphasising community, but in different ways. Besides, the reiteration of rituals of community could not mask the divergences between the constituents and the next chapter takes up an attempt to resolve the difference.

While the two themes discussed above dealt with arbitrations between the differences and the disparity between the constituents of community, the third chapter deals with attempts to stand apart by creating a *community of caste equals*. At the beginning of this century, an elite had emerged among the lower caste of Tiyyas (a significant number among whom were *toddy tappers*), deriving their position from education, employment as lawyers and civil servants, involvement with trade and commerce, and the setting up of factories. In the towns, they had to compete with already established groups and, therefore, they turned to their putative caste brethren in the villages. By emphasising those aspects of rural shrine festivals which reiterated caste identities, this elite tried to draw Tiyyas to new temples in the towns which were to be for Tiyyas alone. This attempt to create a community of equals was premised not only on alternative forms of worship, but the ability to provide credit and employment as well. However, this notion of community was undermined in many ways. Many Tiyyas continued to stay within earlier circuits of shrine worship. Other lower castes and untouchables were not admitted to the new Tiyya temples, which afforded an opportunity to members of tharavadus to assert their links with their dependents and shore up the community around the shrines. More-over, the idea of a community of equals around temples was elevated to another level by the intervention of the Congress.

Nationalism had to conceive of a more universal unity, and here lay the problem. While at a broader level, anti-imperialism and the sense of belonging to a nation could be the basis of an aspiration to community, at the local level, the question of difference was predominant. In Malabar, the Tiyyas had thrown down the gauntlet by raising the question of the inequality between castes and the activities of the Congress in Malabar would confine itself largely to addressing this issue. The initial workings of nationalism, i.e. the civil disobedience movement, in north Malabar, involved mainly members of the Nayar tharavadus. Very often it assumed the nature of an assertion of their authority in the wake of the erosion of rural community occasioned by the setting up of Tiyya temples. Congress activity helped to build a sense of community among the Nayars, without drawing in wider sections of people and this informed the next stage of nationalist activity.

The Congress in Malabar attempted to solve caste inequality by treating it as a problem within religion. Earlier attempts to move away from the shared culture of the shrines were coupled with an effort to gain entry for lower castes into Hindu temples. The limited Tiyya ideal of a community of equals around temples was replaced by the idea of a wider *community of equal Hindus sans* caste difference. This vision of a Hindu community was momentary and the attempt to gain temple entry for lower castes was constrained by two factors. First, the Nayar leaders of the campaign, with their new found unity, transformed it into a personal campaign against the authority of brahmins, limiting its scope and appeal. Secondly, the political conjucture of the Poona Pact with the colonial government necessitated the semblance of the unity of all castes behind the Congress and the potentially divisive campaign for temple entry was abandoned. Many Tiyyas remained loyal to their temples, while the failure of temple entry meant a revival of the shrines in the countryside. The fourth chapter is concerned with this local resolution of the themes of nationalism.

The growth of socialist activity in Malabar reflected, at one level, the nationwide sense of discontent with the moderate programme of Gandhi. At another, and more important level, it was an attempt to resolve, locally, the issue of caste inequality and to renegotiate rural community in the aftermath of the Depression. In the thirties, many of the tharavadus were adversely affected by two pieces of legislation, one allowing the partition of their property and, the other, providing security of tenure for tenants on their lands. Simultaneously, small cultivators who had soared on the profits of cash crops were brought back to earth by the slump in prices and the virtual cessation of exports. Moreover, as more land had been converted to cultivating cash crops to service international demand, the tharavadus came to exercise a monopoly over foodgrains. The balance between independent cultivator and tharavadu which had existed prior to the Depression was upset. Many of the tharavadus attempted to exercise their authority, and at the same time fill their coffers by imposing feudal levies on lower-caste cultivators. A younger generation within the tharavadus, largely from the branches cut adrift by the partition of households, and drawn towards socialism, allied themselves with cultivators and labourers and questioned these excessive demands. The collective activity of peasant unions soon began challenging the imposition of deference on lower castes, and political initiatives were beyond the control of the leaders. In a sense, socialist activity had initiated the challenging of inequality in the countryside, and soon unions and the police were in conflict. The socialists conceived of a *community of peasants* as against *landlords* and this had been useful in the formation of unions. It soon became evident that such a community would prove transient, as caste, class and locality pulled activity in different directions. The fifth chapter considers the efforts of the socialists to renegotiate rural relations with the maintenance of an uneasy balance between peasant union radicalism and the need for community.

At a wider level, tharavadus still controlled wastelands, forests and wetlands, and cultivators would have to negotiate with them. The earlier sense of rural community had been eroded by caste activity, nationalism and the Depression. Now ostensibly, it could only be sustained by the threat of conflict, i.e. the ability of peasant unions to force the hand of tharavadus. Two conjunctures conditioned attempts to build community in the next decade. One was the willingness of the state to use violence to support tharavadus and maintain law and order. The other was the severe crisis of food precipitated by the Second World War which underscored the dependence of cultivators on the tharavadus. The final chapter deals with the decade of the forties which witnessed the limits of rural radicalism. Unions had managed to successfully contest the excesses of authority of the tharavadus, less by concerted activity than divergent initiatives which added an edge of violence to their actions. While caste movements and nationalism had worked within a religious idiom which aspired towards a wider community of equals, socialist activity had confined its horizons and sought to check the secular authority of tharavadus. Demographic pressures, the slump in cash crops, the crisis of food, and the need to bring wastelands under the cultivation of subsistence crops meant that the tharavadus would be calling the shots in this decade. For a brief period between 1942 and 1945 the communists (as in the rest of India, the socialists in Malabar had moved to the communist party in 1939), were able to mediate between cultivators in need of land and tharavadus in need of compliant cultivators. The crisis of food necessitated a conjunctural recreation of community in which tharavadus provided for cultivators, which had ramifications in the revival of the shrine culture as the centre of a community of subsistence as well as of worship. Moreover, by harnessing the land hunger of shifting cultivators, the communists were able to create 'red' villages formally under their control.

However, the pulls of the landless, and the alacrity with which the state acted to put down radical activity meant that community could no longer be negotiated as it had been all along. While the authority of the tharavadus could be contested at the local level, to undermine their power required an engagement with the state. Politics in north Malabar would have to look beyond attempts to create community at the level of the locality.

1   The agrarian economy and households, 1900–1930

In 1927, Malabar was being described by observers as a land of gardens cultivated by prosperous small cultivators. Within a decade, the effects of the Depression had levelled these entrepreneurs and enforced a shift towards subsistence crops. By 1945, Malabar was in the grip of severe food shortage and a storm was brewing over access to cultivable land. These remarkable shifts highlight two seemingly contradictory trends within the agrarian economy. The first was the growth of a class of small cultivators, premised on the availability of land and the high world prices of cash crops, like coconut and pepper. The second trend, heightened by the Depression, was the increasing dependence of these cultivators on the large landowning tharavadus of the region both for subsistence as well as access to land. North Malabar was a region deficient in foodgrains, a fact which had been accentuated by the conversion of wetlands to growing cash crops. The production of subsistence crops like paddy came to be concentrated in the hands of a few, large landowning tharavadus, whose granaries underpinned their authority. With the development of a crisis in food supply, cultivators were forced to shift to growing subsistence crops on the poorer margins. The control exercised by the tharavadus over wastelands and forests introduced a further element of dependence. This determined, to a considerable degree, the trajectory of rural politics between 1900 and 1948, which evidenced a move towards confrontation and conflict over the control of agricultural resources.

With the soaring prices for pepper and coconut in the twenties, the small cultivator producing for the market came to the fore. This degree of integration into the market did not necessarily mean the undermining of patronal, reciprocal relations between large tharavadus and dependent labourers and cultivators. Given the nature of the fluctuating profits from cash crops, determined by the vagaries of international demand, which financed the import of rice into the region,[1] cultivators relied on the tharavadus for the provision of subsistence. This underlay a sense of rural community, fraught with tension, in which

[1] C.A. Innes, *Malabar Gazetteer* (Madras, 1951. First edn 1908), 249.

cultivators expected that they would be provided for in a time of food crisis, and allowed access to agricultural resources. This expectation was offset by the ability, or the willingness, of tharavadus to dispense their obligations. The effects of the Depression rendered negligible the profits from cash crops and precipitated a crisis of food supply. Rural community came to be founded more on the capability of the landowning tharavadus to provide subsistence.

This chapter looks at the economy of north Malabar in the period before the Depression with reference to the cultivation of paddy, coconut and pepper and the relations between landowning tharavadus and cultivators. The incorporation of tharavadus in the revenue bureaucracy, their control over agricultural resources and a near monopoly over wetland made them the focus of authority in the villages of north Malabar. A schematic distinction is made between the eastern, inland regions and the western, coastal regions of Chirakkal, Kottayam and Kurumbranad *taluks*, a region covering 1,668 square miles. The eastern region was characterised by rough terrain, with dense forests to the north and north east, which were controlled by large landowning tharavadus. Pepper was grown on a large scale and both large landowning tharavadus as well as pioneering cultivators were at the forefront of the expansion of cultivation into the forests. Paddy was produced in both the eastern as well as western regions and the control of wetlands tended to be concentrated in the hands of a few large landowners. Shifting cultivators in the east, however, exercised a degree of self-reliance by producing hill rice for themselves.

In the western regions, coconut was the main crop and it was exported, along with pepper, from the port towns of Tellicherry, Cannanore and Badagara. Merchants, mainly Mappila Muslims, were responsible for the import of rice to these ports to feed the regions. The towns along the coast were also the source of casual employment and work in the factories, and credit for petty trade as well as larger ventures. In the aftermath of the Depression, which severely affected the prospects of employment in the towns, and a food crisis aggravated by the Second World War, more cultivators were to become dependent on the land. The eastern regions were to become the site of an increasing conflict between landowners and cultivators over land resources, reaching a climax in 1948.

Nayar tharavadus and the organisation of production

Malabar was wrested by the East India Company from Tipu Sultan in 1792, but it was not until 1806 that the last flicker of resistance was quelled with the defeat of the Pazhassi raja. Following the warfare of the late eighteenth and early nineteenth century, pioneering Nayar tharavadus had managed to carve out areas of influence with the opening up of forests and the expansion of land frontiers. William Logan wrote of 'Nayars of ability' who wrested landholding rights and attracted the great body of cultivators to agricultural production centred on their households. However, he traced this process of the breakdown of communal rights over land in favour of individual 'families' to the fifteenth century.[2] The Nayar tharavadu followed matrilineal inheritance and, over decades of legal redefinition, was presumed to be under the ultimate management of the eldest male known as the *karanavan*.[3] The younger members were entitled to maintenance from the income of the tharavadu from its lands. In south Malabar, the women of dominant Nayar families entered into relationships with Nambudiri brahmins, but often continued to live in their own tharavadus. The children of all such relationships were maintained by the tharavadu of the mother. In the north, Nambudiris were fewer, as was their influence, and Nayar women tended to live with their husbands rather than with their own tharavadus.[4] Over the nineteenth century, the legal profile of the Nayar tharavadu was consolidated, and it came to be defined as an impartible and co-residential unit (eventually decided by the Madras High Court in 1867).[5] However, particularly in north Malabar where land was available for colonisation and profits from pepper were high, tharavadus continued to expand into the interior setting up branches called *tavazhis*, each tracing descent from a female member of the parent tharavadu. Each of these branches was allocated land on improving tenures, and they constituted the cutting edge of the extension of cultivation.

The expansion of dominant tharavadus into the interior brought them into contact with the shifting cultivation practised by tribal groups who produced hill rice and pepper on the foothills. Their random, migratory cultivation was brought under the control of Nayar tharavadus under a system called *cherikallu*. Younger members of the tharavadu were allotted an expanse of forest and, with a Maniyani tribal as supervisor, trees were cleared for the cultivation of pepper

[2] *Malabar Land Tenures Report, 1881-82* (Madras, 1882) (henceforth *MLTR*), I, xv. See K.K.N. Kurup, *Pazhassi samarangal (Pazhassi revolts)* (Trivandrum, 1980).

[3] L. Moore, *Malabar law and custom* (second edn, Madras, 1900), 73, 108. In north Malabar, Tiyyas, Mappilas and some Nambudiri brahmin families in Payyanur followed matrilineal forms of inheritance. See E.K. Gough and D.M. Schneider, *Matrilineal kinship* (Berkeley, CA 1961).

[4] Genealogical data belonging to several families studied by E.J. Miller suggest that for over 300 years, Nayar women of north Malabar had been living with the households of their husbands. E.J. Miller, 'An analysis of the Hindu caste system in its interactions with the total social structure in north Kerala' (unpublished PhD dissertation, University of Cambridge, 1950), 263.

[5] Moore, *Malabar law and custom*, 6-8. For a complex discussion of the structure of the tharavadu and the process of its legal redefinition see G. Arunima, 'Colonialism and the transformation of matriliny in Malabar, 1850-1940' (unpublished PhD dissertation, University of Cambridge, 1992).

and hill rice.[6] Every garden and acre of land in north Malabar was given a name regardless of whether it was unoccupied or cultivated. This constituted a customary claim to title of sorts and could frequently be disputed by both other landowners and enterprising cultivators. Shifting cultivators who were not part of the *cherikallu* system changed their designation according to the name of the tharavadu from which they had leased their land.[7] Vettuvar tribals worked on the coconut plantations of Nayars and other castes and were sometimes employed on the fields during the harvest. They observed death pollution for a period of fifteen days if working on a Nayar's gardens and for ten days if on a Nambudiri's. Their identities were seen as being coterminous with that of their landlords. However, these tribal groups could up and leave if treated harshly, and their lack of 'loyalty' to their masters made their names (*nambuvettuvar*) 'synonymous with ingratitude', according to an early amateur anthropologist.[8] Systematic encroachment on the preserves of the tribals, combined with the attempts at forest conservancy by the Government, had already caused the migration of families of tribals northwards to Mysore and Coorg. In the late nineteenth century, the Conservator of Forests in Malabar found that there were still large tracts of foothills where the local tribes and hillmen gave 'neither dues nor allegiance to anyone' and were for all intents and purposes the owners of the soil 'by rights of long and undisturbed possession'. The Board of Revenue expressed its firm opinion that the sticky question of the rights of tribals should not be raised.[9]

The growth of cash crop cultivation did not necessarily erode patronal ties between the tharavadus and the subordinate tribal labour. Payments of rent were made in kind and subsistence cultivation continued to be dependent on the tharavadus for cash advances and seeds. While tribal production and tribals were being brought under the sway of an export economy, they were also being converted, in most cases, to the status of predial slaves. Thurston had recorded in 1909 that 'in the old days', inhabitants were entered in the contract when forests were sold and that many tribals called themselves 'men of *janmis*'.[10] At the harvest the *janmis* collected their share of the produce and maintained

---

[6] K. Madhavan, *Payaswiniyude teerattu (On the banks of the river Payaswini)* (Trivandrum, 1987), 14.

[7] F. Fawcett, *The Nayars of Malabar* (Madras, 1901), 199.

[8] T.K.G. Panikkar, *Malabar and its folk: a systematic description of the social customs and institutions of Malabar* (second edn, Madras, 1900), 162-3.

[9] *Board of Revenue (L.R.) Proceedings, Forest no. 110 dated 7 March 1888* (Kozhikode Regional Archives) (henceforth KRA); *Board of Revenue (L.R.) Proceedings, Forest no. 635 dated 30 November 1888* (KRA).

[10] E. Thurston and K. Rangachari, *Castes and tribes of southern India*, II (Madras, 1909), 452-3. The enquiries into the existence of slavery in Malabar in the early nineteenth century revealed that even on ordinary leases of land, Mavilan and Karimbalan tribals were sold as part of the contract. Interviews with *mukhyastans* of Chericul and *mukhyastans* of Randaterra, Tellicherry and Irwanaad, *PP, 1828, XXIV (125)*.

patronal relations through gifts and donations on the occasion of festivals, particularly the harvest festival of Onam in September. This practice continued well into the twentieth century on account of the vesting of complete rights over forests and wastelands in the landlords, and the refusal of the Government to consider the vexed question of the rights of tribals over the land they cultivated. Even as late as 1938, volunteers of the Kerala Congress Socialist Party found that Mavilan and Karimbalan tribals were being sold for 10 to 15 measures of grain as cultivators.[11]

Forays by tharavadus, to expand cultivation into forests and wastelands, often created conflict over territories. Dominant tharavadus in the same region were usually in a permanent state of feuding (*kudipaga*) – over territory, water and labour – and some of these feuds were resolved through marriage alliances. It is significant that precisely those families which were involved in *kudipaga* were the ones which tended to cement their truces through marriage. Since the property of matrilineal tharavadus passed through the women, a strategic marriage could bring with it the property in dispute. Madhavan recollects that many of the conflicts over land between his own powerful household Ecchikanam and the neighbouring Kodom were settled by such methods.[12] Alliances could cut across the boundaries of villages, and territorial divisions were covered with webs of property and kinship. The formation of branches of a tharavadu either as a result of internal dissensions or as the cutting edge of cultivation in far-flung areas created filiations of a ritual kind. Those who were members of the parent tharavadu were said to be connected by *mudal sambandham* (community of property) while those who had formed branches were related to each other and to the parent body through *pula sambandham* (community of pollution). The latter meant that the death of any member of the parent tharavadu would necessitate the members of the branches to keep fasts and observe the period of death pollution.[13] Several families in the eastern villages grew powerful in this way, aided by the availability of land which allowed its massing in huge blocks. Kalliattu Chathukutty Nambiar, one of the largest landholders in north Malabar, held over 30,000 acres of land in eastern Chirakkal. The tharavadus of Karakkatitathil and Kalliattu which were related through marriage owned 17,000 acres of the 20,000 or so acres of forest in the revenue division of Kallyad.[14] The degree of control exercised by such landlords, in the veritable little kingdoms they managed to establish, gained for them the popular epithet of *kattu rajakkanmar* or the kings of the forest.

Many large tharavadus built up informal empires, by subordinating tribal

---

[11] *Prabhatham*, 14 November 1938.
[12] K. Madhavan, *Payaswiniyude teerattu*, 18.
[13] Moore, *Malabar law and custom*, 4.
[14] *Malabar Tenancy Committee Report, 1927* (Madras, 1928) (henceforth *MTCR, 1927*), II, Appendix II; *Settlement register of the amsam of Kallyad* (Calicut, 1904).

labour in the forests and through judicious alliances with other powerful tharavadus. Their authority was further buttressed by the control over agricultural resources vested in them by the state. That the landlords in Malabar possessed absolute rights in the soil was recognised as early as 1807. The Board of Revenue had maintained in 1818 that the *janmi* 'possessed a property in the soil more absolute than even that of the landlord in Europe'[15] In 1916, in the landmark Olappamana case, the Madras High Court decreed that the ownership of non-tidal and non-navigable rivers was to be vested in the owners of the banks on either side of the river.[16] The short distance between the hills and the western coast made the courses of rivers brief and therefore difficult to harness for irrigation. Cultivators became dependent on landowners even for watering their crops. Despite the court ruling, actual control over water resources required negotiation with the use of muscle power. Pitched battles between the retainers of rival landlords were common as also the erection of bunds to dam off the flow of water to other fields. The Collector of Malabar observed in some despair that the decision in the Olappamana case meant that there was 'nothing to prevent the riparian *janmi* from reclaiming, damming or diverting rivers at pleasure'.[17]

Control over the ancillaries of agriculture did not necessarily mean that landlords were able to liberate themselves from the bonds of community and customs. Rights were constantly being contested with other landholders as well as recalcitrant tenants who refused to forgo their customary interests in the land. Control over people still mattered more than control over land. The necessity of attracting and keeping agriculturists meant that a landlord never really could exercise monopoly rights. Independent cultivators occupying wasteland were either encouraged or evicted; violence characterised agrarian relations and necessitated the creation of blocks of landlords and their retainers. An early report stated baldly that once a person had got possession of land it was difficult to 'turn him out again except by force of arms'.[18] Well into the twentieth century, village officials sometimes had to resort to murdering squatters to regain possession of fields.[19] Control over agricultural resources

---

[15] *Board of Revenue Proceedings, vol. 2537 dated 5 January 1818*; Thomas Warden, *Report on the Land Tenures in Malabar, 12 September 1815* (Calicut, 1910), paras. 3-8. See also, T.C. Varghese, *Agrarian change and economic consequences: land tenures in Kerala, 1850-1960* (Calcutta, 1970), 20-2, 53-5.

[16] *Revenue Department G.O. 2564 dated 9 December 1929* (India Office Library and Records) (henceforth IOL).

[17] *Revenue Department G.O. 2425 dated 23 November 1921* (IOL); The Board of Revenue was forced to recognise that unless they could lay stress on the fact that the rights of a landlord in Malabar were not more extensive than those of a *ryotwari* proprietor, the position of the Government was 'hopeless'. *Revenue R.Dis. 6525/20 dated 18 September 1920* (KRA).

[18] William Thackeray, *A Report on the revenue affairs of Malabar and Canara dated 7 September 1807* (Calicut, 1911), 6.

[19] *Report on the administration of the Police Department of the Madras Presidency* (henceforth RAPMP), 1936, 15. On 21 February 1932, A.C. Kannan Nayar, a landlord from Hosdrug,

had to be negotiated and rights granted by the law were blunted by local circumstance.

The possibility of migration gave cultivators a relative degree of independence and blunted, to an extent, the authority exercised by large landowners. In 1931, we find Kannan Nayar recording in his diary that sixteen Cherumas had migrated from the neighbouring village to his lands, because they were 'unable to bear the oppression of their *janmis*'.[20] Availability of land and a shortage of labour meant that agricultural wages in the interior continued to be high as late as 1930. Short-term migrants from Malabar provided most of the labour for the plantations in Coorg to the north.[21] After cultivating the fields before the onset of the monsoons in July–August, labourers would leave for the plantations, returning home just before the harvest in September. Those with single crop lands worked on the plantations for five or six months a year. In the two decades before the Depression, there was a considerable outflow of emigrants to the tea estates in Ceylon and rubber plantations in Malaya.[22] By the mid twenties, Ceylon had reached the saturation point for Indian labour and in 1931, with the depression in the rubber trade, recruitment to Malaya was completely stopped.[23] Thus, by 1930, the alternative of emigration had virtually ceased. With the unfavourable ratio of labour to land in the aftermath of the Depression, the authority exercised by tharavadus was to increase. However, many of the lower caste emigrants who returned to Malabar found themselves at odds with local authority and notions of hierarchy. Their experience of anonymity and, therefore, a degree of equality, in the countries where they had worked underlay their pamphleteering against caste restrictions. A pamphlet of 1927 spoke of the 'absence of caste in Singapore, Penang, and even in savage Africa'.[24]

The authority of the tharavadu

Migration and the independence afforded by the cultivation of cash crops meant that tharavadus could not exercise absolute control over their tenants and labourers. In the last instance, however, their control over wastelands, water

recorded in his diary the shooting dead of a member of his tharavadu in a dispute over land. *Diaries of A.C. Kannan Nayar*, Nehru Memorial Museum and Library (henceforth NMML).
[20] *Diaries of Kannan Nayar*, 25 October 1931; see also entry for 19 March 1938.
[21] *Census of India, 1911, XII, Madras, part I, Report*, 27.
[22] Most of the emigrants to Ceylon were untouchables and about 10,000 Parayans had emigrated between 1900 and 1921. *Census of India, 1921, XIII, Madras, part I, Report*, 49.
[23] In 1926, 10,572 persons emigrated from Malabar to the Straits Settlements and Malaya. In 1931, the number had dropped to 2,807. *Public Works and Labour Dept. G.O. 1257 L dated 7 May 1931* (IOL).
[24] K.S. Narayanan, *Teendalvairi (Against untouchability)* (Calicut, 1927), verses 43-5.

and granaries was to increase their authority. Tharavadus formed the foci of settlement in north Malabar on account of the rough terrain which enforced scattered occupation. Authority was exercised by individual tharavadus over those who held land from it, laboured on its fields and performed specialised services. Whereas the Nayar tharavadus exercised powers of arbitration over inferiors, there was no local authority above them capable of regulating their relation with their inferiors.[25]

The incorporation of heads of tharavadus in the lower echelons of the revenue bureaucracy further extended their authority. This was done partly because of the exigencies of the situation arising after pensioning off the rajas in 1801. The Joint Commissioners appointed to look into the conditions in the newly acquired region observed that these 'lesser rajas', or heads of tharavadus, possessed 'in their different districts the same rights as to justice and revenue which the rajas had themselves and were totally exempted from tribute'.[26] In 1822, H.S. Graeme organised the district into revenue divisions called *amsams* which were further subdivided into *desams*. A hereditary official called the *adhikari* was made responsible for the collection of revenue from the *amsams*, and he was chosen from an influential landholding family, usually one dominating several *desams*.[27] This had profound implications since settlement tended to be clustered around powerful tharavadus particularly in the eastern region. The revenue division in most cases came to be congruent with the sphere of influence of a family. In 1896, when the government escheated the Kannoth lands in Chirakkal it was found that the entire *desam* of Kannothumchala had belonged to one Kannoth Kelappan, the head of the now extinct family.[28] Regulation XI of 1816 had placed the village police under the heads of villages, adding on the coercive powers of the state to the traditional authority of the *adhikari*. There were complaints late into the nineteenth century that the *adhikaris* were a law unto themselves and rarely, if ever, reported offences to magistrates, preferring instead to exercise their own authority.[29] Moreover, by the mid 1880s, it became one of the cardinal principles of police recruitment that lower castes were to be chosen only where other recruits were unobtainable. In Malabar, Nayars came to comprise two-thirds of the constabulary by 1920.[30]

As the younger sons from prominent tharavadus went in for education and jobs in the colonial bureaucracy, local influence came to be buttressed by extra

[25] J.P. Mencher, 'Kerala and Madras: a comparative study of ecology and social structure', *Ethnology*, 5, 2 (1966), 135-71.

[26] W.G. Farmer to Taylor, October 1792, quoted by B.S.W. Swai, 'The British in Malabar, 1792-1806' (unpublished D Phil dissertation, University of Sussex, 1975), 146.

[27] William Logan, *Malabar Manual*, I (3 volumes, London, 1887), 89; *Report on the revenue administration of Malabar dated 14 January 1822* (Calicut, 1898), 4.

[28] *Revenue R. Dis. 162/Rev. 1896 dated 25 January 1896* (KRA).

[29] *DR Magisterial 122.M/GL dated 11 March 1891* (KRA).

[30] David Arnold, *Police power and colonial rule: Madras, 1859-1947* (Delhi, 1986), 41.

local authority. In 1899, members of the Legislative Council pointed out in debates over the passing of the compensation for tenants' improvements bill that the 'illiberal treatment of tenants' could be attributed to the fact that the District Munsifs were 'nearly all of them junior members of tharavadus'. A Nayar inebriated with 'Western education' and the progress made under British rule observed at the beginning of this century that society was now under the guidance of 'that marvellous piece of legislation, the IPC [Indian Penal Code]'.[31] However, at the level of the *amsam* the long arm of the law was a wooden one and the *adhikaris* held the strings. As late as 1950, the erstwhile revenue divisions were held together by the allegiance to formerly powerful families and the selection of *adhikaris* from these families.[32]

The influence of a landowning tharavadu was not restricted only to the *desam* in which it was physically situated. Many of the largest landholders owned land in several *desams* which were at times managed by its branches. For their tenants, in such cases, it was not so much the fact of the land which they occupied being in a particular area, but their relation with the tharavadu which was of prime importance. When the first settlement operations were undertaken in Malabar, it was found that the five wealthiest *janmis* held lands in 149 *desams*.[33] Rural political activity in the late thirties was facilitated by this as the resentment towards one landowner necessarily had a significant geographical spread.

Rural settlement tended to be centred on a Nayar or Tiyya tharavadu and the lands and labourers it commanded. More specifically, the word tharavadu also meant the family house; the land where the ashes of the ancestors lay (which was usually within the compound of the house).[34] It incorporated both the immediate members of the tharavadu as well as labourers working on its lands who were identified with the tharavadu they worked for. Around each major tharavadu there were families of service castes – oil pressers, washer people, potters and barbers – who held hereditary rights and privileges in the produce as well as the family and local shrine.[35] In 1901, the settlement register for Karivellur *amsam* recorded nine oil pressers (Vaniyans), ten washermen (Vannan/Mannan), two weavers (Chaliyan), eight shrine priests and oracles (Komaram/Velichapad), four astrologers (Kanisans), two barbers for castes below Nayars (Kavutiyan) and two traditional teachers (Panikkar/Vadhyar), who held land from shrines managed by dominant Nayar tharavadus.[36] Traditionally,

---

[31] Panikkar, *Malabar and its folk*, 266.
[32] E.J. Miller, 'Village structure in north Kerala', in M.N. Srinivas ed., *India's villages* (Bombay, 1960), 49.
[33] *Revenue Dept. G.O. 477 dated 22 December 1904* (IOL), 17.
[34] Fawcett, *The Nayars of Malabar*, 199.
[35] E.K. Gough, 'Changing kinship usages in the setting of political and economic change among the Nayars of Malabar', *Journal of the Royal Anthropological Institute*, 82, 1 (1952), 72.
[36] *Settlement Register for Karivellur amsam*, Chirakkal taluk (Calicut, 1904).

Nayar tharavadus had charged a tax called *kudicillara* which was collected on the implements of the profession of the potters, blacksmiths and the like.[37] Within a village, Mappilas too shared a right in the services of artisans and other lower castes and the occupations of these latter groups reflected more a secular, community obligation rather than their position within a religious framework of responsibilities towards Nayar tharavadus alone. Some of the dominant Nayar tharavadus had Tiyya retainers called *adiyans* who rendered service in personal quarrels, acted as the private armies of landlords, and 'policed' the castes below them to prevent any infringement of caste mores.[38]

The tharavadu in north Malabar tended to be more paternalistic and had the authority to settle civil disputes as well as conflicts between the castes clustered around them unlike south Malabar where assemblies constituted by several Nayar tharavadus were more powerful.[39] In some parts of Chirakkal and Kottayam where the Tiyyas were in a majority, dominant Tiyya tharavadus, whose control extended over three or four revenue divisions, exercised powers of civil jurisdiction. The four major Nayar or Tiyya families in a region decided on questions of caste precedence and petty quarrels and imposed traditional punishments like the stopping of the services of the washer people, preventing an individual or group from participating in community ceremonies or imposing the ultimate sanction of excommunication. When a branch of a dominant tharavadu was set up in another region, it would sometimes assume rights of caste jurisdiction over the inhabitants of that region.[40] Where a Nayar tharavadu was more powerful, the headman of the Tiyya caste assembly (*thandan*) acted as the intermediary between his community and the ultimate appellate authority of the Nayar. The prominent Nayar *yajamanan* families, particularly those in Kottayam, decided disputes among their Mappila tenants as well and as a measure of their patronage donated rice to the local mosque. Miller records an interesting incident from 1937 when a group of Mappilas decided to become Ahmadiyyas. The *yajamanan* refused to accept gifts from them (which necessarily involved the concomitant denial of patronage to the heretic body) and rescinded the right to use the common Muslim burial ground.[41] As yet, in the early decades of this century, the secular authority of the tharavadu over a region was not seen as detrimental to the influence exercised by the mosque and Mappila *ulemas*. Religious difference seemed to count for little. In Tellicherry, the Muthur tharavadu had four *tavazhis*; all the descendants of one had converted to Islam. The *karanavan* of the branch was

---

[37] Logan, *Malabar Manual*, II, Appendix XIII, clxviii-xix, cxcviii.
[38] A. Aiyappan, *Iravas and culture change* (Madras, 1944), 49; Miller, 'Village structure in north Kerala', 50.
[39] E.J. Miller, 'An analysis of the Hindu caste system', 121-2.
[40] Manuscript of unfinished autobiography of Murkkoth Kumaran (1937) (In author's possession).
[41] Miller, 'An analysis of the Hindu caste system', 158-9.

a Hindu and the tharavadu continued to function as before without any censure of the *tavazhi*.[42]

The authority exercised by tharavadus was also manifested in the degree of restrictions placed on the movement, dress and speech of lower caste tenants and labourers. Significantly, such restraints fell more heavily on the backs of those working on a tharavadu's wetlands, mainly Cherumas and Pulayas, and those dependent on it for lands or sustenance. It was not so much the operation of an abstract set of caste rules which is evident in the restrictions but the fact that deference was embedded in quotidian routines of speech, dress and manner. It was in the *practice* of certain actions and modes of behaviour within a specific situation, i.e. the interaction between high and low castes, that the relations of power were emphasised. The enforced repetition of gestures and of speech forms sought to make seem natural what was arbitrary and imposed.

Lower caste agricultural labourers were expected to keep a certain distance from upper castes, as Pulayas and Cherumas were believed to 'pollute' from a distance. In 1929, Congress activists took up the cause of Pulaya labourers in Pappinisseri and Kalliasseri villages, who were not allowed to use the narrow paths between fields when a Nayar was walking on them. Some of the Pulayas had to backtrack a distance of two to three furlongs to give way to higher castes so that they would not have to step into the marshy fields.[43] Other restrictions provide an arbitrary and wide-ranging list. Tenants were not allowed to tile their roofs and had to be content with thatched ones. In parts of Chirakkal, every lower caste labourer's hut had to have a chair for the local landlord when he visited, an event as rare as would, otherwise, have been the presence of a chair in a hut. Different castes had to call their houses by different names; Parayas called theirs *cheri*, Cherumas called theirs *chala* and the artisan castes, *pura*. In speaking with a person of higher caste, therefore, these castes had to use debasing terms about themselves and all that was associated with them. It was made evident in the way people dressed whether they belonged to the upper or lower castes. Nayar landlords wore silk waistcloths (*mundus*) reaching their ankles. Artisans, washermen and the like wore them reaching midway between the ankle and the knees and the lowest castes wore them above the knee. Kanakkans shaved their heads clean, Pulayas and Cherumas retained frontal tufts of hair, Nayars grew their hair long and tied it in a knot on the side of the head. While walking on the road, lower castes had to take off their head cloths in the presence of Nayars or Nambudiris. Nayars and Nambudiris had to be addressed in an elaborate manner. The headcloth had to be taken off, tucked under the armpit and with one hand covering the mouth and eyes fixed on the ground a lower caste would make the sound *R-r-a-n* (a shortening of *thampuran* or lord). Each caste addressed a Nayar differently;

[42] Hamid Ali, *Custom and law in Anglo-Muslim jurisprudence* (Calcutta, 1938), 50.
[43] *Mathrubhumi*, 26 November 1929.

Tiyyas as *yashamanan*, Vaniyars (oil pressers) and Vannans (washermen) as *nayanar* and Malayan tribals and the lowest castes as *thampuran*.[44] Adherence to such 'rules' was the only means of telling people apart, a breach of rules often served as a disguise. As early as 1822, it was observed that slaves escaping from Malabar to Coorg disguised themselves by putting on a larger quantity of clothing and altering their headdress.[45]

The maintenance of marks of subordination did not necessarily lead to an internalisation of feelings of lowness. Explanations which seek to link a lower-caste world view of acceptance of inequality with textual concepts of *karma* or the station of people within a structured hierarchy overplay the aspect of consensus within society.[46] Moreover, they presume an almost unmediated dissemination and acceptance of ideas of acquiescent subordination. Eric Miller, who conducted his field work in Malabar in the late 1940s, found that ideas such as *karma* and its relation to cycles of life were familiar only to those 'informants' who belonged to the upper castes and had a knowledge of 'all Indian Hinduism'.[47] There does not seem to have been an unquestioning acceptance, by lower castes, of prescribed modes of behaviour. In 1800, Buchanan recorded that Nayars would cut down lower-caste men who ventured on to the main road, which seems to indicate less a consensus than something maintained by force.[48] In 1901, Fawcett wrote about a Tiyya tenant who was murdered by his Nayar landlord when the former refused to present some sweets as token of his allegiance.[49] Genuflection and self abasement were extorted as much by the use of power as they came to be, if at all, instilled as habit. Dumont with his model of consensual hierarchy was hard put to explain the necessity for force in Kerala. He therefore maintained that the situation here was a contradiction of the hierarchical principle because what should have been admitted as custom had to be imposed by power.[50]

However, to understand relations between tharavadus and their cultivators, particularly in the context of subsequent political mobilisation we need to look at the idea of deference. Authority, and its acceptance, was rooted not solely in cultural constructs, but was born out of the sense of an occupational

---

[44] Written evidence of T. Chathu, Schoolmaster, Badagara, *MTCR, 1927*, II, 346-7; Madhavan, *Payaswiniyude teerattu*, 15-27; Logan, *Malabar Manual*, I, 85; Innes, *Malabar Gazetteer*, 143; Panikkar, *Malabar and its folk*, 156.

[45] Extract from Mr. Graeme's report on Malabar, 14 January 1822, *PP 1828, XXIV (125)*, 920.

[46] Kathleen Gough sees the Brahmins as the subtle elaborators of the unequal social structure who then reconciled the lower orders to their existence by instilling a belief in notions of *karma, dharma*, and the like. E. Kathleen Gough, *Rural society in south east India* (Cambridge, 1981), 26-7. See also M. Moffatt, *An untouchable community in South India* (Princeton, NJ, 1979).

[47] Miller, 'An analysis of the Hindu caste system', 140.

[48] Quoted in Fawcett, *The Nayars of Malabar*, 254.

[49] *Ibid.*, 311.

[50] L. Dumont, *Homo Hierarchicus: the caste system and its implications*, trans. Mark Sainsbury *et al.* (Chicago, IL, 1980), 82.

community consisting of landowners and cultivators. Many of the younger members of tharavadus were involved in the actual work of cultivation, while the older men and women were either employed in supervisory functions or at various stages in the harvest. Moyyarath Sankaran, who was from one of the larger tharavadus in north Malabar, recalled how his mother used to winnow during harvests and his grandmother transplanted and tied haystacks in her time.[51] Younger men worked alongside household labourers on the fields, and led forays to divert water supplies or lay claim over disputed land. The degree of interaction between tharavadus and cultivators was extensive, and there may have been less of a feeling of 'us' and 'them'. At the end of a working day, and more often on the occasion of festivals, the men of all castes would gather at the local toddy shop and experience a temporary camaraderie with their workmates. This is not to posit an Arcadia where master and servant lived as equals. Precisely because of everyday association at work, the maintenance of the deferential demeanour of cultivators was important. Personal contact produced familiarity but also allowed for the passing of strictures on unusual, or unacceptable behaviour. Moreover, charity and indulgences, marking the benevolence of the superior, were as much part of this quotidian interaction as the regulating of the behaviour of lower castes. Deference emerged out of and was maintained by the nature of work relations. This mix of uneasy intimacy and formal hierarchy was accentuated by the dependence of labourers on the tharavadu for subsistence within an agrarian economy short of foodgrains. Rural agitation in the 1930s would define deferential behaviour as an arbitrary imposition by upper castes, but the initial leadership came from the tharavadus.

The economy of pepper and coconut

The economy of Malabar has hitherto been depicted in gloomy terms and a characteristic evaluation has it that the 'peasantry in Malabar . . . lived and worked in conditions of extreme penury entailed by the twin exactions of lord and state'.[52] Such judgements stem from a model of the economy, which is more concerned to explain that favourite conundrum of historians of Malabar: who are the Mappilas and why do they rebel? Even though the agitations in the nineteenth century of the Mappila peasantry and the final upsurge in 1921 have been provided with ideological underpinnings, the consensus seems to be that these outbreaks had predominantly agrarian origins. Despite the fact that the

[51] Moyyarath Sankaran, *Ente jivithakatha (An autobiography)* (Calicut, 1965), 205.
[52] Panikkar, *Against lord and state*, 48. For characteristic statements see also K.P. Kannan, *Of rural proletarian struggles: mobilisation and organisation of rural workers in south-west India* (Delhi, 1988) and Varghese, *Agrarian change and economic consequences*.

Mappila outbreaks were restricted to three of the eight taluks of Malabar, and that too in the south, this has not prevented a tendentious extrapolation for the economy of Malabar as a whole. Rack renting, insecurity of tenure, evictions, the British 'policy of pauperizing the peasantry' through exorbitant revenue demands and a stagnant wetland economy which led cultivators to cultivate cash crops out of desperation; these are the broad outlines of the picture. Kannan goes so far as to state that the major characteristic of the economy till the Depression was 'a majority of landless labourers attached to their masters'.[53]

This section will elaborate a different approach which does not see cultivators as trapped within a torpid economy and at the mercy of big landlords. The main theme will be that of commercialized agriculture, fuelled by international demand, in which small cultivators participated willingly, and to their profit. It was this eagerness to cultivate pepper and coconuts for an export market, and the shift away from subsistence cultivation which was to highlight the latent flaw in the nature of the agrarian economy: Malabar did not produce sufficient paddy to feed itself. Thus, instead of a tale of consistent poverty within a subsistence economy, we have the picture of fragile affluence created by a cash crop economy. Seen in this light Malabar does not seem to be an anomaly within the larger south Indian economy, for which recent work suggests that the region should be seen as one characterised by independent market-oriented small farmers rather than of agrarian dependents under the sway of rural magnates.[54] Moreover, we need to revise the picture of the cultivator dulled by the revenue exactions of the state into an inability to innovate or respond to the lure of the export market. As Washbrook has shown, the proportion of total revenues represented by land revenue dropped by over half in the period between 1880 and 1920. In addition, a 'real property revolution' may have been occasioned by the fact that the weight of land revenue in relation to the value of agricultural produce may have declined by as much as two-thirds in the same period.[55]

The first settlement report of Malabar, completed in 1904, found that jungles and hills occupied more than half the classified area. Practically all of

---

[53] Kannan, *Rural proletarian struggles*, 48-9.

[54] See David Ludden, *Peasant history in south India* (Princeton, NJ, 1985), ch.5 and 'Productive power in agriculture: a survey of work on the local history of British India' in M. Desai, S.H. Rudolph and A. Rudra eds., *Agrarian power and agricultural productivity in south Asia* (Delhi, 1984), 51-99. B. Robert, in 'Economic change and agrarian reorganisation in "dry" south India, 1890-1940: a reinterpretation', *Modern Asian Studies*, 17, 1 (1983), 59-78 offers a comprehensive critique of Washbrook's formulation overplaying the role of big landlords as the sole movers of the economy. See D.A. Washbrook, 'Country politics: Madras, 1880-1930', *Modern Asian Studies*, 7, 3 (1973), 475-531.

[55] D.A. Washbrook, *The emergence of provincial politics: the Madras Presidency, 1870-1920* (Cambridge, 1976), 50-2 and 'Law, state and agrarian society in colonial India,' in G. Johnson *et al.* eds., *Power, profit and politics* (Cambridge, 1981), 677-9.

these, and the wastelands, were under the control of landowners and only 5,000 acres were available to the government, for any schemes it wished to implement.[56] The region was badly off for roads, and at the beginning of the century the north east was inaccessible except on foot, making the enforcement of law and order by the government a problem. Kottayam had been opened up only at the turn of the nineteenth century when the East India Company had driven roads through the intractable terrain during its campaigns against the rebellious raja of Pazhassi.[57] Communications and trade utilised the rivers and streams, and boats were the only means of transport from Chirakkal northwards to Kasergode in south Kanara. Trade along the rivers was mainly in the hands of Mappilas, who, though they were concentrated in the port towns, had major settlements in Irikkur and Valapattanam to the interior, on the banks of navigable rivers.

The boom in world prices for pepper in the twenties underlay the prosperity of the few, large tharavadus with plantations and of small entrepreneurial cultivators. However, two significant factors conditioned the profits accruing from exports of pepper. Malabar was a secondary supplier to the world market and prices were determined, in the last instance, by the availability or failure of crops from the plantations in south-east Asia. Secondly, Malabar could not avail itself of the economies of scale that these plantations possessed since cultivation was largely in the hands of small cultivators. While this allowed flexible responses to fluctuations in world demand, in the long run, Malabar pepper was relegated to the sidelines.

In the years before the Depression there was a spurt in land colonisation, particularly in Kottayam where the wastelands and forests to the north-east were encroached upon.[58] The availability of land and the necessity of ensuring that there was a constant production for the market gave a particular character to the tenures on the frontiers. In the eastern *desams* of Chirakkal, wasteland was given on improving tenures or *kuzhikanam* for periods ranging from forty to ninety-six years.[59] In real terms this meant that the cultivators would not be uprooted from their plots; what was required in a period of profits was that there should be no hindrance to the extension of cropping. Deforestation and the expansion of cultivation were going on even in the second decade of the twentieth century when pepper prices were at their highest; new clearings were opened up in the forested hillocks of Chirakkal and Kottayam. The line of

[56] *Revenue Dept. G.O. 477 dated 22 December 1904* (IOL), 11.
[57] Innes, *Malabar Gazetteer*, 268–9.
[58] The average increase in cultivated area for Malabar was 37.5 per cent between the years 1911–51. The figures for the period 1913–30 were Chirakkal–30.1 per cent; Kottayam–50.06 per cent; Kurumbranad– 34.27 per cent. Varghese, *Agrarian change and economic consequences*, 123; *Statistical atlas of Malabar for the decennium 1920-30* (Calicut, 1933).
[59] Note of visit by the President and others to Mattanur *desam*, 14 October 1927, *MTCR, 1927*, I, 140.

expansion followed the major routes of communication, like the road leading from Tellicherry to Coorg, and pushed into the forested territory on either side.[60] Smaller cultivators, responding to the soaring prices of pepper, were responsible for this thrust forward. Landlords made large sums of money yearly by leasing out areas from the unsurveyed parts of their forests for cultivation.[61]

At times, tenants took a large plot of dry land on lease along with garden land to make what they could from cultivation of pepper, plantains, coconuts and other cash crops. In small, overcrowded plots, pepper vines were trained on standing areca or coconut trees and plantains were grown to provide shade for the new vines. In Kottayam and Chirakkal, pepper was the chief commercial crop, occupying about 18 per cent and 14 per cent respectively of the cultivated area in 1925.[62] On the larger plantations the Nayar tharavadus bore the expenses of cultivation. The smaller growers, who were in the majority, borrowed money from the agents of the Mappila traders on the coast. The crop was the security offered and it was usually sold to the agents at less than the market rates at least a year before it had formed.[63] Since the landlord had to be paid a fifth of the gross produce and the rest of the crop was usually pledged to a merchant, small cultivators made huge profits only when there were swings in the world prices of pepper to their advantage. Mappila traders were the crucial nexus between production and the market and even the larger Nayar tharavadus depended on them for selling their produce. Merchants or their agents visited the hamlets lying near important market towns regularly and purchased paddy, coconut and pepper directly from the cultivators. Srikandapuram, in north-east Chirakkal, had a large *bazaar* where the produce of the hill cultivation was collected, and sent down the river to Tellicherry for export. Tellicherry was the terminus of feeder roads, from the interior to the railway and to its port, from where the whole of the pepper crop from Chirakkal and Kottayam was exported.

The warfare of the late eighteenth century had resulted in the large scale destruction of vines and reduced the production of pepper by almost half. By the time Malabar became part of the Madras Presidency, 'the golden days of the pepper trade were over', and in 1800 only 8 per cent of the pepper produced in the East was grown here whereas Sumatra alone produced more than 50 per cent.[64] However, by 1836, the 'peculiarly indulgent system' of land revenue,

[60] *Revenue R.Dis.12A/1930 dated 5 March 1930* (KRA), 26.
[61] *Revenue Dept.G.O.477 dated 22 December 1904* (IOL), 11.
[62] *Revenue R.Dis.12A/1930 dated 5 March 1930* (KRA), Appendix VI.
[63] Written evidence of Chellarian Karuvan, Member, District Board, Madras Provincial Banking Enquiry Commission, 1930-31 (henceforth MPBEC), II, 193; letter of N. MacMichael, Special Settlement Officer, Malabar, *Proceedings of the Board of Revenue 477 dated 22 December 1904* (IOL), 20.
[64] Francis Buchanan, *A journey from Madras through the countries of Mysore, Canara and*

whereby the wastelands of the interior were not as heavily assessed as the lands near the coast, had allowed the extension of pepper cultivation to the forests, and restored export levels to the heights of the mid eighteenth century.[65] Although growing pepper was highly profitable, it was not classified as 'garden' produce and, therefore, charged a lower rate of assessment. This meant that well into the twentieth century a large part of the cultivation was still being carried on by tenants who took improvement leases on jungle land at the foothills of the Western Ghats.[66]

Until the Depression, the pressure of demand from European markets and the fluctuations in supply from the Malay Peninsula and the Straits Settlements were to determine the price of pepper. Pepper vines, once planted, started to bear only in three to four years. This made cultivation a risky business as there was no guarantee of a steady demand over such a long period. For example, in 1905-06, a bumper crop in Malabar coupled with a poor one in the Straits Settlements and Java saw exports to Germany, Italy and the USA touch Rs. 35 lakhs. The very next year as a result of overstocked markets in Europe and the indiscriminate plantation of infertile vines in Malabar, exports to these countries fell by 66 per cent.[67] Till the beginning of the war in 1914, there had been an artificial spurt in demand due to the activities of speculators, but through the war there was a steady decrease in exports. The period between 1925 and 1929 again saw a rise in the exports of pepper as a result of a failure of crops in the East Indies. If we assume a base price of Rs. 100 per cwt of pepper in 1900-01, by 1928 prices had rocketed to Rs. 274.78 per cwt. This sparked off a manic renovation, by small cultivators, of old pepper gardens and the planting of new ones all over north Malabar.[68] The enthusiastic response of cultivators is reflected in the extent of land under the cultivation of pepper which rose from 23,857 acres in 1903 to 111,057 acres in 1928.[69] From the early thirties, the effects of the Depression combined with increasing competition from plantations in south-east Asia, led to a steady decline in demand from Europe. By 1935, Italy had become the only country which continued to import pepper

Malabar, II (London, 1807, 3 volumes), 531; Pamela Nightingale, *Trade and empire in western India, 1784-1806* (Cambridge, 1970), 84.

[65] P. Clementson, *A Report on Revenue and other matters connected with Malabar dated 31 December 1838* (Calicut, 1916), 8; Sullivan, *Report on the Provinces of Malabar and Canara, 1841* (Calicut, 1911), 2.

[66] *Revenue R.Dis.12A/1930 dated 5 March 1930* (KRA), 63.

[67] *Review of the sea-borne trade of the Madras Presidency* (henceforth *RSTMP*), 1905-06, 16; 1906-07, 16.

[68] *RSTMP*, 1916-26; *Report of the operations of the department of agriculture in the Madras Presidency* (henceforth *RDAMP*), 1928; *RSTMP*, 1930-31; *Report on the Working of the Department of Industry in the Madras Presidency* (henceforth *RDIMP*), 1932-33, 10.

[69] Returns of agricultural statistics for the year 1891-92, *Public Dept. Madras Board of Revenue (R.S., L.R. and A) Proceedings no. 145 dated 21 April 1893* (Tamil Nadu Archives) (henceforth TNA); *Season and Crop Report of the Madras Presidency* (henceforth *SCRMP*), 1902-03, 1920-21, 1927-28.

from Malabar.[70] From the mid thirties, the small cultivators who had spear-headed the pepper boom would be forced to shift to the cultivation of subsistence crops. They were to become dependent on the large tharavadus, as cultivation expanded into the poorer margins.

Coconut was the main cash crop in the gardens along the west, largely because the palm grew best on sandy soils. All along the western coast, land revenue was paid from the sales of coconut crops between January and May. The coconut palm needed to be tended and manured for the first ten years after which with a minimum of maintenance it would continue to bear for another forty years. This left individual cultivators with the time to engage in petty trade or pursue a variety of occupations like toddy tapping, making coir, and manufacturing oil from copra involving their crop. When women were not employed on the fields, they would take coir to the market and barter it for rice, chillies and other necessities. Tiyyas, Mappilas and Vettuvans along the coast engaged in making coir ropes and mats for the market, and some banks were willing to lend money on the mortgage of coir yarn.[71] Tenants on improving leases, unlike their eastern counterparts, were not dependent on the profits from the sale of their crop alone, and would be hit less hard by the crash in prices in the thirties. The port towns of Cannanore, Tellicherry and Badagara handled both the exports of coconut as well as the vital imports of paddy which fed the region. Mappilas – merchants, petty traders and moneylenders – clustered along the coast and constituted a significant proportion of the population of these towns.[72] Badagara exported most of the coconut and copra crop and this trade was the monopoly of the Mappilas.

The profits from coconut followed a trajectory similar to that from pepper, rising to a peak in the mid twenties and collapsing by the middle of the next decade. Here again, small cultivators producing for the market from their homesteads were unable to face the competition from plantations in south-east Asia and, nearer home, Ceylon.[73] The problem was aggravated by a tenancy act which was initially beneficial, providing security of tenure for cultivators by requiring the payment of compensation for improvements on eviction. However, cultivators increasingly resorted to overplantation on their plots in the hope of pricing their holdings beyond the payment of compensation. This

[70] *RDIMP*, 1934-35, 31; 1935-36, 38; *RSTMP*, 1929-30, 1935-36. An indication of how sensitive prices in Malabar were to events in Europe is the fact that on the very next day after Italy declared war on Abyssinia, the price of pepper fell in the Calicut and Tellicherry markets. *Mathrubhumi*, 9 October 1935.

[71] D. Narayana Rao, *Report on the Survey of Cottage Industries in the Madras Presidency* (Madras, 1929), 133-6.

[72] In 1921, the percentage of Mappilas in the population was forty-two in Cannanore, thirty-eight in Tellicherry and fifty in Badagara. *Census of India 1921, XIII, Madras*, Table 4 and 5.

[73] P.J. Thomas and N. Sundararama Sastry, *Commodity prices in south India* (Madras, 1940), 18.

led to poorer quality of the crop as well as an occasionally disastrous glut in the market.

The first two decades of the twentieth century saw a boom in coconut cultivation as Malabar copra became the leader in the world market because of its higher oil content. The prices for coconut reached their peak in 1928 with a thousand coconuts selling for Rs. 49-2-10. By 1931, the rate was well below the average price over the previous decades, having fallen to Rs. 27 for a thousand nuts.[74] In 1930, Chirakkal, Kottayam and Kurumbranad had 20 per cent, 26 per cent and 42 per cent respectively of their cultivated area devoted to growing coconut.[75] Lands were converted from paddy cultivation to the growing of coconut, and many leases on wetland were beginning to include the stipulation that they should be converted to coconut gardens.[76] A definite geographical profile was emerging in north Malabar, and one respondent to the Tenancy Committee of 1927 described the region as a 'land of *parambas* [gardens]'. The ambition of every aspiring cultivator was to build a house in a garden plot of half to one acre in area and plant coconut and areca palms.[77] As plots decreased in size, there was a fall in productivity on account of overcrowding.

Before 1914, coconut oil was exported mainly to Germany, France, Holland and Austria-Hungary both for the manufacture of soap and margarine as well as for industrial uses. Home demand was as great as foreign demand, and Indian buyers were prepared to buy as much; figures for coastwise trade to Bombay and Karachi sometimes exceeded exports to Europe. Therefore a cessation of international demand would be less unsettling for the economy than in the case of pepper, most of which was exported to the European market. The increase of Indian import tariffs during the war opened up a line to the oil mills in Bombay and Karachi which drew the surplus of copra from Malabar.[78] It was this lifeline which would prove to be of great importance when, by a combination of circumstances in the mid twenties, the demand for coconut oil from Malabar declined. In 1918, the export of coconut oil from Malabar to Europe touched 4 million gallons. By 1937 oil exports had dwindled to almost nothing, while those of copra had virtually ceased as early as 1930.[79] The rise of large-scale plantations in the Dutch East Indies, the Philippines and Ceylon meant that they could export at far more competitive prices, and Kerala became the dumping ground for coconuts from Ceylon, taking 35-40 per cent of her exports

[74] *Revenue Department G.O.493 dated 4 March 1931* (KS).
[75] *Revenue R.Dis.12A/1930 dated 5 March 1930* (KRA), 58 and Appendix 6.
[76] Written evidence of M. Anantan Nayar, Dy. Collector (retd.) and oral evidence of Paloran Koran, *MTCR, 1927-28*, II, 185, 243; written evidence of M. Giriappa, Dy. Registrar of Cooperative Societies, *MPBEC, 1930-31*, III, 844. By 1930, the value of land growing coconuts along the coast had risen to well over 300 per cent of that of wetlands.
[77] Written evidence of E.G. Nair, High Court *vakil*, Tellicherry, *MTCR, 1927-28*, II, 151.
[78] *RSTMP*, 1914-15, 18; *RSTMP*, 1917-18, 16.
[79] *RDIMP*, 1936-7, 35; Thomas and Sastry, *Commodity prices in south India*, 16-18.

between 1930 to 1935.[80] By the mid thirties a combination of cultivation on overcrowded gardens, competition from the plantations of east Asia and the decline of exports to Europe had seriously hit the small cultivators.

The Compensation for Tenant's Improvements Act, 1900

Tenancy legislation was partly responsible for the rise of the small cultivator sensitive to the market. A rise in agricultural prices in the late nineteenth century had led to an increase in evictions of tenants.[81] Even though prosperous tenants had enough money to renew their leases, landlords did not wish to entrench a class of tenants at a time when there were more profits to be derived from soliciting higher payments of rent. The continuing unrest among the Mappila cultivators in south Malabar, made the government aware of the fact that evictions needed to be curtailed. This view was stated with great force in the tenancy report of the Collector, William Logan, who argued that the roots of unrest lay in the fact that cultivators did not have security of occupation.[82] In 1887, an act was passed, giving tenants the right to compensation on eviction. Instead of checking evictions, it resulted in the prevalence of the *melcharth*, or overlease, whereby the person receiving the overlease agreed to bear the costs of evicting the incumbent tenant and pay the landlord an enchanced rent. There was consternation about the fact that the *kanajanma maryada*, the customary relations between landlords and tenants, were being eroded and *janmis* were acting in 'utter disregard of the moral, unwritten law'.[83]

The Compensation for Tenant's Improvements Act of 1900 sought to plug this loophole and was comprehensive in its scope. It included not only those who were lessees or mortgagees of land but also those who, without the permission of the landowner, had brought land under cultivation 'with the bonafide intention of attorning and paying the customary rent to the person entitled to cultivate or let wasteland'. In order to entitle the tenant to compensation it was not necessary that the improvements had to have been done by the tenant.[84] It was deemed sufficient that, at the time of eviction, improvements

[80] Thomas and Sastry, *Commodity prices in south India*, 15; *Mathrubhumi*, 11 January 1936.
[81] *MLTR, 1881*, I, lxxv.
[82] *MLTR, 1881*, I, lxxviiii. For the influence of Mappila unrest on tenancy legislation, see Panikkar, *Against lord and state*, ch. 3.
[83] Explanatory note by V. Krishna Menon, *MTCR, 1927-28*, I, 95.
[84] The tenant on an improvement lease, the *kuzhikanam*, was expected to effect improvements of three kinds: *kuzhikkur* – on the usufruct, including the planting of coconut, areca and jack trees, pepper vines; *chamayam* – the erection of buildings; *vettuchamayam* – the improvement of the soil. *MLTR, 1881*, I, xliv; *Legislative Dept. G.O.89 dated 20 April 1886* (TNA).

had been made, even if by a previous occupant. Court decisions took cognisance of the increasing tendency towards the cultivation of cash crops and decreed that even the conversion of paddy land to the growing of coconut would be deemed to be an 'improvement'.[85]

Apart from an increase in litigation (by 1910, Malabar had become the most litigious district in the Presidency) the Act created new opportunities for the small cultivator on the improving lease; the majority of them gained *de facto* permanency of occupation.[86] Their lessors found the rates of compensation for improvements too high at a time of soaring prices for cash crops. Even the larger landlords found their vast holdings a liability as any attempt at evicting tenants usually involved phenomenal payments. A respondent to the Malabar Tenancy Committee of 1927 stated that the rajas of Kadathunad and Chirakkal were unable in many cases to pay off the value of improvements and the latter had had to borrow Rs. 75,000 to settle claims.[87] It has been argued that the actions of the state in the nineteenth century which entrenched 'resident cultivators' meant that 'large accumulations of capital' found it difficult to gain access and control over agricultural production. Since 'small-holding farmers' came to control production, 'the agrarian base remained insensitive to market changes'.[88] However, in Malabar, it was these very 'small-holding farmers' who responded with alacrity to the needs of the market, and as we have argued with grievous consequences for themselves.

The MCTI Act provided a fillip to the aspirations of small cultivators who now saw their salvation in the growing of pepper or coconut. By the first decade of the twentieth century it had become the practice for agricultural labourers as well as new tenants to request plots for the cultivation of cash crops as a safety net against the occasional failure of paddy crops.[89] In the inter-war years there was a tenfold increase in occupied garden land with a sudden spurt in the twenties when the prices of cash crops peaked.[90] The flip side of the boom was that fluctuations in prices on the world market and the inexperience of new cultivators in dealing with local cartels of merchants meant that many fell by the wayside. By 1927, revenue officials had begun to notice the existence of 'thousands' of impecunious small landowners who owned one to two acres and were deeply in debt and in arrears with their revenue payments.[91] Apart from the strengthening of the small cultivator, the major consequence of the passing

[85] *Malabar Compensation for Tenants' Improvements Act, 1900 (Madras Act I of 1900) and commentary*, (Madras, 1933), 24–33.
[86] Innes, *Malabar Gazetteer*, 385.
[87] Oral evidence of E.G. Nair, High Court *vakil*, Tellicherry. *MTCR, 1927-28*, II, 180–81.
[88] Washbrook, 'Law, state and agrarian society', 677–9.
[89] Letter from A.R. Mac Ewen, Special Settlement Officer, 25 March 1927, *Revenue Dept. G.O. 1609 dated 19 August 1927* (IOL); ARDMP, 1900-02, 3–4.
[90] *Revenue R.Dis.3431/36 dated 2 April 1936* (KRA).
[91] Minute of dissent by H.R. Pate, *MTCR, 1927-28*, I, 91.

of the MCTI Act of 1900 was overplantation on plots, as tenants tried to increase the value of the plot beyond what the landlord could afford to pay as compensation. Customary strictures on the improving lease stating that a tenant should plant palms not less than twelve yards from each other were quickly jettisoned. Poor quality coconuts, the competition from plantations in Ceylon, and the fall in prices from 1930 undermined the relative independence of the small cultivator.

The cultivation of paddy

The fluctuating profits from the production of pepper and coconut gave cultivators a degree of independence and money in their pockets. Yet it also increased their dependence on landlords for subsistence in moments of crisis as they moved away from cultivating paddy in search of quick profits. Large tharavadus were beginning to acquire a near monopoly over wetlands and stocks of grain. In the months of July and August when the torrential monsoons prevented agriculture or any occupation whatsoever, agricultural labourers and small cultivators were forced to exhaust their reserves of foodgrains and seed for the next crop. Some landlords lent grain at phenomenal rates of interest which had to be repaid in grain at the next harvest.[92] Landlords controlling scarce wet lands were able to wield considerable clout. Kurumathur Parameswaran Nambudiripad owned all the 93 acres of wetland in Aticheri and S. Mammi Supi owned over half the wetland in Kolanta.[93] Ultimately, cultivators were dependent on tharavadus which acted as a safety net in times of a crisis in the supply of food. It is not without significance that the granaries of the dominant tharavadus were the centres of authority in the countryside and it was here that Nayar landlords sat to administer justice in local cases.[94]

The amount of paddy produced by smaller cultivators was just sufficient for consumption, and the payment of revenue had to be done out of the profits of pepper and coconut crops. Large tharavadus could retain paddy for domestic consumption, paying the wages of agricultural labourers, and still have enough to stock their granaries.[95] A greater part of the cultivation was carried out with

---

[92] These loans, called *kadam vaypadharam*, were made in grain and had to be repaid at the rate of thirteen measures for every measure borrowed. Written evidence of V.V.G. Nayar, Member, Excise Board, MPBEC, 1930-31, II, 83.

[93] *Settlement Registers* of Aticheri *desam*, Malapattam *amsam* and Kolanta *desam*, Irikkur *amsam*. (Calicut, 1904). T.W. Shea Jr, 'Economic study of a Malabar village', *Economic Weekly*, 7 (1955), 997-1003.

[94] Testimony of Pokkan Gurikkal *et al. File on the oral history of Kasergode taluk* (A.K. Gopalan Centre, Trivandrum).

[95] *Revenue Dept. G.O.477 dated 22 December 1904* (IOL).

the help of hired labour – Nayars, Mappilas or Tiyyas – who were at liberty to change their service when they wished. Only the larger landlords and tharavadus owning extensive wetlands had families of labourers who worked primarily on these lands. Such labourers were shared between branches of tharavadus as part of kinship obligation and members of the tharavadu themselves worked on their relatives' plots.[96] Powerful tharavadus had patronal relations with their dependent labourers and cultivators premised, to a large extent, on their control over scarce resources of paddy and their ability to provide subsistence. An inchoate community of subsistence existed, comprised of two concentric circles. There was the wider and more fluctuating circle of small market-oriented cultivators who were dependent on the tharavadus only at a time of crisis of food. The more immediate and constant circle consisted of labourers and service castes who held wetlands from the tharavadus and whose dependence was less conjunctural.

The idea of a community of subsistence requires some elaboration. It was not premised on the idea of an all powerful, bountiful patron from whom largesse, in the form of paddy, flowed down to helpless dependents. The demand for subsistence, and the obligation to provide, arose only in exigent situations when there was dearth and tharavadus were then expected to sustain the community out of reserves held in trust.[97] In the final chapter, we shall explore this idea of paddy as community property in political practice. The argument is similar to that of James Scott's notion of a 'subsistence ethic', i.e. that landowners should provide, and that the State's exactions should not encroach upon, the 'minimum needs' of cultivators. Scott, however, reifies the idea as the bottom line of peasant expectations: a moral principle binding landlord and labourer. In north Malabar, cultivators responded more flexibly, and in the face of the inability and reluctance of households to provide subsistence during the food shortage of the forties, they bargained for access to land instead.[98] The understanding that the tharavadus would provide subsistence at a time of crisis was manifested in both charity as well as ritual assertions. Tharavadus made a show of paternalist benevolence at the new year festival of Vishu when they distributed grain, cloth and money to labourers and dependents. During the period of torrential monsoons in July and August, the

---

[96] A.C. Mayer, *Land and society in Malabar* (Bombay, 1952), 72-3.

[97] Paul Greenough employs several metaphors in elaborating the subsistence bond between landlords and labourers in Bengal: that of gods and humans, parents and children, and stresses the 'idiom of indulgence' in hierarchical relationships. It is not clear, however, that these ahistorical, often metaphysical (the Bengali conception of prosperity resembles 'poetry, alchemy, and ritual') constructs help us understand the nuances of an agrarian work ethic. Paul R. Greenough, *Prosperity and misery in modern Bengal: the famine of 1943-1944* (New York, 1982), 14-32, 38, 42.

[98] See James C. Scott, *The moral economy of the peasant: rebellion and subsistence in south east Asia* (New Haven, CT, 1976), 1-10.

poorer sections were forced to draw on stocks of tapioca for food and get grain loans from landlords. At such times, tharavadus would very often set up temporary structures called *tannir pandals* for distributing gruel to the starving.[99] Very often, poor families living in the vicinity of a tharavadu would solicit rice and oil regularly, performing occasional services in return.[100] Moreover, during the monsoons, there was a ritual assertion of community when Malayan tribals would visit a tharavadu and the houses of dependents within a region dressed as the god Siva in his manifestation as hunter. They were received with a bowl of charcoal water and a lamp; the idea was that evils like dearth and death would be drawn into the blackness of the charcoal. The same houses would later be visited by Vannans (washermen) who would 'wash away' the dearth by pouring water mixed with charcoal on the northern side, the direction associated with Lakshmi, the goddess of prosperity.[101]

Cultivation on the paddy fields was concentrated around April and May for the *kanni* crop and August and September for the *magaram* crop. Wooden ploughs were used and very often the plots were too small to allow the employment of animals. A tiller pulling the plough managed to break not more than three to four inches of the surface soil and the customary method was to plough and cross plough between two to fifty times to pulverise the soil. The buffaloes used in ploughing were usually undersized and the good cattle imported from Mysore and Coimbatore could be afforded only by the more prosperous cultivators.[102] Men ploughed the land, levelled, sowed, and manured it, while the women broke the clods into a fine dust and played the major part in transplanting and threshing. The back-breaking labour involved in producing a meagre paddy crop rendered the prospect of converting the land to growing cash crops very attractive.[103] The difficulty of getting labourers solely to work on wetlands was responsible for a peculiarity in the wetland tenure or *verumpattam* in north Malabar. It was normally held for a period of four to five years, and sometimes even up to thirty years. In south Malabar the pressure on wet-lands had made the *verumpattam* a yearly tenure.[104]

The smaller cultivators who continued to grow paddy on their small plots

[99] Aiyappan, *Iravas and culture change*, 34, 115.
[100] See Kalamandalam Krishnan Nair, *Ente jivitham: arangilum aniyarayilum (My life: between the greenroom and the stage)* (Trivandrum, 1991). In K. Damodaran's political play of the 1930s, Pattabakki (*Rent arrears*), he draws a rich picture of the networks of charity and loans in which the poor in the village survived. *Pattabakki* (Trivandrum, 1987).
[101] A.M.A. Ayrookuzhiel, *The sacred in popular Hinduism* (Madras, 1983), 116-17.
[102] Innes, *Malabar Gazetteer*, 212; *RDAMP*, 1927, 3.
[103] In the first three decades of the twentieth century, there was a 50 per cent increase in cultivated area in Kottayam. However, the number of working buffaloes decreased by 75 per cent between 1904-05 and 1940, while the number of ploughs decreased by 50 per cent. *Statistical atlas of Malabar for the year 1904-05* (Calicut, 1907); *Statistical atlas of Malabar for the decade ending 1940* (Calicut, 1941).
[104] Note of visit to Edakkat *amsam*, Chirakkal, 15 October 1927, *MTCR, 1927*, I, 142.

were dependent on the forests of landowning tharavadus for green leaves and dry sticks used as manure. Immediately after the harvest of the kanni crop, heaps of green manure were dotted over the field and left to decay after which further ploughing and levelling took place.[105] Sometimes, a tenant would take wetland on a lease which included the adjoining unoccupied dryland in the agreement. The latter would be used as a source of green manure and, at times, sublet to an agricultural labourer.[106] The collection of dry and green leaves and sticks was essential for the second crop. Access to the forests was based more on custom, since landlords had complete rights over all forests.

The cultivation of hill rice by shifting cultivation, *punam*, did not involve as much labour. The seeds were sown in April, after a clearing had been made with axe and billhook.[107] Beyond occasional weeding not much attention was paid to the crop until it was reaped in September. As in the case of pepper, plots were cleared in the forest for cultivation, and after every two or three years, land was allowed to lie fallow for a similar period. Another crop called *modan* was grown on the open hilltops in the less-forested villages of the east. Since the yield was minimal and just enough for subsistence no extra rent was charged on this crop. Though the *punam* crop had a higher yield, partly on account of its being grown on virgin, fertile soil, often there was only enough for consumption by the cultivators. Both *modan* and *punam* were classed as 'fugitive cultivation' by the Board of Revenue and no revenue was charged since the land was not continuously under cultivation for more than three years.[108] Though loans had to be taken from landlords for seeds and implements, both forms of hill cultivation allowed the small cultivator to exert some independence as they could avoid complete dependence on the dominant family in the region for subsistence.

In the long run, however, the landlord exercised control over wasteland and forest as shifting cultivators did not enjoy security of tenure under the law. Matters reached a head only in the latter years of the thirties. Landlords tried to lease their forests for the cultivation of lucrative plantation crops, even as a food crisis made the crop from shifting cultivation a necessity to supplement inadequate imports of paddy. The number of small cultivators growing paddy decreased steadily over the years and there was an increasing polarisation between the large landlords with a monopoly of wetland in their villages and shifting cultivators on the hills and in the forests. As cultivators responded to the market and grew crops for profit, they became ultimately dependent on the larger landlords and dominant tharavadus for subsistence. In Bengal, the other

---

[105] *Revenue DR8153/34 dated 24 January 1934* (KRA).
[106] *Revenue R.Dis.12A/1930 dated 5 March 1930* (KRA).
[107] *MLTR, 1881*, I, Report, xx.
[108] *Revenue Dept. G.O.883 dated 29 August 1900* (TNA); *Board of Revenue Proceedings no. 3 dated 5 January 1901* (IOL); *Revenue R.Dis.12A/1930 dated 5 March 1930* (KRA).

major rice-producing area, a similar picture emerges of a potentially disastrous shift from subsistence to cash crops in this century, though the search for profits occurred more in the context of agrarian overpopulation.[109]

North Malabar had never produced enough paddy for its subsistence and was dependent on imports, both from south Malabar, as well as from other parts of the Presidency. British observers, however, were sanguine about Malabar. The crystal clear backwaters, lush vegetation and swaying palms which were so much in contrast to the more arid areas of the Madras Presidency lulled them into overlooking the fragile balance of the economy. The 1911 Census waxed eloquent about Malabar: conditions, it said, 'may recall the great and jolly nation of the Do-as-you-likes who sat beneath the wild Flapdoodle tree'.[110]

From the nineteenth century, rice had been exported from Palghat and Ponnani in the south by land to the northern region and Coimbatore and by sea to the ports of Tellicherry and Cannanore. By 1918, the major supply of rice to the region came from south Malabar, south Kanara and particularly Burma through the port at Calicut. A large proportion of the trade at the northern ports consisted of the collection of rice by merchants, who then retailed the produce throughout the hinterland.[111] Two groups of importers and merchants dominated the trade in rice, one of which consisted of Cutchi Memons and Mappilas who had agents in every port in Burma. The other was an importer's syndicate of Hindu merchants who had agents only in the main port at Rangoon.[112] These merchants were quick to respond to fluctuations in prices and supply and were able, by functioning as a cartel, to commandeer finances to exploit a situation for profit. An instance of the flexibility of their response was the financing, in 1918, of the building of over 50 sailing ships ranging from 30 to 300 tons. This was in response to the crisis of a shortage of rice coupled with the decrease in the number of coasting steamers on account of the war.[113] Before the war there had been occasional exports of rice to Ceylon and Mauritius from south Malabar, particularly when there was a shortage of supplies from Bengal and Assam. After 1918, imports from Burma were becoming the norm and the traders on the coast relied for profits on the movement of grain within Malabar, exporting grain from areas of dearth to regions where prices were higher. Merchants and their agents purchased grain directly from the bigger producers

[109] Greenough notes that the net cropped area for foodgrains in Bengal remained static from 1891 to 1947, and between 1901 and 1947 the output of foodgrains decreased by 38 per cent. See Greenough, *Prosperity and misery*, 68-9, 81-3 and S. Bose, *Agrarian Bengal: economy, social structure and politics, 1919-49* (Cambridge, 1986), 52-3.

[110] *Census of India, 1911*, XII, Madras, part I, 8.

[111] The distribution of foodgrains and other articles of daily consumption was carried on by means of small boats called *pathamars* trading up and down the coast. *Revenue R.Dis.12A/ 1930 dated 5 March 1930* (KRA), 19.

[112] *Development Department G.O.356 dated 25 February 1945* (KS).

[113] *Revenue (Special) Department G.O.584 dated 22 October 1918* (KRA).

of the interior and grain came to be massed at the ports, the nexus of the trade network.

During the First World War, as in the rest of the Presidency, there were attempts to start licensing imports of rice from Rangoon, and place restrictions on the sale and import of rice from ports. The Collector of Malabar attempted to get the merchants operating at Calicut and the northern ports to sign a bond which would place all exportable stocks of rice at his disposal. Inevitably this broke down, because of the merchants' unwillingness both to reveal their holdings and allow themselves to be placed under any restraint. The merchants got their security deposits back; some of them lodged complaints that they should have got interest on their deposits as well![114] The Government's reluctance to interfere with private enterprise meant that the merchants exercised a near monopoly over distribution, which the increasing reliance on imports from Burma only served to augment.[115] The control exercised by the Cutchi and Mappila merchants in providing foodgrains was increased in 1942, when the Japanese laid siege to Rangoon, since the Hindu importers did not have access to the other ports. It was only with the introduction of rationing in 1944 that their stranglehold would be relaxed.

Credit and the structure of landholding

There were two distinct kinds of credit relations in the interior. Large tharavadus and well-off peasants provided credit to dependent labourers and cultivators working on wetlands. A second group consisting of pepper cultivators, shifting cultivators of hill rice, and those who grew subsistence crops as also coconut and pepper on their homesteads, relied to a lesser degree on tharavadus. They borrowed from Mappila traders, the landowners on whose land they grew their crops, as well as from each other. Some of the larger tharavadus, with pepper plantations, borrowed money at a customary rate of 10 per cent, called the *maryada palisa*, from the traders who sold their crops.[116] They lent to their tenants as well as the smaller tharavadus, and this could, at times, act as a method of extending their ownership of land. As we shall see later, in the context of the Depression, the larger tharavadus managed to extend their land holdings considerably by taking over the lands of their debtors. Tenants and sub-tenants borrowed cultivation expenses from landowners and these loans had to be repaid in paddy. Any arrears were collected with interest whenever

[114] *Public DR.D.Dis.5223/19 dated 22 September 1918* (KRA).
[115] See David Arnold, 'Looting, grain riots and government policy in south India, 1918', *Past and Present*, 84 (1979), 136-8.
[116] Oral evidence of M. Giriappa, Dy. Registrar of co-operative societies, MPBEC, II, 550, 553.

there was a good crop.[117] Collection of loan repayments in kind underwrote the authority of the tharavadus by strengthening their role as the repositories of grain in a region deficient in paddy.

An informal system of credit prevailed among cultivators who exercised a relative degree of independence by producing for the market. They built up casual loan networks amongst themselves. These were called *kuris* and consisted of a certain number of people coming together, each contributing a certain sum of money. The total sum of money thus collected would go in turn to each individual over a period of time. The time period of a *kuri* could be between one to five years, and the total sums could be as high as Rs. 20,000. *Kuris* were a flexible form of saving and, in their simplest form, they were an informal method of investment to get a lump sum after a period of time. More often than not, such savings went towards purchasing a small plot of land and acquiring the status of a landholder and sometimes even the title of *janmi*. *Kuris* could not always function at the level of cooperation between cultivators. At times, landowning tharavadus held feasts called *Kuri kalyanams* to which all their tenants and cultivators were 'invited' on the payment of a fee.[118] Landowners with huge debts would sometimes put up their land as security and conduct a *kuri* to help clear the debt.[119]

Along the coast there were diverse sources of credit and money could be found for anything ranging from the setting up of a teashop to the financing of a consignment to Europe. There were several rungs on the ladder of the credit hierarchy. The Imperial Bank at Tellicherry and the branches of the Nedungadi Bank lent only to those who had 'property and credit', and their main customers were merchants and moneylenders who lent at a higher rate of interest the money they themselves had taken on loan. Cooperative credit banks and smaller banks allowed the pledging of ornaments and lent money on the strength of promissory notes and even on the security of mortgages. Petty trading was financed by cooperative banks, moneylenders and professionals in the towns with money to lend.[120]

In the distribution of landholdings while there may have been a polarisation between a dominant landlord and agricultural labourer, in the middle there were small landowners who were tenants and cultivators of the wetlands of other landowners, while holding usufructuary rights on a plot. An individual

[117] Written evidence of M.A. Kesavan, Registrar, Tellicherry, MPBEC, III, 952.
[118] There were instances, early this century, of landlords who had collected sums as high as Rs. 30,000 from their tenants. Note by C.A. Innes, *Revenue Dept. G.O.3021 (Confdl.) dated 26 September 1917* (IOL).
[119] Presidential address by T.M. Appu Nedungadi, Tellicherry tenants conference, May 1919. *Revenue Dept. G.O.2510 dated 3 November 1919* (TNA).
[120] Written evidence of V.V. Govindan Nayar, Member, Excise Licensing Board, MPBEC, II, 83; Oral evidence of V.K. Menon, President, The Malabar District Cooperative Federation Ltd., Calicut, MPBEC, IV, 530-1.

could be absentee landhold, cultivating landowner, tenant, intermediary as well as cultivator all rolled into one.[121] In most cases, landowning rights were held on the plot of land where a person lived (on which coconut palms, plantains, jack trees and a few pepper vines were grown for the market) and for their subsistence they would cultivate, as tenant or labourer, the lands of several landowners scattered over a very wide area.[122] Moreover, it is difficult to establish an absolute correspondence between the land tenure structure and the 'social–ritual status structure', as some analysts of political change in Malabar have done. R.J. Herring argues that a close coincidence of caste and class was 'an important explanation for the mobilisation of the rural poor by the left' in the thirties and forties.[123] However, this appears to be less true than the fact that a slogan such as 'land to the tiller' could attract cultivating landowners, tenants and labourers of all castes. This seems to be true right through from 1828, when the Collector observed that a 'higher casteman not infrequently cultivates as a hired man the land of another of inferior caste' to 1927, when the Tenancy committee found that *janmis* could be tenants of people 'occupying a low position socially and materially'.[124] Higher castes like the Nayars as well as lower ones like the Tiyyas could be, to different degrees, landowners, tenants and cultivators.

The author of the report on the second resettlement of Malabar in 1930, observed that distinctions between cultivating and non-cultivating and land-owner and tenant were misleading and not of much value – a person could be the *janmi* of a plot of wetland and a tenant of their garden and house.[125] However, there was a clear distinction between the *janmam* (landholding) right on a plot on land and the right of being called a *janmi*. Thomas Munro had observed, in 1820, that the title of *janmi* had 'a dignity beyond the possession of land', and that the 'price' of the 'empty' name of *janmi* was worth half the price at which the productiveness of his land was valued.[126] This continued to be true into the twentieth century and land was seldom sold outright by impecunious but proud landowners since 'parting with the full *janmam* title [was] considered dishonourable'. A system of complicated sub-tenures came into being whereby the *janmi* divested himself of rights in the soil while retaining the title of honour.[127]

---

[121] T.W. Shea Jr., 'The land tenure structure of Malabar and its influence upon capital formation in agriculture' (unpublished PhD dissertation, University of Pennsylvania 1959), 221-2.

[122] Note of a visit by the President and others to Mattanur *desam*, 14 October 1927. *MTCR, 1927,* II, 141.

[123] See Herring, *Land to the tiller,* 158.

[124] Letter to the Board of Revenue from J. Vaughan, Collector, 2 September 1822, *PP 1828, XXIV (125);* written statement of K.T. Kammaran Nambiyar, Koodali, *MTCR, 1927-28,* II, 299.

[125] *Revenue Dept. R.Dis.12A/1930 dated 5 March 1930* (KRA), 14.

[126] Quoted in *MLTR, 1881,* I, xiv.

[127] *Statistical atlas for the Malabar district for the decennium ending 1940-41,* 13.

Small cultivators possessing an acre or two, and tilling their homestead, were the norm in north Malabar.[128] When the first comprehensive settlement of Malabar was completed in 1904, it was found that over 75 per cent of the title holders paid a revenue assessment of Rs.10 or less, the figures for Chirakkal and Kottayam being 83 per cent and 84 per cent respectively.[129] House sites were not exempted from assessment and they accounted for the bulk of the titles paying Rs.10 or less, and it was in these minute plots that pepper and coconut were cultivated for the market. The frontiers of expansion of cultivation were set by the dominant landowning tharavadus like those of the Vengayil Nayanar, who held two *lakh* acres of land and the Kalliattu Nambiar who held over 36,000 acres in Kottayam.[130] However, this disparity was of not much consequence during a period of high prices for cash crops, and it was the small size of the holdings rather than the inequality in their distribution which was the major problem.

The Depression upset the balance that had been maintained between independent cultivators and dominant landowners at a time of land availability, high prices for cash crops and the possibility of employment on the coast. As more cultivators were forced to depend solely on the land and move away from cash crops towards subsistence, they were forced to encroach on to wastelands and the poorer margins controlled by dominant landowners. In 1904-05, 43.98 per cent and 33.52 per cent of the total arable land in Chirakkal and Kottayam respectively had been occupied. This shot up to 62.09 per cent and 63.43 per cent by 1940.[131] The population pressure per 1,000 acres of cultivated land, between 1911 and 1941, rose dramatically from 701 to 2,418 (244.9 per cent) in Chirakkal and from 1,441 to 2,422 (68 per cent) in Kottayam.[132] The polarisation between large landowners and the landless became starker, providing an edge to the rhetoric of rural politics in the late thirties.

Conclusion

The tharavadus were involved in a network of relationships with a welter of agrarian entities: shifting cultivators, tenant cultivators on homesteads, artisanal groups who held land in return for services, ritual performers who held rent free land from shrines and temples managed by tharavadus and untouchable castes

[128] D.Dis.9222/21. Collector to Secretary, Law (General), 23 January 1922. *Law (General) Dept. G.O.2732 dated 13 November 1923* (Kerala Secretariat Records) (henceforth KS).
[129] *Revenue Dept. G.O.477 dated 22 December 1904* (IOL), Appendix N.
[130] *MTCR, 1927*, Appendix II.
[131] *Statistical Atlases of the Malabar district*, 1904-05 and 1940-41.
[132] *SCRMP*, 1911, 8; *SCRMP*, 1941, 13.

who worked on the paddy fields. Dependence on the tharavadu ranged from the peripheral (cash and seed advances) as in the case of the shifting cultivators, to the absolute as in the case of the untouchable labourers. At the centre of these fluctuating relationships stood the *pathayapura* or the granary of the tharavadu representing the possibility of a still point in a fragile economy. The promise of sustenance was a resource, the existence of which was reiterated ritually in agricultural practice and religious ceremony during the boom years of the twenties. The enthusiastic response of cultivators to the market need not be seen as contradictory to the presence and continuation of patronal relations. It has been convincingly argued for nineteenth-century north India that the *jajmani* mode of relations between rural patrons and dependents was not subverted by the forces of the market. It was in fact strengthened in the conditions of population growth and price inflation that prevailed. More recently, Fuller has pressed for a more holistic understanding of the economy in which market exchange as well as patronal relations should be seen as 'major features of the economic system as a whole'.[133] In Malabar, patronal relations were the outcome of relations within an agrarian economy unable to provide food for itself. The crash in prices following the Depression, the decline of international demand, and a crisis in the supply of food were to not only undermine the self-reliance of the small cultivators but to call into question the ability and willingness of the tharavadus to provide subsistence. Landowners and cultivators came to be bound together in an uneasy community. However, there was another and more intangible emphasis on interdependence. This was rooted in a shared religious culture incorporating upper and lower castes, as well as landowning tharavadus and cultivators. However, here too there was a recognition of the differential access to, and control of, material resources between their constituents. The next chapter looks at how a religious culture centred on shrines provided the space for negotiation of the disparity in power between the components of rural community.

[133] S. Commander, 'The Jajmani system in north India: an examination of its logic and status across two centuries', *Modern Asian Studies*, 17, 2 (1983), 307-8 and C.J. Fuller, 'Misconceiving the grain heap: a critique of the concept of the Indian jajmani system' in M. Bloch and J.P. Parry eds., *Money and the morality of exchange* (Cambridge, 1989), 51.

2 Shrines and the community of worship, 1900–1910

In north Malabar, a fragile community of subsistence was sustained by the fact that the control of a tharavadu over agricultural resources was offset by its obligations to dependents. Moreover, such control was premised as much on the use of benevolence as of guile and violence. If the nature of the economy promoted dependence on tharavadus and enforced a community of subsistence, there was space for negotiation within a community of worship centred on shrines. It was a religious culture shared by both upper and lower castes but understood and appropriated differently. In this chapter, we shall consider the community of worshippers around local shrines in north Malabar. This was composed of dominant Nayar and Tiyya tharavadus and the other castes who lived around the shrine and worked on the lands of the tharavadus or performed specialised services for them.

It has been argued for the Madras Presidency that, following the colonial land settlement, local elites had little to do with the sustaining of community other than 'the application of credit, employment and revenue sanctions and of unchecked physical force'.[1] In Malabar, unlike the rest of the Madras Presidency, landowning tharavadus continued to play an important role in the management of temples and shrines. The *melkoyma*, or the right of kings and landlords to superintend religious endowments was not taken over by the government. Tharavadus played a complex role in the religious practices of the region. In their capacity as overseers of the wetlands which maintained shrines and temples, they supervised large stocks of paddy. Moreover, worshippers brought offerings of grain on the occasion of festivals, and consequently the tharavadu-shrine complex too, reiterated the community of subsistence. The tharavadu and shrine were also at the centre of a community of worship which emphasised *inter alia* the interdependence between castes.

A sense of community arose out of diverse religious practices; in the

[1] D.A. Washbrook, 'The development of caste organisation in south India', in C.J. Baker and D.A. Washbrook eds., *South India: political institutions and political change* (Delhi, 1975), 166. For a general overview of the Presidency see Burton Stein, 'The integration of the agrarian system of south India', in R.E. Frykenberg ed., *Land control and social structure in Indian history* (California, 1968), 201-3.

immediate physical sense of community it involved a definable body of worshippers at a certain shrine managed by a certain tharavadu. In another sense, tharavadus and cultivators, upper castes and low, shared an eclectic pantheon of worship. In the process of the expansion of tharavadus into the interior, their ancestors, local heroes and heroines, spirits, and brahminical deities began to rub shoulders in shrines. Within this community of worship there was also a recognition of the fact that its constituents were not equal either in terms of status or access to resources. This gave rise to distinct forms of religious practice premised on different notions of community. First, there were festivals centred on the tharavadu-shrine complex, which emphasised interdependence and obligations. Secondly, there were pilgrimages to shrines which emphasised the possibility of interaction as equals despite differences in caste status. In the third form of worship, there was a direct recognition of the skewed balance of the relations of power between tharavadu and cultivators. Lower caste victims of upper caste authority were deified in certain shrines and thus, the limits of authority were defined to an extent.

The current orthodoxy on south Indian religious festivals and worship at temples tends to see them both as a microcosm of social relations as well as the means by which such relations are reproduced over time.[2] Such explanations of ritual have origins in 'correspondence theory', with a lineage going back to Durkheim, which seeks to establish a direct correlation between symbolic representations of the social world and actual patterns of conduct.[3] Rules of caste hierarchy are elaborated, and enacted, at temple festivals which then help to keep the 'system', so to speak, functioning. Within temple rituals, specific functions are allocated to castes which ostensibly signify as well as reiterate their position in the hierarchy. The relation between the deity and worshippers parallels, and is the model for, the relation between higher and lower castes and, more generally, between superior and inferior.[4] Too little attention has been paid to Stein's judicious formulation that a temple is a 'complex and *transitory* outcome of an extraordinary range of relationships ... (emphasis added)'[5] An argument needs to be constructed which allows for dissonance and difference and assumes that individuals may be involved in several religious and social

[2] See for instance the works of Appadurai, *Worship and conflict*, 35-6; Dirks, *The hollow crown*; Appadurai and Breckenridge, 'The south Indian temple', 190. Appadurai provides a self-critique in a recent article, arguing against a 'holism that snares anthropologists in the image of the microcosm, the part that stands perfectly ... for the whole'. 'Is homo hierarchicus?', *American Ethnologist*, 13, 4 (1986), 745-61.
[3] For a critique of 'correspondence theory', see R.P. Werbner, 'Introduction', *Regional cults* (London, 1977).
[4] E.J. Miller, 'Caste and territory in Malabar', *American Anthropologist*, 56 (1954), 410-20. See also Dirks, *The hollow crown*, 47-8 and Ludden, *Peasant history in south India* (New Jersey, 1985), 65.
[5] Burton Stein, 'Introduction', in Stein ed., *South Indian temples: an analytical introduction* (Delhi, 1978), 3.

practices not all of which purvey the unitary idea of a hierarchical society. Some religious festivals may assert, at particular junctures, hierarchy and the interdependence of castes. Others may convey an altogether opposed conception of social relations. The assumption of the existence of options within any given 'system' of belief, in which a host of identities are asserted and transformed over time would make our understanding of social change more nuanced. Looking at a religious culture which is shared by lower and upper castes but understood, and appropriated, differently over time, would help in historicising the experience of culture.

Tharavadus and temples

When the Madras Endowments and Escheat Regulation relating to the control of charitable endowments and trusts (temples were regarded as trusts) was passed in 1817, it was not made applicable to Malabar. The Collector of Malabar maintained that temples in the region were more in the nature of 'private endowments' than sites of public worship. When the question was raised again in 1915, the then Collector, C.A. Innes, observed that, 'having regard to the usage of a hundred years ... Government cannot apply these Regulations'.[6] In the rest of the Presidency, temples came to be supervised by the judiciary, and subsequently the executive, rather than the king or local lord whose ritual authorities were undermined.[7]

The head of a dominant Nayar or Tiyya tharavadu, who was also, in many cases the head of the *desam*, or the smallest revenue paying division, possessed a complex of religious and secular powers. Rights of a seat of honour at the temple and the superintendence of its affairs were vested only in the village headman and the *karanavan*. The proprietary right of the whole of the revenue division (*desam*) and of representing political authority in the area formed the second set of rights.[8] The traditional investiture of these rights in a tharavadu cemented its local dominance, giving some *desams* the character of little kingdoms. Moreover, major Nayar tharavadus and their branches were connected to each other through a community of property and a community of pollution involving the common observance of death pollution rituals. Local authority was combined with links with powerful tharavadus in contiguous regions.

[6] *Revenue DR D191/R15 dated 16* February 1916 (KRA).
[7] Appadurai, *Worship and conflict*, 105, 162-3. There is a nice irony in the fact that when the Hindu Religious Endowment Board was established in 1926, and the executive assumed control, this was represented by the Government as a reversion to the ancient south Indian practice of state 'protection' of temples. See F. Presler, *Religion under bureaucracy: policy and administration for Hindu temples in south India* (Cambridge, 1987), 24-9.
[8] Logan, *Malabar manual*, II, Appendix XIII, clxviii.

There was thus, a constellation of tharavadus possessing religious and secular powers over a wide area. Some like the Ayillyath in Chirakkal were so powerful that when a member died, the whole region observed pollution rituals.[9] It was not necessary that tharavadus should have possessed, over generations, the *uraima*, or the right to administer the affairs of local shrines and temples. At times they founded temples and appointed themselves as managers. In other cases, the actual possession of a temple or a shrine and its properties over a period of twelve years was considered enough for a possessory title to the *uraima*.[10] Tharavadus without access to governmental power, or a place in the revenue bureaucracy, could extend their local influence by assuming the rights of overlordship and maintenance over a local shrine or temple.

Control over a temple did not only mean the exercise of influence over an imagined or actual community of worshippers. It also meant an access to the stocks of grain a temple commanded, thus underwriting the authority of a tharavadu. The Koothali Nayar, one of the big landowners of Kurumbranad, had the right of overlordship over four temples and the tenants of the paddy lands held from these temples paid their rent in paddy. At one of the temples, the annual demand was 32,000 measures of grain and the proceeds went towards maintaining temple officiants – the priest, drummer and ritual dancer among others.[11] Rents on temple lands were always paid in grain and even during the food shortage of the forties, rents continued to be collected in kind. The settlement register for Karivellur in 1904 gives the details of lands held by twelve temples and eleven shrines. Both service and ritual castes were given *janmam* rights on wet or garden lands and rent was collected in kind.[12] Of course, the dues paid to the temple were no different from the rents collected by the landlord on other lands; they had to be collected with the use of force at times. An enquiry at the end of the nineteenth century into the special dues charged on lands held by temples observed that tenants, in former times, had paid 'out of respect for the Diety [*sic*]', but now only the 'fear of the *janmi*' could make them fulfil their obligations.[13] There were a whole range of special dues collected by landlords for the maintenance of the temples and shrines and, notionally, the ownership of temple lands was vested in the deity. Customarily, the temple would 'send men' to watch over the fields during the harvest,

[9] C.H. Kunhappa, *Smaranakal matram* (*Memoirs*) (Calicut, 1981), 3.
[10] Moore, *Malabar law and custom*, 276-7.
[11] *Revenue R.Dis. 7034/39 dated 23 January 1941* (KRA); Report of the special duty *tehsildar*, 15 August 1939.
[12] The list includes nine oil pressers (Vaniyans), ten washermen (Vannan/Mannan), two weavers (Chaliyan), eight shrine priests and oracles (Komaram/Velichapad), four astrologers (Kanisans), two barbers for castes below Nayars (Kavutiyan) and two traditional teachers (Panikkar/Vadhyar). *Settlement Register for Karivellur amsam*, Chirakkal taluk (Calicut, 1904).
[13] Report on the *pattonnu* assessment from the *tahsildar*, Chirakkal taluk, *Revenue R.Dis.126-R dated 22 May 1894* (KRA).

receiving a certain sum from the tenants for this service.

Though most of the shrines and temples were managed by Nayar tharavadus, in Chirakkal there were a certain number of temples under the control of the small yet powerful Nambudiri community.[14] Institutions like the Tali temple at Taliparamba and the Perul Siva temple in Eramam were sustained by lands set aside for their maintenance and the extravagances of the annual ceremonies. A network of minor temples in the immediate vicinage held lands from which an annual rent was paid to the major temple.[15] Worship and religious ceremonies at these temples were conducted solely by Nambudiris and even the higher caste Nayars were given only restricted access within the temple and not allowed to enter the inner courtyard surrounding the *sanctum sanctorum*. Within north Malabar, the higher groups of Nayars were broadly divided into the *Purathu charna* Nayars – the 'martial' clans, and the *Agathu charna* Nayars – the clerks, domestics, and revenue officers.[16] Those Nayars who were permitted inside were prohibited from ringing the bells hanging from the ceiling as this was a privilege allowed only to Nambudiris.[17]

A large majority of the temples, however, were those owned by individual tharavadus and managed by their heads (*karanavanmar*). They were private temples in the sense that only members of the tharavadu worshipped there. Officials at these temples were usually senior members of the family, who had given themselves up to a religious life.[18] Annual ceremonies were held at other temples, which allowed entry to all castes. On such occasions alone, Brahmin priests officiated and used fish and toddy in the rituals; most of the temples being devoted to Siva or *shakti*, the use of alcohol and meat was common.

Shrines and shared worship

The basic distinction between temples (*kshetrams*) and shrines (*kavus*) was that only the Nayar landholders and Nambudiri Brahmins were allowed to pray at

---

[14] It has been argued that the Nambudiris in their migration from the north some time in the early centuries AD (the date remains in dispute) settled in areas where wetland cultivation could be practised. See K. Veluthat, *Brahmin settlements in Kerala* (Calicut, 1978). Chirakkal was the main rice-producing area in north Malabar, which could explain the large number of Nambudiris in the region.

[15] *Revenue R.Dis.126-R dated 22 May 1894* (KRA); *Public DR D918/Pub. dated 24 June 1903* (KRA). The Perul Siva temple had nine items of land set aside for temple expenses alone which had an annual yield of 2,500 *seers*.

[16] See Fawcett, *The Nayars of Malabar*, 188-9.

[17] Vishnu Bharateeyan, *Adimakal engane udamakalayi* (*How the slaves became masters*) (Trivandrum, 1980), 25.

[18] Kunhappa, *Smaranakal matram*, 41. Kunhappa's grandfather acted as priest at the family shrine and devoted himself to the study of the *Vedanta*, hunting and breeding dogs.

the former. *Kavus* were of various kinds, but generally they were the focus of worship of a community of lower and upper castes within a region defined by the sphere of overlordship (*melkoyma*) of the dominant family or families managing the shrine. Shrines were the characteristic site of worship and in 1881, of the 240 religious institutions belonging to superior castes, only forty-five were to be found in north Malabar.[19]

Kavu literally means a grove of trees, and many tharavadus had a few stone idols situated in a wooded corner of their backyards, where snake deities and other nature spirits were worshipped. At times, a *kavu* consisted of a stone idol under the vast, leafy, expanse of a *banyan (ficus indicus)* or *pipal (ficus religiosa)* tree beside the road. The more formalised *kavus* were built along the lines of temples, and the structure which housed the deity had a circumambulatory path running around it. The whole complex could be surrounded by four walls (*chuttambalam*), on the outside of which were rows of lamps which were lit during festivals. Even in such formal structures, there were holes in the roof just above the image, to indicate that originally, the deity was exposed to the elements.[20] It was at the level of the shrines that a greater degree of integration of the complex of tharavadu, shrine and lower caste adherents was visible. The sphere of worship at shrines could correspond at one level with the tharavadu, its branches, and their labourers. Therefore, apart from the religious domain, the adherents of a shrine could reflect the pattern of shared irrigation networks, shared labour and so on. Neither loyalties nor devotion to a particular shrine stemmed from primordial allegiances, and could constantly shift. It was perhaps only the members of tharavadus and their tied labourers – Pulayas and Cherumas – who may have constituted a hard core of worshippers. In every Nayar tharavadu, some form of ancestor worship was practised, the most common being the setting apart of a room in the house as the abode of the ancestors. The symbol of the ancestor – a sword if the person had been of a martial temperament, and beads and slippers if they had been spiritually oriented – was worshipped in an outhouse and one of the male members of the family acted as a priest. Worship of these ancestors and the goddess of the tharavadu was linked, and together, they represented a check on morality within the tharavadu.[21] Sometimes, these family shrines were thrown open to the public if offerings to the ancestor were seen as effective in preventing or curing diseases. In times of epidemics (smallpox continued to be prevalent in

[19] *MLTR, 1881-82,* lix.
[20] See C. Achutha Menon, *Kali worship in Kerala* (Madras, 1943), 8-16 for a discussion on the historical development of the *kavu* from grove to established shrine.
[21] K.R. Pisharoti, 'Notes on ancestor worship current in Kerala', *Man*, 60 (1923), 99-102; E.K. Gough, 'Cults of the dead among the Nayars', *Journal of American Folklore*, 71 (1958), 447-52. Gough makes an interesting comparison with the princely state of Cochin to the south where compact village settlement led to ancestor worship within a household being linked to the goddess, impinging on a wider sphere of morality.

Malabar as late as the forties), the shrine of the Nayar ancestor and therefore the tharavadu itself became a focus of the community.[22] Such shrines came to be seen over time as being shared in common between those residing in the vicinity (*kavuvattam*) and daily expenses – rice, coconuts, oil – were met by those living around it.

Some Nayar tharavadus set up a revered ancestor in a local shrine merging the family cult with a local cult. The reverse could happen when local heroes and heroines, usually victims of perceived injustice at the hands of members of the tharavadu, were deified and worshipped along with the ancestors.[23] Thus, even as Nayar tharavadus attempted to increase their sphere of authority by transposing their ancestors in local shrines, they themselves had to constantly attest their legitimacy by 'atoning' for excesses committed. Deceased ancestors, local heroes and heroines, gods of the Vedic pantheon, and nature gods all rubbed shoulders in a seamless fabric of worship. Membership in a community of worship defined a collectivity to some extent but the dissonances were evident. The punishment or killing of lower castes clearly indicated that tharavadus possessed authority, and would use it. That atonement was necessary defined, to some extent, the limits of an exercise of authority. For instance, at the beginning of this century, when the head of the Manakampat family put a Pulaya youth to death, suspecting him of practising sorcery, he had to be deified and worshipped alongside the ancestors of the Nayar tharavadu.[24]

The expansion of tharavadus into the forests, incorporating tribal groups into production for the market, created an interface between two belief systems. Very often, the deity at a family temple (Siva, Vishnu or Bhagavathi) was merged with a local deity. At Pandicode, in a temple managed by the Koothali tharavadu, the local goddess of the mountains, Payyormala paradevata, had become the family deity and was worshipped alongside Siva.[25] Questions of cognition are difficult to resolve but, it is possible that over a period of time these two entities might have merged and Siva would have become as much a folk deity as the Payyormala devata a goddess of the Nayars. This merger of the gods of the upper caste landholders and those of the lower caste or tribal adherents was another facet of the presumed community around the temples or shrines. The word 'presumed' is important in this context as it was only on the occasion of worship, festivals, or dearth which entailed dependence on the temple granary that a sense of community may have been summoned up. In

---

[22] Achutha Menon, *Kali worship in Kerala*, 82.

[23] V.K.R. Menon, 'Ancestor worship among the Nayars', *Man*, 25 (1920), 42-3; Gough, 'Cults of the dead', 467; M. Unni Nair, *My Malabar* (Bombay, 1952).

[24] Unni Nair, *My Malabar*. Kathleen Gough writes of a prominent Nayar household in Kottayam which had shrines for six to eight 'alien ghosts' in its compound. Gough, 'Cults of the dead', 467.

[25] *Revenue R.Dis.7034/39 dated 23 January 1941* (KRA).

Mattanur, Nayars took offerings to the annual *nercha* (festival) at the local mosque but this was a more fragile link renewed only once a year.[26]

Thurston records a striking instance of the melange of beliefs created between castes and religious communities. He writes of the houses of a large number of Tiyyas in Malabar, where regular offerings were made to a person called Kunnath Nayar and his Mappila friend Kunhi Rayan. The former was believed to have control over all the snakes in the land. Near Mannarghat, Mappila devotees collected alms for a snake mosque.[27] If lower castes were beginning to worship higher deities, upper castes had to acknowledge lower deities. In Gyan Prakash's study of relations between *kamias* (bonded labour) and *maliks* (landlords) in south Bihar, he shows how the landlords by subordinating the spirit cults of their bonded labour to 'Hindu beliefs', reproduced the caste hierarchy.[28] In Malabar, as we have seen, there is a two-way process and landlords are as much under the sway of lower caste spirits and gods. A community of worship was sustained by this tension between integration and the possibility of deities retaining their separate identities for different groups of worshippers. For example, at a shrine in Kunuthur, the characters of the Mahabharata have been transformed by the local religious idiom. Kunti and Panchali (Draupadi) are portrayed as mother and daughter (not as mother-in-law and daughter-in-law). Together with the five Pandavas, they are worshipped as gods in the form of leopards.[29] Historians and anthropologists, working within different theoretical paradigms argue that lower caste culture consists of replication and imitation of the dominant culture of the upper castes.[30] Looking at the process of the formation, expansion and intermingling of the shrines of Nayar ancestors, goddesses and local heroes and heroines, the social order appears to be far more dynamic.

Shrine festivals – interdependence and obligation

A study of the shrine festival at Pishari *kavu*, near the port town of Quilandy in Kurumbranad will help to illustrate the reiteration of caste identity as well

[26] E.J. Miller, 'An analysis of the Hindu caste system', 164.
[27] E. Thurston, *Omens and superstitions of southern India* (London, 1912), 128-9.
[28] See Gyan Prakash, 'Reproducing inequality: spirit cults and labour relations in colonial eastern India', *Modern Asian Studies*, 20, 2 (1986), 216-21.
[29] Chanthera, *Kaliyattam*, 47.
[30] Michael Moffatt argues for replication on the grounds of the permeating structure of purity and pollution inbuilt into an undifferentiated caste culture. Dirks, though more processual and willing to historicise the notion of culture, again stresses the cultural apathy or inefficacy of client castes who 'had minimal control over the articulation of their social order'. Moffatt, *An untouchable community*, 9; Dirks, *The hollow crown*, 269.

as a sense of community.[31] A Mussad (Nambudiri) performed worship in the shrine and castes below the Nayars were prohibited entry into the shrine. During festivals, washermen, tribals and oracles were an integral part of the ceremonies. Most of the ritual officiants and religious performers held rent free land from the shrine and the annual yield from the small plots provided a bare subsistence. The festival at Pishari *kavu* was held over seven days in the months of April and an account of the ceremonies on each of the seven days shows how different castes were associated at different stages with the festival.

First day – The Mussad (Nambudiri) swept the shrine and five Nambudiris bore the five products of the cow and sacred grass for use in worship at the shrine. The heads of the four trustee Nayar families presented the shrine flag to the shrine servant (*pisharodi*) who hoisted it on the eastern side.

Next three days – The image of the goddess (*bhagavathi*) was carried in procession round the *desam*.

Fifth day – A washerman (*vannan*), who held a hereditary landholding office with the shrine announced the procession of the *bhagavathi*. Accompanied by a tribal (*munnuttan*) carrying an umbrella, he led devotees to the shrine.

Sixth day – The headman of the fisherpeople (*mukkuvar*) arrived at the shrine together with the blacksmith and the goldsmith. The goldsmith 'repaired' the silver umbrella of the shrine which was then given to the headman along with half a sack of rice. Meanwhile, the blacksmith 'repaired' the shrine sword. In the afternoon, the headman of the Tiyyas arrived with two of his castemen carrying bunches of young coconuts. They led a procession followed by the blacksmith and the goldsmith carrying the shrine sword while the chief of the fisherpeople brought up the rear holding the shrine umbrella.

Seventh day – After the daily procession, an umbrella maker (*panan*), danced before the shrine carrying a small umbrella. In the afternoon, the oracles (*velichapad*) danced before the shrine cutting their foreheads with swords.

Nine Tiyyas bearing pots of milk and toddy ran around the shrine and received five measures of rice and a piece of the sacrificial goat. Then a procession of eight caparisoned elephants, preceded by a Nayar bearing a sword, set out with a priest seated on the leading elephant. As the procession left, a washerman performed a ritual dance at the main gate while a Munnuttan tribal performed at the eastern gate. When the procession returned, cocks were flung to the dancers who wrung the heads off and tossed them to the crowd.

The Tiyyas gave their pots of toddy to the shrine servants and collected rice for themselves from a pit which devotees had filled with their offerings. The principal ritual dancers flung rice towards the gathered crowd and then moved to the houses of the four Nayar trustees. Each tharavadu put out a measure of grain which was then carried to the shrine. At the shrine, the priest on the elephant and the sword in his hand both began to tremble and he was carried inside the shrine where sacred water was

[31] This account is taken from a description of the festival in 1901. Fawcett, *Nayars of Malabar*, 255-64.

poured on the sword. The chief dancer made an oracular announcement about the prospects for the future and the crowd departed.

After this, four goats and several cocks were sacrificed on behalf of the four Nayar tharavadus. The flesh of the sacrificed animals was cooked with rice and the priests recited prayers over it. The next day the Nambudiris performed worship thrice at the shrine.[32]

During the course of the festival, each caste performed the role traditionally associated with it: the blacksmith repaired the sword, the umbrella maker supplied umbrellas, the fisherpeople brought salt from the coast and the Tiyyas brought coconut and toddy. It is significant that service castes, those most intimately associated with tharavadus, were the ones who played a major role in the rituals. Perhaps, we can make a distinction between those for whom participation was an obligation – the service castes who actually played a part in the ritual – and those for whom it was a matter of personal devotion. And, religiosity need not have stemmed from, nor did it emphasise in a particular way, the devotees' position in a caste hierarchy. What was being emphasised was possibly the fact of a community of worship sustaining the shrine which was the centre of the community of subsistence along with the Nayar tharavadus. The four major Nayar tharavadus of the area donated rice to the shrine and the devotees received quantities of rice as offerings from the shrine. The processions took a definite route embracing the presumed sphere of religious authority of the Nayar families. It was quite common for shrines to be supported by donations of produce from worshippers, particularly in festivals coinciding with the harvest in April. At the main shrine in Taliparamba, the *puttari* (new rice) festival was held after each harvest and worshippers of all castes, as well as tenants of the shrine, brought offerings of grain and vegetables.[33] It is significant that prestations go both up and down the caste hierarchy and what seems to be emphasised is more a secular notion of contribution to a collective pool of scarce resources, i.e. grain.

Every shrine festival was thus a reiteration of the community of worship as well as of subsistence marked in the giving and receiving of paddy. Just as the roles performed by each of the castes was emphasised, so was the duty of the Nayar tharavadus and the temple to provide for the community of worshippers. It would be simplistic to argue that such festivals simply reiterated and reproduced caste hierarchy or caste identity. In the first chapter, we spoke of two concentric circles of dependence on tharavadus, an inner one of greater dependence, including the service castes and labourers, and an outer and more flexible one of cultivators. Here too, service castes formed the inner ring of worship and their caste identity was emphasised by their association at

[32] Fawcett, *Nayars of Malabar*, 255-64.
[33] Vishnu Bharateeyan, *Adimakal engane udamakalayi*, 79.

particular stages of the ritual. The washermen, ritual dancers, oracles and potters were completely dependent on the tharavadu shrine complex since they held land from the shrine and performed services primarily for it and the controlling families. It would be possible to argue, even in the case of the 'service castes', that their primary loyalty, as such, would have been towards the dominant tharavadus rather than towards their 'caste' people over a wider region.[34] As for the other castes, it was the more intangible aspect of worship which drew them to the festivals, and they were on the peripheries of the ritual rather than central to them. Besides, it is possible to argue that rituals at the festivals were both opaque as well as of little interest to most of the putative beneficiaries. This poses further problems for any analysis that reads off social hierarchy from enactments of ritual hierarchy.

The community around the shrines was premised on the interdependence of those living and worshipping there as well as the fact that in times of dearth, the stocks of the tharavadu and the shrine helped tide them over the crisis. Shrine festivals such as the one at Pishari *kavu* emphasised the obligation of the tharavadus to provide grain to their dependents. However, we cannot stop at a purely functional and materialist level of explanation. There were also the intangible elements of devotion, respect, loyalty and fear which kept the community together when the tharavadu was on the decline and, at times, even when the shrine had ceased to exist. In 1939, the temples belonging to the Koothali family were escheated along with their lands and other properties after the death of the last member of the family. Within a year, there were petitions from the local inhabitants to the Collector asking for the temple festivals to be renewed.[35]

Shrine festivals – community of equals?

While the festival at Pishari *kavu* may have emphasised dependence and ob-ligations, it was only one of the diverse religious practices that persons were involved in. People moved within various spheres of worship, the experience of each informing their participation in others. The pilgrimage to the shrine at Kottiyur provides an illustration of another kind of religious practice at shrines. Here the central theme was the temporary dissolution of differences between the participants and the transgression of the limits imposed on interaction between high and low castes.

[34] Miller argues this for all castes however. As we have seen in the first chapter, cultivators could have held land under several landlords. It would be difficult to argue that loyalty towards any one particular landlord or household would prevail. Miller, 'Village structure in north Kerala', 43.

[35] *Revenue R.Dis.7034/39 dated 23 January 1941* (KRA).

Situated in the Wynaad foothills, the Kottiyur shrine was kept closed throughout the year except for a brief period between the fifteenth of May and the eleventh of June. The shrine was managed by a few Nayar tharavadus, though the pilgrims who travelled there were of all castes. Between the twenty-first and the twenty-fourth of May, Tiyyas, a large minority among whom were toddy tappers, would bring traditional offerings of tender coconuts and pots of toddy. Pilgrims came from different regions in groups based on neighbourhoods, work communities and villages, led by men called *thandans*. On the way to the shrine it was customary to 'insult anyone they came across' and break and cause damage to property beside the pilgrimage route.[36] The pilgrims found their way into reports by the local police and magistrates who invariably described them as 'rural illiterates' from Chirakkal, Kottayam and Kurumbranad. Policing was, therefore, restricted to the fringes of the crowds. Only the pilgrims were allowed in the vicinity of the shrine, and the crowds doing the last lap of the trek from Manathana to Kottiyur were free of any surveillance. They followed an order of precedence initially; the Nayars would arrive first, followed by the Tiyyas and so on. Once the Nayars, Tiyyas and other castes reached the shrine, they abused one another, sang bawdy songs and occasionally came to blows. Worship was tempered with gaiety as the pots of toddy were diverted for secular consumption.[37]

Before the festival began, a Tiyya would perform worship at the shrine, only after which were Nayars and Nambudiris allowed to worship. The chief representative of the Nambudiris paid a certain amount of money as *dakshina* (offering) to the Tiyya priest and received charge of the temple from him. On the last day of the festival, a washerman, in the guise of the mountain god Muthappan, 'arrived' near Kottiyur and was received by a Nambudiri priest who offered him sandalwood paste.[38] Seemingly, the caste hierarchy was stood on its head as upper castes could worship only after receiving permission from a Tiyya. Similarly, a washerman, exalted on account of being possessed by a deity (significantly, a non-brahminical deity), was temporarily superior to a Brahmin. The specific context blurred questions of hierarchy and allowed for the adoption of roles which did not replicate everyday norms of behaviour. The Nambudiri brahmin offered *dakshina* to a Tiyya, reversing the kind of 'trans-action' usually seen as obtaining between 'higher' and 'lower' in which 'grosser material elements go up' from those of lower status and 'more refined symbolic elements go down' from those of higher status.[39] The Brahmin paid

[36] *Public DR1585/P.08 dated 17 October 1908* (KRA).

[37] Fawcett, *Nayars of Malabar*, 268; Report of the second class Magistrate, Kuthuparamba, 27 June 1908 and Superintendent of Police, Tellicherry, 14 June 1908. *Public DR1585/P.08 dated 17 October 1908* (KRA).

[38] Miller, 'An analysis of the Hindu caste system', 344–5.

[39] The *puja*, occasioning the transfer of superior substances downward from superiors is seen as a metaphor for social relations in Ludden, *Peasant history in south India*, 65; Dirks, *The*

money to the Tiyya for the intangible, symbolic benefit of his blessing, just as the washerman was anointed with sandalwood paste, so that the brahmin could share in a 'lower' caste's temporary divinity. All the other actions were seemingly contained within the parenthetical ceremonies in which the Tiyya handed over the temple to the Nambudiri and the washerman was received as a 'god' by another Nambudiri at the beginning and end of the festival. However, in both these instances, a reversal of roles was implied and they marked a continuity with the rest of the activities during the festival.

A similar festival was held in the month of April at the Kodungallur temple in the neighbouring state of Cochin. Nayars and lower castes from north Malabar made a pilgrimage to the temple and, once there, drank alcohol, sacrificed cocks and goats and sang lewd songs both about the goddess of the temple as well as hapless passersby. The culmination of the revelries was marked by the raiding of the *sanctum sanctorum* by washermen, otherwise denied entry in the temple, who then belaboured the idol of the goddess with sticks.[40] No overt distinctions of caste were maintained during the pilgrimage to Kottiyur, but even within this ephemeral sense of community created by religion, secular concerns could, at times, be prominent. In 1908, for the first time, the spirit of revelry and latent violence found an outlet against an external authority. On the twenty-second of May, when over 5,000 pilgrims had gathered at Manathana, they moved in a body to the office of the forester, a Christian named Lobo. They accused him of desecrating the shrine by being in the vicinity and also insisted that he was aiding private timber merchants to cut down the forest. Meanwhile, some members of the crowd broke into the office and set fire to some of the lists after 'mockingly calling out names as from a roll'.[41] Under cover of being pilgrims, the participants, or some of them, infringed both caste and legal norms transforming a seemingly 'ritual', repetitive event by investing it with unexpected conflict and contest. Profane and sacred, high and low, and superior and subordinate identities were subsumed within the space of these shrine festivals. A fragile sense of community was created, tempered by the tensions between the different caste

hollow crown, 47-8. In this they draw upon the work of Marriott and Inden, to argue that 'transactions', i.e. interactions between castes are characterised by the exchange of 'substances' from the 'superior' to the 'inferior'. See McKim Marriott and R.B. Inden, 'Towards an ethnosociology of south Asian caste systems', in K. David ed., *The new wind: changing identities in south Asia* (Hague, 1977). For a critique see S. Barnett, A. Ostor and L. Fruzzetti, 'Hierarchy purified: notes on Dumont and his critics', *Journal of Asian Studies*, 35, 4 (1976), 633-7.

[40] The degree of licence on such occasions was presumably extravagant, as contemporary observers like Fawcett, in 1901, maintained a prim silence about goings on. Fawcett, *Nayars of Malabar*, 268. A reformer's pamphlet of the twenties (?), describes scenes of seduction, bloody sacrifice and drunkenness with great enthusiasm. T.V. Das, *Kodungallur bharani (The Kondungallur festival)* (Calicut, nd).

[41] *Public DR 1585/P.08 dated 17 October 1908* (KRA). Only one file of the incident survives at the Kozhikode Regional Archives and it is not clear what the 'lists' contained.

groups which could surface in squabbles and fights during the festivals. What was important here was the fact that it was not so much a caste identity which was being asserted on these occasions but the possibility of concerted behaviour regardless of distinctions.

There was no presumed physical community of worship around these shrines, nor was there any clear ritual demarcation of territory. Both at Kottiyur and Kodungallur, the imagined terrain of worshippers theoretically embraced all of Malabar. In the crowds that surged to these festivals anonymity was the key feature and their joint participation as pilgrims was the unifying factor. At festivals associated with particular shrines in the countryside, there was less anonymity and the premise was of different castes working together. However, hierarchies persisted: between the Nayar *uralars* of the temple and the pilgrims, between the heads of pilgrimage groups from different regions and the pilgrims under them and between the pilgrim groups themselves. The variety of affiliations and resentments engendered by neighbourhood, locality and, not least, of caste, may have continued into the space of the ritual: hence, the riot of 1908. Thus, there was less a forgetting, or suspension, of differences in the space of the pilgrimage and more a pragmatic attempt to work out relations in spite of discord. Thus, as has recently been argued, it is community rather than Turner's *communitas* – a liminal space of equality – which can be seen as the hallmark of pilgrimage.[42] Within the pilgrimage social interactions can take place afresh within a new setting; both worship and licence binding together the participants.

Shrine festivals – the moral community?

There was another rung of shrines managed exclusively by Tiyya families, service castes, fisherpeople and untouchable castes like the Pulayas. Nayar landlords of the immediate locality were deemed to be members of the religious community, and though they never worshipped at these shrines, they had an important role to play in annual festivals. It was at shrines like these that the *teyyattam*, or the divine dance, was performed. The *teyyattam* was a performance which incorporated the telling of the story of a lower or upper caste victim of perceived injustice and the circumstances of their deification. Shrines grew up around these deified victims and they were never worshipped in

---

[42] V. Turner, *The ritual process: structure and anti-structure* (Harmondsworth, Middlesex, 1974), 119-54 and *Dramas, fields and metaphors: symbolic action in human society* (Ithaca, NY, 1974), 166-231. M. Sallnow, '*Communitas* reconsidered: the sociology of Andean pilgrimages', *Man* (ns) 16, 2 (1981), 163-82. See also P.S. Sangren, *History and magical power in a Chinese community* (California, 1987).

person, but incorporated either within local cults, existing *bhagavathi* shrines, or the worship of ancestors in Nayar tharavadus. Performances were always localised geographically and if the plot of land where a *teyyattam* was performed was sold, it was up to the new purchaser to continue holding the ceremony.[43] This level of shrines served as physical markers of an imagined area of community as well as reminders of the ever-present relations of power.

Performances of the *teyyattam* were held at shrines managed by Nayars, Tiyyas or castes lower to them. The incorporation of local heroes, the ancestors of the Nayar families, and the *bhagavathi*, in the sphere of worship defined a cosmology particular to every tharavadu–shrine complex. The distinctive form of worship at these shrines also emphasised the conviviality of the religious community. Toddy and meat were an essential part of the ceremonies and very often the performer himself was stoked up with alcohol. The essential spiritual ideal in all the ceremonies was not so much the transcendence of the world as enjoyment within it.

Before we move to a consideration of the two kinds of *teyyattam* festivals and particular performances, we must look at the performers themselves. Malayan tribals, many of whom practised shifting cultivation on the foothills of the western hills, and Vannans (washermen) were the two main groups who performed at the shrines.[44] Both these groups occupied a special place in the social structure. Malayans were not tied to any particular tharavadu, and even though they were sometimes dependent on landlords for money and seeds, they enjoyed a relative freedom from the direct authority which other labouring castes were subjected to. Vannans performed the role of implementing social sanctions on the community. Every Nayar family had to have the clothes of their menstruating women washed by the washerwoman (Vannathi), and it was only after she had collected and delivered the fresh clothes that the tharavadu was deemed to be free of pollution. A tharavadu, or a caste assembly which wished to impose sanctions on a family for errant behaviour, would withhold the services of the washerwoman to their house. This was called the *vannathimattu* and it was very effective in regulating and, at times controlling the behaviour of groups in the village, as no one would have anything to do with a house under the cloud of pollution. Both the groups performing the *teyyattam* occupied a position of relative power within the social structure, the Vannans in their role as whips of the community, and the Malayans on account of their being at the fringes of the authority exercised by dominant tharavadus.

A week before any performance, the priest (*komaram*) of the particular shrine visited every house within the presumed area of influence of the religious

[43] Joan Mencher, 'Possession, dance and religion in north Malabar, Kerala, India', *Collected papers of the VII congress of anthropology and ethnographic sciences*, Moscow (1964), 340.
[44] Thurston and Rangachari, *Castes and tribes of southern India*; Vannan: VII, 318-20; Malayan: IV, 436-9.

community. The procession was received at each house with drumming and showers of rice (probably an enactment of the thunder which augured heavy rains and a good crop). If an epidemic was raging, the *teyyattam* was performed to placate the goddess and the priest appeared as her representative to every tharavadu summoning them to prayer.[45] Whether in prosperity or dearth, health or sickness, the interdependence of tharavadu, shrines and worshippers was emphasised. Individual performances of the *teyyattam* could be held at any time of the year at a shrine or in the compound of a Nayar, Nambudiri or Tiyya house. Grand performances coinciding with shrine festivals tended to be concentrated in the period between December and March when there was a lull in agricultural activity prior to the harvest in April.[46] Some of the larger festivals were similar to the temple festivals at which the contributory and particular role of each caste was emphasised. These festivals could be of two kinds: those hosted once a year by powerful Nayar tharavadus and the others hosted once in a decade or every twenty-five years. The latter were usually held in areas where the Tiyyas were a numerically or economically powerful caste, but where, over time, the shrine had come under the sway of the locally powerful Nayar tharavadus.[47]

Local Nayar tharavadus were Janus faced in their religious attitudes. On the one hand, they contributed towards the cost of the temple festivals at which only the Nambudiris and they had the right to attend. On the other, they subsidised the festivals at shrines belonging to the lower castes and played a part in the rituals. At the yearly performance of a *teyyattam* held at Kottayam, the material needed for the ceremonies was supplied by the service castes around the shrine, and the tenant families. Tiyyas provided coconuts and toddy; the Vaniyans (oilpressers) oil for the lamps; Chaliyans (weavers) wove fine cloth for the goddess; and the blacksmith sharpened the swords. Before the festival began, the Nayar family priest, two Nayars from the Vaniyan subcaste, the Tiyya priests of the shrine and the head of the Nayar tharavadu offered prayers. During the festival six Malayans, four Munnuttan tribals and three Vannans (distinguished performers bearing the title *peruvannan*) performed the *teyyattam*.[48] The Vannans came from three different *desams*: an indication of the fact that the community of worship was not restricted within a single village, and the shrine could have a wide network of adherents. Here

[45] C.M.S. Chanthera, *Kaliyattam*, 41.
[46] *Census of India, 1961*, VII, vii b (ii) – Report on fairs and festivals in Kerala. Of a total of 304 festivals held annually at temples and shrines in north Malabar, 75 per cent were held between December and April. The *teyyattam* was performed at 49 per cent of these festivals. Crowds of a *lakh* in number attended the grand festivals held every twelve years at the Muchilot shrines in Karivellur and Eramam.
[47] K.K.N. Kurup, *Aryan and Dravidian elements in Malabar folklore: a case study of Ramavilliam kazhakam* (Trivandrum, 1979), 2-3.
[48] Miller, 'An analysis of the Hindu caste system', 123-4.

again, there was an emphasis on the specific roles played by castes in the rituals of the shrine. What is significant is the fact that the Nayar received offerings from the Tiyya priest who was lower in the 'caste' hierarchy. At a temple, the Nayar would have accepted offerings only from a Nambudiri priest. In both instances, however, it was in the specific context of the ritual that the secular status and authority of the Nayar was subordinated to the ritual authority of the Nambudiri or Tiyya priest. Status was not unequivocal and was in the same state of flux that the pantheon of deities was.

The performance of the *teyyattam* discussed here was situated within the context of a festival in which its enactment was an adjunct to the reassertion of community and interdependence. What about individual performances of the *teyyattam* held at local shrines? The cosmology of worship had the nature of a palimpsest, with earlier imprints blurred, but still visible. The predominant characteristic was that of community: a community of past beliefs, of gods and humans, of ancestors and the present generation and during the space of the performance, of upper and lower castes. We can broadly distinguish between four categories of gods in the *teyyattam*. The first category was predominantly female; the powerful, bloodthirsty aspects of *shakti* were personified in the *bhagavathi* and her manifestation as Raktachamundi and Kurathi. The second category included a small number of male divinities who were aspects of Siva – Pottan, Gulikan and Bhairavan. Here too, a considerable degree of mixture was evident with ghosts, spirits and heroes performed as manifestations of Siva. A third was the minuscule category of the manifestations of Vishnu, though Vishnumurti or Vishnu in his incarnation as Narasimha (half man and half lion), had acquired general acceptance as a village deity. The fourth category of local heroes and heroines was absorbed into the earlier categories and they were always performed as aspects of one of the main deities. Earlier practices continued within the space of the *teyyattam*, as for example both tree and snake worship. Shrines were usually situated in groves of trees and the performances of the *teyyattam* were done beneath *banyan* or *peepul* trees. Serpent worship, which continued among Nayar families well into the twentieth century, was evidenced in the worship of serpent *teyyams*.[49]

During a performance of the *teyyattam*, the performer (*kolam*) was possessed by the spirit of the local hero or heroine who had been deified as a form of the *bhagavathi* or Siva. While the *kolam* was waiting to be possessed by the deity, the *thottam* was sung relating the circumstances of the life and death of the deified victims. The word *thottam* is derived from the verb *thonnuka* meaning to create.[50] At times, the performer himself was called the *thottam*, no distinction being made between the creator and his creation. During the space

---

[49] Raghavan Payyanadu, *Teyyavum thottampattum (The Teyyam and its literature)* (Kottayam, 1979), 39, 44-5.

[50] H. Gundert, *Malayalam nighandu (Malayalam dictionary)* (Kottayam, 1962 edn), 474-5.

of the performance, the hero or heroine was brought alive in the body of the *kolam*, who was at the same time possessed by the deity. The *kolam* therefore, was at the same time human as well as divine, the creator as well as the creation, lower caste as well as being god. When he was in a state of possession, he castigated the upper caste members of the audience for acts of commission and omission towards their servants or labourers. In a sense the performance was a lengthy rebuke; the retelling of the story of the unjust killing of a lower caste was a criticism of the power exercised by upper castes in general. During the period of the performance, Nambudiri and Nayar landlords would seek the advice of the performer as it was believed that his prophecies as well as his curses came true.[51]

An important strand in the *teyyattam* is that of a notion of a moral community – of a recognition of mutual spaces and the resentment of the arbitrary exercise of power. The dominant tharavadus, their labourers or dependent castes, and the amorphous community of worshippers were expected not to transgress certain limits. It is significant that *thottams* usually began with the performer saying, 'I do not know the name of the village [where the incident happened] that I could inform or enlighten you. I do not know the name of the person.'[52] This stanza, taken from the *thottam* of Vishnumurti (an incarnation of Vishnu) into which is woven the story of a Tiyya youth murdered by a Nayar landlord, is suggestive. It is as if there is an incipient understanding of the fact that regardless of the person or place, a Tiyya or Pulaya would have experienced the oppression of a landlord. Moreover, by not specifying persons or places, the story carried by the wandering performer began to assume the character of a type, allowing for a filling in of detail in different localities. A collective memory of incidents was created, scattered in time and place but flattened into the moment of the performance.

A study of the more important *teyyams* would give us an idea of the components of this moral community.[53] Kathivanur Viran was born in Cannanore and, during his youth, engaged himself in the study of martial arts to become an expert archer. When asked to work to feed himself and his parents, he

---

[51] Mencher, 'Possession, dance and religion', 344. The reverent attitude of the upper castes and the feeling of power invested in the Malayan surely outlasted the space of the performance. There is a proverb in Malayalam which says of those showing false humility that they are like performing Malayans. For proverbs derived from the *teyyattam* see Chanthera, *Kaliyattam*, 290-1.

[52] M.V.V. Nambudiri, *Uttara keralathile thottam pattukal (The thottams of north Kerala)* (Trichur, 1981), 271.

[53] Most of the *thottam* were committed to writing on palm leaf manuscripts and jealously guarded by performers. Recently, collections have been made by amateur anthropologists, the more important of them being Nambudiri, *Uttara keralathile thottam pattukal* and Chirakkal T.B. Nayar, *Kerala bhashaganangal (Folk songs of Kerala)* (2 volumes, Trichur, 1979). There remains the serious problem of dating these *thottams* which has yet to be done. Some of them go back as far as the seventeenth century, though new *teyyams* were being created as late as the third decade of this century. Chanthera, *Kaliyattam*, 285.

refused to take part in the transplantation of rice which he saw as women's work, or carry burdens which he saw as demeaning. His father threw him out of the house saying that manliness was not enough; if the community was to be fed men had to do 'women's' work as well. An agricultural community living from hand to mouth could not indulge someone who believed in living for pleasure. People had an obligation to the community which necessarily involved an obligation also to the Nayar tharavadu on whose lands they worked. Kathivanur Viran left for Coorg (the destination of every migrant from north Malabar), and decided to marry and settle down there after refusing the option of being a priest at a shrine. The only other course was to opt for a religious life out of the secular world of production and reproduction. While living as a householder in Coorg, he died defending his adopted village against marauding robbers. Having thus redeemed himself by his becoming part of the community through marriage, filial responsibility and heroism, the Viran was deified.[54]

Another *teyyam* is that of Palantayi Kannan, a young Tiyya boy who fell in love with the daughter of the Nayar who had given him shelter. Kannan was banished from the village and migrated to Coorg, but feeling homesick he returned, only to be killed by the Nayar, Kuruvadan Kurup. Immediately the Nayar tharavadu was visited by pestilence and the Nayar had to deify Kannan as an aspect of Vishnu to atone for his sins.[55] The story of Kannan reveals that he practised several deceits on people while he was in exile. In addition, he had infringed on caste norms by falling in love with a woman of higher caste. Thus, while he was a victim, he was also a rule breaker and could be redeemed only by his death. However, the excessive nature of his punishment necessitated retribution. The Nayar could not exercise his power arbitrarily, and had to observe definite limits.[56] Stuart Blackburn has pointed out the geographical spread of such performances: the *bhomiya* in Rajasthan; the *khambha* in Gujarat; the *paddana* in south west Karnataka; and the *vilpattu* in southern Tamil Nadu, all belong to a tradition of deification of lower caste martyrs. Both the performances as well as the texts of these forms turn on the death of the local hero or heroine; the death being violent, premature and unjustified. The victims are deified, partly representing a triumph over death, and partly creating an access to the 'power' seen to be possessed by the violently killed.[57]

An analysis of one of the *thottams* will help highlight some of the key themes within the *teyyattam*. We shall take up the narrative of Vishnumurti, or Vishnu in the incarnation of half man and half lion. It is the form in which he kills the

[54] Nayar, *Kerala bhashaganangal*, 446-70; Payyanadu, *Teyyavum thottampattum*, 91-2.
[55] Nambudiri, *Uttara keralathile thottampattukal*, 270-333; Chanthera, *Kaliyattam*, 103-05.
[56] For a more detailed discussion see Dilip Menon, 'The moral community of the teyyattam: popular culture in late colonial Malabar', forthcoming *Studies in History*, IX, 2 (1993).
[57] S.H. Blackburn, 'Death and deification: folk cults in Hinduism', *History of Religions*, 24, 3 (1985), 255-74.

demon king Hiranyakashipu, both to protect the world as well as to defend his devotee, and Hiranyakashipu's son, Prahlad. Into this story is woven the circumstances of the death of Palantayi Kannan, a Tiyya youth, killed by the Nayar Kuruvadan Kurup.[58] The sparse, unadorned narrative of the account of Kannan provides a contrast to the ornate telling of the conflict between Vishnu, Hiranyakashipu and Prahlad, in which several philosophical ideas such as *karma* and the transmigration of souls appear. Kannan's story was known more in unrecorded tradition and collective memory than ensconced in texts; the very sparseness of details provided in the performance presumes a knowing audience. The *thottam* begins 'The brave Palantayi Kannan of the Tiyya caste/ Performed many deceits on several people/ Once, having annoyed Kuruvadan Kurup/ He left his family and village and went north.'[59]

We are told nothing beyond the fact that he was brave, perhaps foolishly so, for having annoyed an upper caste overlord. We are also told that he was a trickster, something which may not have endeared him to many in his village. When he returned home after his exile, he stopped to bathe in the village pond and was killed by the Kurup. But even as the Kurup flung the blood-stained sword into the water, 'he knew in his heart that disaster would strike'. His cattle are killed in an epidemic and the astrologers tell him that 'a powerful god is on the loose'; 'quick retribution was needed for the murder'. If the Kurup tried to escape doing penance, the gods would wreak havoc. An anguished and repentant Kurup cries, 'Alas! Alas! O lord of Payyanur, save me!/ Do not raze my family and village to the ground.'[60]

The consequences of the Kurup's act are spelled out in detail; his transgressions as an individual bring harm not only to himself and his family but to the entire village. A revengeful act has to be followed by restitution. If in rebelling against the mores of the presumed community, lower castes are punished more severely than they deserve, they are deified, and thus an example made of the arbitrariness of those who possess authority. We do not seem to have an acceptance of the skewed relations of power here, legitimised by an overarching ideology of the proper place and duties of persons within a hierarchical society. It may be possible to speculate, as Juergensmeyer does in the context of the religion of the untouchables in Punjab, that the living presence of good and evil spirits not only vitiates Hindu notions of *dharma* but replaces it.[61]

[58] Nambudiri, *Uttara keralathile thottam pattukal*, 270-333.
[59] *Ibid.*, 283-4.
[60] *Ibid.*, 284.
[61] M. Juergensmeyer, *Religion as social vision: the movement against untouchability in twentieth century Punjab* (Berkeley, CA, 1982), 100. He provides a critique of Dumontian conceptions of lower caste religion, and maintains that objects and events in the social firmament seem to be charged with degrees of moral force rather than degrees of ritual purity or cleanliness.

The sections of the Vishnumurti *thottam* which deal with the conflict between Prahlad and Hiranyakashipu, paralleling the clash between Kannan and Kurup, are told in great detail. All sections take place in the foreground: Prahlad's gentle piety, Hiranyakashipu's towering rage and Vishnu's terrifying roars as he manifests himself in his half-man, half-lion incarnation. Whereas the telling of Kannan's story presumes a knowing audience, who would place a bare outline within a context, these sections are proselytising in tone. They dilate on life and death, the necessity for authority, the virtues of forbearance and the notion of the world as a vale of suffering from which one is delivered by religiosity or death. There is a plea for the worship of Vishnu 'who is present within all the creations on this earth' a monotheism unadulterated by the worship of *bhagavathis* or deified humans.[62] Further on in the *thottam*, Hiranyakashipu expatiates on the notion of transmigration of souls, to console his mother on the death of her other son at the hands of Vishnu. The body is but a vehicle for the soul.[63] Kannan's *thottam* demands revenge for his death, whereas this section seems to imply that it is only Kannan's shell which has ceased to exist; his essence lives on. The Kurup, in a sense, has only delivered Kannan's soul from bondage. It is as if a struggle is taking place within the text between two opposed conceptions of death. One sees it as a release for the soul; the other evaluates the circumstances of the death and then considers it just, or unjust.[64]

To posit too sharp a distinction between the ideas in the story of Kannan and that of Hiranyakashipu might suggest that these sections functioned autonomously within the narrative. Then it could be argued that since the *teyyattam* was situated within a community of upper and lower castes, different sections appealed to different understandings. However, this would negate the intermediary role of the Vannan or Malayan, who bring their own understanding as well as constructive misunderstandings into the performance. Moreover, while they may be 'divine' in the context of the ritual, as professional performers they are open to the influences of Sanskritic epics and ideas purveyed by the dominant literary and upper caste performers.[65] The process of dissemination, furthermore, subjects ideas to creative distortions. Vishnu is absorbed into the pre-existing tradition of animal worship, hence the popularity of the incarnation in which he is half lion. Moreover, there are other transformations: one verse

[62] Nambudiri, *Uttara keralathile thottam pattukal*, 280-1.

[63] *Ibid.*, 287.

[64] As George Hart points out, while devotional south Indian Hinduism may pay lip service to the doctrine of reincarnation, popular manifestations 'never make very much of that theory'. George L. Hart III, 'Theory of reincarnation among the Tamils' in W.D. O'Flaherty ed., *Karma and rebirth in classical Indian tradition* (Berkeley, CA, 1980), 123.

[65] Narayana Rao refers to this as the process of 'secondary epic formations', i.e. the accretion of Sanskritic ideas onto 'folk' narratives. V. Narayana Rao, 'Epics and ideologies: six Telugu folk epics' in S.H. Blackburn and A.K. Ramanujam eds, *Another harmony: new essays on the folklore of India* (Berkeley, CA, 1986), 149-60.

mentions Vishnu as a 'devotee of Siva' and another depicts him astride a leopard and holding its tail like the popular image of a *bhagavathi*.[66]

Conclusion

Tharavadus and cultivators, upper castes and lower castes were bound together in a shared religious culture which was understood and appropriated differently. This was evident in the enactment of religious festivals which reflected varying conceptions of the relations between castes. Alcohol and blood sacrifice were part of both upper and lower caste culture and the deities worshipped spanned cosmologies. The Tiyya, Palantayi Kannan was as much a part of the Nayar pantheon as Vishnu was of the lower caste pantheon. Over a period of time the boundaries between beliefs and deities became blurred and in north Malabar a composite culture arose, shared by upper and lower castes. The cosmology was defined as much by the lower castes, as in the absorption of local heroes and heroines, as by the upper castes, witnessed in the absorption of their ancestors in a general pantheon of worship.

The first two decades of the twentieth century, saw attempts by lower and upper caste reformers to move away from shrines towards worship at temples. At one level, the assumption of subsistence which incorporated tharavadus, shrines and worshippers underlay a physical sense of community. This would be attenuated only by the inability, or unwillingness, of tharavadus to dispense their obligations. At another level, the community of worship around the shrines possessed ambivalent characteristics. Some festivals emphasised casteness and the place of castes within a hierarchy. Others afforded a vision of a sphere in which all castes mingled despite their differences. The next chapter looks at the attempts of reformers to move away from aspects of shrine community which emphasised caste subordination and to recreate a sense of a community of equals around temples. This was a limited conception in that this equality was to be only between members of one caste category – the Tiyyas. However, it sought to combine several aspects of the rural community – common worship, mutual help and interdependence. The community of worship was sought to be extended by flattening all variation and thus bringing about an equality between castes in the sphere of worship.

[66] Nambudiri, *Uttara keralathile thottam pattukal*, 271, 277.

3　Shrines, temples and politics, 1900–1930

Tharavadus, shrines and cultivators were bound together in a complex community of worship. There was an implicit recognition of the disparity between its constituents while, at the same time, there were attempts to transcend these differences. The first two decades of the twentieth century witnessed efforts by an emergent, urban Tiyya elite to draw away worshippers from the shared culture of the shrines. Shrines were typified as the sites of blood sacrifices and rituals involving the use of alcohol, as distinct from the 'higher' religious practices at the new Tiyya temples. More significant, in its consequences for the trajectory of politics, was a re-evaluation of the complex nature of shrine festivals to emphasise only those aspects which reproduced caste inequality. The new Tiyya temples were portrayed as the foci of a community of equals, as opposed to the shrines which were represented as buttressing the dominance of the upper caste tharavadus. This movement among the Tiyyas sought to create an inward looking community which attempted not so much to move upwards within a putative social hierarchy, but to opt out of the extant hierarchy altogether. There were no appeals to the statuses parcelled out by Censuses, nor was this a knee-jerk reaction of creating a 'caste constituency' to take advantage of the inclusion of caste groups in municipal and local administration from the late nineteenth century.[1]

The motives behind the building of the new temples as well as the responses to the call for community stemmed from varying causes. In the face of the commercial power of the Mappilas and the control they exercised over land in the towns, the nascent Tiyya elite needed to create cohesion within its own

[1] For caste movements reacting to Censuses see the seminal essay by B.S. Cohn, 'The Census, social structure and objectification in south Asia' in *An anthropologist among the historians and other essays* (Delhi, 1987), 224-54. See also L.I. Rudolph and S.H. Rudolph, *The modernity of tradition: political development in India* (Chicago, IL, 1967), 118-19 and for a recent restatement, K.W. Jones, 'Religious identity and the Indian census' in N.G. Barrier ed., *The Census in British India* (Delhi, 1981), 75. For an effective critique see L.M. Carroll, 'Colonial perceptions of Indian society and the emergence of caste(s) associations', *Journal of Asian Studies* 37, 2 (1978), 249. For links of caste associations with municipal administration see D.A. Washbrook, 'The development of caste organisations in south India, 1880-1925' in Baker and Washbrook, *South India: political institutions and political change,* 184-7.

ranks as well as forge alliances. They were able to draw upon the migrants to the towns by setting themselves up as alternative sources of credit and employment. The advocacy of temperance and the jettisoning of the use of alcohol in religious rituals had resonances for those Tiyyas in the interior who had begun to resent their roles as suppliers of toddy to shrine festivals. Moreover, in an indirect way, the actions of the state helped to strengthen the emergent sense of Tiyya community. A harsh excise policy made the Tiyyas' traditional occupation of toddy tapping increasingly unprofitable, driving impoverished tappers to the towns. Further, with the incorporation of locally powerful tharavadus in the excise administration, and the role they played in policing infringements, relations with their dependents were undermined.

Meanwhile, a political conjuncture helped to project the idea of a community of equals around temples to a much wider forum. In the aftermath of the Mappila rebellion of 1921, Congress politics in Malabar developed an introspective, Hindu idiom. Faced with the dilemma of creating a unity between unequal castes, the Congress elevated the Tiyya ideal of building a community of equals around temples to the level of building Hindu unity through admission into temples for all castes. Gandhi's definition of the inequality between castes, as partly arising from differences in cleanliness and hygiene, added another dimension to the search for equality. It provided a new generation of reformers within Nayar tharavadus with a programme which allowed them to try and rebuild a sense of rural community by working with their lower caste dependents. Moreover, they could again present themselves in the role of arbiters between castes in the face of Tiyya reluctance to include other castes within their conception of community. The campaign to enter Vaikkam temple in 1923 allowed a confluence of the disparate themes of temperance, cleanliness and caste inequality; they converged in the idea of a Hindu community of clean castes trooping through the portals of a temple towards unity. The political rhetoric of a community of equals which underlay the efforts of Tiyya elites as well as the Congress, employed a predominantly religious idiom. Neither confronted the issue of the secular component of inequality between the constituents of their proposed communities.

The growth of a Tiyya elite, 1900-20

In the aftermath of the MCTI Act, 1900, many landlords had begun to resort to overleases, putting the costs of evicting the incumbent tenant on the overlessee (*melkanakkaran*). A large number of these overlessees were drawn from the class of newly rich and influential Tiyyas, either professionals or emigrants investing in land in their ancestral country.[2] A typical example was the Tiyya lawyer, C. Krishnan, who supplemented his fluctuating professional earnings by collecting the rent on lands which his father had bought on overleases.[3] This new elite was also born out of the colonial and missionary presence in north Malabar. The Basel Evangelical Mission, established in Switzerland in 1815, began its activities in north Malabar a quarter of a century later, establishing a network of elementary and high schools by the end of the nineteenth century.[4] The Tiyyas were among the first to join these institutions and a significant minority had subsequently worked their way into the colonial administration as *tehsildars*, lawyers, pleaders, sub-judges and up to the ranks of deputy collectors. Though there were two colleges in Malabar at the time (Zamorin's College, Calicut [established, 1879] and Brennen College, Tellicherry [established, 1891]), Tiyyas were denied admission till as late as 1918. A few went to Madras for a university education and Tiyyas constituted slightly more than a tenth of the migrants from Malabar between 1906-20.[5]

A rung below these entrepreneurs in social status but matching them in terms of wealth were those Tiyyas who, from the days of the East India Company, had served as produce brokers, suppliers of provisions to the cantonments, and monopolists of toddy and arrack distribution. In the early nineteenth century, the Excise Department had not yet come into existence and the rights to sell and tap toddy were auctioned by the Revenue Department of the government of Madras. Speculators and contractors were given a free hand in administering this ramshackle system and sections among the Tiyyas, who monopolised the toddy tapping profession, created informal empires criss-crossing the countryside. A few Tiyya families came to dominate the toddy and arrack business by buying up the rights for a whole taluk and, in the mid nineteenth century, Murkkoth Ramunni was the head of a company controlling all the shops in Malabar.[6] The fortunes of three generations of the Murkkoth family in Tellicherry provide an illustration of Tiyya mobility. Murkkoth Ramunny's father worked as a butler at the house of a senior employee of the East India Company and Ramunny rose from toddy shopowner to the foremost toddy magnate of his time. His son Murkkoth Kumaran began his life as a

[2] *MTCR, 1927-28*, I, 51.
[3] K. Achuthan, *C. Krishnan* (Kottayam, 1971), 70-1.
[4] E.J. Edona, *The economic conditions of the Protestant Christians of Malabar with special reference to the Basel Mission Church* (Calicut, 1940).
[5] K.K.N. Kurup, '*Inglish vidyabhyasavum samuhya purogatiyum malabarile tiyyaril*' (English education and social progress among the Tiyyas of Malabar) in *Adhunika Keralam: charitra gaveshana prabandhangal* (*Modern Kerala: essays in historical research*) (Trivandrum, 1982), 31-2; Susan Lewandowski, *Migration and ethnicity in urban India: Kerala migrants in the city of Madras, 1870-1940* (Delhi, 1980), 59-60.
[6] MSS of Murkkoth Kumaran's autobiography, 5-6.

school teacher but became a journalist, novelist and, ironically, a campaigner for temperance.[7]

The Basel Mission was responsible for setting up the first weaving and tile factories in Malabar, largely to provide employment for its converts. There seems to have been a direct link between the ability of the Mission to provide employment and the numbers of its converts. The setting up of a tile factory at Chombala in 1890 led to 153 conversions. Between 1914 and 1921, the lean war years, when the mission was classified as 'alien' and the running of its factories was stalled, over 900 members of the congregation departed.[8] A few enterprising Tiyya converts maintained their links with their families while working their way through the mission factories and became factory owners in their own right. One such convert was Churikkat Samuel, who began work in a weaving establishment of the Basel Mission, rose to become foreman and, with help from the Mission, set up his own weaving factory.[9] There was considerable cooperation between Tiyya entrepreneurs and the mission since the factories set up by the Tiyyas tended to manufacture cloth for local consumption while the Mission factories were geared to an export market. In 1908, the 'Tiers of Cannanore' organised an Agricultural and Industrial exhibition which was intended to be both a celebration of their achievement as well as an inspiration to other communities.[10]

Profits from the boom in cash crop prices were diverted into investment in factories, particularly weaving establishments. In the war years, there was a rise in demand for cloth, particularly from the armed forces, which the factories of the 'alien' mission could not meet. A rash of weaving factories sprang up in north Malabar. These 'factories' employed between five and ten weavers and it is difficult to estimate their numbers as the Factories Act of 1911 did not extend to such ramshackle establishments. Samuel Aaron, the proprietor of Aaron mills estimated that between 100 and 150 'factories' were founded in this period, mainly by Tiyya entrepreneurs.[11] These factories provided a source of employment in the agricultural off season for those living near the port towns. Increasingly, Tellicherry and Cannanore attracted petty traders, casual labourers and weavers from the hinterland. In 1909, C. Krishnan founded the Calicut Bank, catering primarily for other Tiyya professionals and merchants. Unlike the other established banks, money was lent primarily on the security

---

[7] Karayi Bappu, one of Murkkoth Ramunny's associates in the toddy trade had two sons in the colonial administration, one a *tehsildar* and the other a sub-registrar. MSS of Murkkoth Kumaran's autobiography, 12–13; Interview with Murkkoth Kunhappa (son of Murkkoth Kumaran), Calicut, March 1989.

[8] Edona, *Economic conditions of the Protestant Christians*, 52–3.

[9] C. Samuel Aaron, *Jeevithasmaranakal (Memoirs)* (Cannanore, 1974), 18, 28.

[10] *Revenue Dept. G.O.1518 dated 24 June 1920* (TNA).

[11] Aaron, *Jeevithasmaranakal*, 45–8. The spiralling prices of cotton twist had affected the handloom weavers severely and these 'factories' took over the manufacture of cheap cloth. *Revenue DR6431/16 dated 27 April 1919* (KRA).

of promissory notes and pledged ornaments. Over the years, its activity was extended to financing the small tea shops and stalls set up in the towns.[12]

The emergence of alternative sources of income and patronage had repercussions in the interior as well. Some Tiyyas began moving away from wholly agricultural occupations to casual work in the towns, during the off season, to supplement their income. This was not such a sharp break because most individuals continued to cling on to their small homesteads with palm and jack trees. Their involvement in the earlier circuits of worship at shrines was undiminished and they were in many cases ultimately dependent on the dominant tharavadus for paddy in times of crisis. However, tensions were on the increase. Some among them sought to move away from the networks of deferential association with a tharavadu, and these resentments began intruding into 'ritual' spaces like the mock fights between Nayars and Tiyyas at Mavila *kavu* in Kottayam. The festival had to be suspended for a few years after Tiyya participants bloodied the noses of Nayars in what the latter thought would be another 'ritual' encounter.[13] By 1920, observers had begun to speak of a 'communal split' between Nayars and Tiyyas, particularly in Chirakkal taluk.[14] Relations between Nayar social reformers and the Tiyya elites were far more ambivalent. Nayars contributed to the Tiyya journal *Mithavadi*, founded in 1913 by C. Krishnan, dilating on the 'present condition of the Tiyyas and the road to advancement'. These articles typically advised Tiyyas to become more like the 'Hindu' Nayars by giving up the worship of low gods, reading the Puranas regularly and going on pilgrimages to Varanasi.[15]

Tiyya temples and the search for community

The establishment of separate temples by castes within the Madras Presidency has been studied only within the narrow framework of municipal and local politics. The fashioning of caste unity is seen as nothing more than the attempt to create a political lobby.[16] However, the Tiyyas were considered to be on a par with other 'non Brahmins' like the Nayars, and therefore could not scramble for caste concessions from the state.[17] A study of their efforts to establish separate temples will not only temper an understanding of caste politics as nothing more than political opportunism, but also allow us to see

[12] Achuthan, *C. Krishnan*, 72-3.
[13] Kunhappa, *Smaranakal matram*, 5-6, 26.
[14] Written evidence of K.V. Krishnan Nair, High Court *vakil*, Tellicherry, *MTCR, 1927-28*, II, 396; Kunhappa, *Smaranakal matram*, 26.
[15] *Mithavadi*, September, 1913.
[16] See Washbrook, *The emergence of provincial politics*, 282.
[17] *Public (Political) Dept. G.O.1997 (Confidential) dated 7 December 1936* (IOL).

how it represented a strategy towards equality. Temple building activities were given a cohesiveness by the social message of the Sri Narayana movement in Travancore led by the Ezhava, Narayana Guru. The movement was institutionalised with the formation of the Sri Narayana Dharma Paripalana Yogam (society for the propagation of the religion of Sri Narayana) in 1903.[18] First, it argued against differences in society based on caste. Narayana Guru made a direct connection between the 'low' social and religious practices of the Ezhavas and their low social status. They could attain equality with others by becoming like the upper castes – an idea which found expression in the realm of worship in the setting up of Ezhava temples devoted to gods regarded as belonging to the Brahminical pantheon. The entrance to an equal society lay through common worship. Secondly, the SNDP Yogam sought to create self esteem within the Ezhava community by building their economic strength and propagating a vigorous self-help ethic.[19]

The SNDP's message of equality and economic self reliance found a resonance in the activities of Tiyya elites along the coast in north Malabar. In July 1906, Kottieth Ramunni, a lawyer at the Tellicherry courts and K. Chantan, a retired deputy Collector founded the Sri Gnanodaya Yogam (the society for the awakening of knowledge). The Yogam, which was comprised mainly of the Tiyya professional classes and lesser civil servants, stressed that they should organise alongside the SNDP 'under the themes of religion, business, education, and social reform'. In 1908, the Yogam proposed the building of temples for the Tiyyas of north Malabar to which they alone would have access. The same year Narayana Guru himself laid the foundation of the Jagannatha temple at Tellicherry. By 1916, two more temples had been built; the Srikanteswara at Calicut and the Sundareswara at Cannanore. From the very beginning the new temples represented a departure from the idea of community envisaged by the rural shrines. All of them were financed wholly by donations from prosperous Tiyyas and the names of the prominent donors were inscribed on tablets put up on the walls.[20] What these temples needed was to gain general acceptance, and adherents who could sustain the temple with something more tangible than worship. There were two immediate constraints to contend with. First, the new community could only be a limited one. Nayars

[18] The Ezhavas in Travancore were regarded as belonging to the same caste category as the Tiyyas. Narayana Guru himself tried to foster cooperation between the two caste groups.
[19] See Robin Jeffrey, 'The social origins of a caste association, 1875-1905: the founding of the SNDP Yogam', *South Asia*, 4 (1974), 59-78; M.S.A. Rao, *Social movements and social transformation: a study of two backward classes movements in Malabar* (Delhi, 1979). For a comprehensive analysis of the sources of Narayana Guru's philosophy see V.T. Samuel, '"One caste, one religion and one God for man": a study of Sree Narayana Guru (1854-1928) of Kerala, India' (unpublished PhD dissertation, Hartford Seminary Foundation, 1973).
[20] When subscriptions for the Sundareswara temple were being raised, Aaron Senior (who though a Christian convert, maintained his links with the Tiyya community) donated a 'large sum' to Narayana Guru. Aaron, *Jeevithasmaranakal*, 56.

would not worship at what were seen as Tiyya establishments, and untouchable castes like Cherumas and Pulayas were prevented from doing so by the managers of the temple. Secondly, in the countryside and the hinterland of the towns, a significant number of Nayars, Tiyyas and Pulayas continued to be involved in a more universal, vital and vibrant culture around shrines.

In 1918, a Tiyya conference was held in Calicut. It called upon all Tiyyas to break away from worshipping at temples and shrines, to which they supplied offerings, but, which denied entrance to them. A resolution stated that there was an overwhelming 'need to eschew all ideas of the lowness of Tiyyas and the superiority of the upper castes'.[21] Sundareswara and Jagannatha temples were represented as being of, for, and by the Tiyyas and the self esteem of the community was to be built around these. An attempt was made to demarcate the sphere of influence of the new temples, in very much the same way that the processions of rural shrine festivals had done. The latter charted routes which passed through one or a few *desams*, taking in subsidiary shrines as well as a realm of worshippers. Moreover, they defined the space in which a dominant tharavadu exercised its sway. The establishment of the Jagannatha and the Sundareswara temples was an attempt to construct just such a community of members. But, if these temples had to vie with other shrines for worshippers, they needed to pull themselves out of purely local circuits and aspire to become centres of pilgrimage, like Kottiyur. By presenting itself as a rival pilgrimage centre, the Jagannatha temple could try to draw upon wider loyalties as well as try and create a sense of Tiyya community. Kottiyur, the shrine to which Tiyyas and Nayars made annual pilgrimages, was represented as a temple managed by and for Nayars; Jagannatha, on the other hand, was for and of the Tiyyas.[22] But there was a problem. Kottiyur, like any other centre of pilgrimage was not and could not be a centre of daily loyalty. It drew upon a number of pilgrims of all castes, from different regions and asserted itself only annually as a focus of worship.

The Gnanodaya Yogam exhorted Tiyyas to make a pilgrimage to the Jagannatha temple rather than the one at Kottiyur. This movement was represented as the eschewing, in rituals, of toddy and blood sacrifices, for a purer form of worship. It was an espousal of the teaching of Sri Narayana Guru in that 'low' practices were to be jettisoned to cast off a 'low' status. It was also an expression of the economic well-being of the worshippers. A pamphlet contrasted the 'pure way' in which rites were performed at Jagannatha temple as a result of the influence of Narayana Guru: 'Without any mercy we killed

---

[21] *Mithavadi*, November 1918.
[22] Oral evidence of K.V. Krishnan Nair, vakil, High Court, Taliparamba and oral evidence of M. Anandan, member of the Bar, Tellicherry, *MTCR 1927-28*, II, 382, 396.

cocks for worshipping God/With the smell of blood, our temples became like markets.'[23]

Thus, purists with sensitive nostrils, those who wished to display their wealth in their form of worship, and those desiring to make Jagannatha a Tiyya bastion, each for their different reasons began moving to Tellicherry. There was a steadily increasing trickle from the countryside for other reasons. The shrine at Kottiyur, managed by Nayar tharavadus, became the focus of resentment of large numbers of Tiyyas, who began to see their relation to the shrine purely as suppliers of toddy and cocks to festivals. In 1921, Tiyyas in Chirakkal refused to take the traditional pots of toddy decorated with flowers and red silk to the temple festival. They described the festival 'as an occasion for the upper castes to get free liquor'. When the *teyyattam* was performed, it had been customary for the Vannan washerman to help carry the heavy, tall head-dress of the goddess. That year, the Nayars themselves did it.[24]

Toddy came to signify not only the Tiyyas' subordination to the Nayars, but also the 'lowness' of the Tiyya through association with what was increasingly characterised as an 'impure' profession. This was a remarkable shift as toddy possessed a ritual virtue for most Tiyyas in the countryside. If a man was too ill to bathe after death pollution, the custom was to make him touch a pot of toddy to 'cleanse' him.[25] Moreover, alcohol had always played an important part in religion; in a sense, toddy sanctified the ritual. Kottiyur and Kodungallur marked periods of heavy drinking and, in the case of the *teyyattam*, the degree of devotion of the performer was measured by the extent of his intoxication. Drinking during religious ceremonies affirmed local community; at Kottiyur, inebriation was the premise of the equal interaction between upper and lower castes. Moreover, consumption of alcohol in ritual conditions even to the point of saturation was accepted as moderate. In a secular context too, after a day's work in the fields it had been customary to repair to the toddy shop. The toddy drawer's work gave him great leisure and as the supplier of alcohol he enjoyed great popularity with Nayars as well as Tiyyas and Cherumas.[26] The new re-forming zeal did not allow for nuances; it saw toddy only as the marker of lowness and exploitation.

In the attempt to draw worshippers to the new temples, the Tiyya elite had consciously redefined the shrine culture by identifying it with its animistic and purely local aspects. However, not all were in agreement about the alternative proposed. Some believed that a religious system centred on temples was a

---

[23] P. Govindan, *Adidravidarude ambalapravesanam (The entry of the Adi-Dravidas into temples)* (Calicut, 1915), 7. He pointed out how the temple had *puja, kirtanams* (communal singing), *naivedyam* (offering of clarified butter), *deeparadhana* (worship of the idol with lamps) and other wholesome forms of worship.

[24] *Mithavadi*, May 1921.

[25] Aiyappan, *Iravas and culture change*, 110.

[26] *Ibid.*, 107.

replication of the religion of Brahmins. There was no consensus on this question and the *Mithavadi* itself sought to portray the diversity within opinions and attitudes. It published articles on the eating habits of the Brahmins and the suggestions of correspondents that the lower castes had a lot to learn from the Brahmins. There were frequent letters soliciting more information on brahminical rites of passage.[27] In Kurumbranad some Tiyyas discarded what they now called their 'animistic religion' and set up *bhajana samajams* (prayer societies) where the praises of Saraswati, Vishnu and other 'brahminical' deities were sung.[28] The complex pantheon of shrine worship was in the process of reinterpretation, and a sharp division emerged between 'brahminical' and 'non-Brahminical' deities, at least within the discourse of reform.

Ostensibly, the building of temples and the establishment of prayer societies had one common aim. Historians have tended to subsume such attempts within the category of 'sanskritisation'. Their main aim, according to the most recent analyst, was 'to obtain access to the high gods for lower castes'.[29] However, it is not *emulation* which we are dealing with here; an idea presuming a filtering downward of the ideas and practices of a social elite which acts as the primary element of change in an otherwise static system. In the context of shrine worship and the cosmology of the *teyyattam*, categories of worship were miscible. Siva was as much part of a 'lower caste' pantheon as any local heroine was of an 'upper caste' pantheon. Different castes in north Malabar had always had 'access' to all gods, ancestors and spirits. When Siva or Vishnu, in their forms as Sundareswara and Jagannatha, were installed at Tiyya temples, it was less a move *up* a religious hierarchy as a move *sideways*. Local deities had always possessed this manifold aspect – the local hero Palantayi Kannan was also Vishnumurti and *vice versa*.

While moving away from the religious framework of the shrine festivals, some Tiyyas also distanced themselves from secular obligations placed on them. At Palayad, near Tellicherry, Tiyya tenants refused to perform the traditional role of couriers bearing the news of the Nayar landlord's death.[30] The community of worship and sustenance, around the Nayar tharavadu and shrines, presumed the involvement of its constituents in the crucial rites of passage. Tiyya tenants were usually called upon to cut down a mango tree for the funeral pyre whenever there was a death in the family of a Nayar landlord. Increasingly, around Tellicherry and Cannanore, Tiyyas refused to perform these traditional caste obligations.[31] It was a conflict which arose both from the

---

[27] *Mithavadi*, May 1915.
[28] *Mithavadi*, February 1915.
[29] G. Lemercinier, *Religion and ideology in Kerala*, trans. Y. Rendel (Delhi, 1984), 248. For earlier analyses on the same model see M.S.A. Rao, *Social change in Malabar* (Bombay, 1957) and *Social movements and social transformation*.
[30] *Mithavadi*, May 1921.
[31] Oral evidence of E.G. Nair, High Court *vakil*, Tellicherry, *MTCR, 1927-28*, II, 163.

possibility of moving out of a relation of deference and obligation, as well as the existence of an alternative sphere of involvement. The Jagannatha and Sundareswara temples at least recognised a formal equality between their worshippers – as members of one caste. Moreover, the move to the new temples reflected the attitude of a younger generation working as petty traders and casual labour in the towns, who no longer felt wholly dependent on the land, and therefore the dominant tharavadus, for a living. Joseph Muliyil, a second generation Tiyya convert and pleader in Tellicherry, spoke with a resentful contempt of the attitudes among the younger generation. Even the 'sons of pedlars [*sic*] etc.', he observed, abhorred the idea of manual labour for fear of being thrown out of the vague, yet charmed 'circle of the middle class'.[32] However, this movement away from caste obligations was not uniform. In Puthur and Kalavallur *desams*, there were two groups among the Tiyyas, and the 'conservatives' were supported by, and continued to work with, the Nayar landlords.[33]

Tiyya temples and Mappila shrines

Prosperous Mappilas had begun to acquire land near existing temples and shrines by investing in overleases in the towns. Nayar tharavadus, with lands on the coast, and faced with competition from both Tiyyas and Muslims, preferred to retire from the fray and let the rival contenders battle it out among themselves.[34] M. Anandan, a Tiyya pleader at Tellicherry was given a lease to convert wetlands to garden to prevent the encroachment of Mappila landlords who were annexing plots adjoining theirs. By 1915, there was acute rivalry between Tiyya and Mappila traders. There were complaints that Tiyya merchants and professionals like C. Krishnan had begun to 'poach into the commercial preserves of the Mappilas'. Kottieth Ramunni, a prominent Tiyya lawyer in Tellicherry, was asked to form a conciliation board. He felt that a 'spirit of mere commercial jealousy' was being aggravated because the Chamber of Commerce was unwilling to open its doors to all merchants.[35]

Mappilas had begun to establish *srambis* (wayside shrines) and existing *srambis* were enlarged into mosques where prayers were held on Fridays. About 1914, there was a movement among sections of the Mappilas of north Malabar to create a sense of community in very much the same way that Tiyya

[32] Evidence of Joseph Muliyil, Calicut, *Report of the Unemployment Commission, 1927*, 343-4.
[33] Oral evidence of E.G. Nair, High Court *vakil*, Tellicherry. *MTCR, 1927-28*, II, 163.
[34] Oral evidence of A.K. Sankara Varma raja, Valiya raja of Kadathunad, *MTCR, 1927-28*, II, 318; oral evidence of M. Anandan, Member of the Bar, Tellicherry, *MTCR, 1927-28*, II, 377.
[35] *DR Magisterial D 298/M.15 dated 13 June 1915* (KRA).

elites were attempting to do. Just after the outbreak of the war, there seems to have been a degree of empathy for the fate of Turkey among *kazis* and Muslim notables. Pamphlets were distributed in Chirakkal taluk emphasising that the British government in declaring war against Turkey 'were in no sense fighting against the Muhammadan religion'. It is possible that the distribution of the pamphlets helped create the situation the administration was trying to avoid.[36] Meetings conducted by *kazis* and *maulvis* tried to define the differences between the Hindu and Mappila communities, and called upon all Mappilas in north Malabar to reject the matrilineal system of inheritance. Those who continued to follow matriliny were to be 'condemned as *kafirs*'. In a memorial to the Governor of Madras, the 'Moplah residents of Cannanore' state categorically that the '*marumakkathayam* law of inheritance is opposed to the spirit and teachings of Islam'.[37] The mushrooming of *srambis*, coupled with the calls for community, portended trouble. A generation earlier, the Collector of Malabar had written confidently that 'processions involving religious antagonism are here few and far between' largely because routes did not overlap and shrines tended to be concentrated in the interior.[38] Processional conflicts would emerge but without the sharpness they would acquire in the thirties. At this juncture the efforts of the Gnanodaya Yogam and the Mappila publicists did not manage to create more than an ill-defined sense of community among their respective constituencies.

In February 1915, a shrine in Tellicherry, managed by Nayar *uralars*, with a Tiyya priest and a mixture of worshippers decided to take out a festival procession. It made no attempt to mask its other than religious concerns. Traditionally, the procession had been nothing more than a parade with lamps following a time-honoured route. On this occasion, drummers accompanied the procession, there were several Tiyya 'volunteers' in uniform and the route traversed the major mosques in Tellicherry town, and the new Pilakod mosque in particular. The Inspector of Police was not far wrong when he observed that the procession seemed to want to 'establish a precedent'. Kottieth Ramunni, the founder of the Gnanodaya Yogam, was consulted for his opinion on the matter, both as a lawyer and as a prominent Tiyya, and he made good use of this opportunity. In a report, he stated that Hindu religious processions took place only twice a year in north Malabar – one was the *arat* procession taken from the Jagannatha temple at Tellicherry and the other from the now defunct regimental temple at Cannanore.[39]

[36] *DR Public 185/P-16 dated 31 January 1916* (KRA).
[37] *DR Public 497/Pub.15 dated 9 March 1915* (KRA).
[38] William Logan had written that all that was needed was to 'leave the thing to the good sense of the processionaries...'. *Revenue R.Dis. Magisterial R7/M82* (KRA).
[39] Petition from Imdadul Islam Association, Tellicherry, 28 February 1915; Report of the Inspector of Police, Tellicherry, 22 March 1915; Report of K. Ramunni, President, Sri Gnanodaya Yogam, Tellicherry. *DR Magisterial D 298/M.15 dated 13 June 1915* (KRA).

It was quite clear that there was a tussle over urban space; the Tiyya procession deliberately charted a route passing in front of new Mappila mosques. It was a flexing of territorial muscle, which did not engender real conflict despite the provocative presence of Tiyya 'volunteers' in uniform. The reactions of both the authorities and Kottieth Ramunni are interesting in that each wished to define the issue as one of law and order, but for different reasons altogether. The District Magistrate saw it essentially as a matter for negotiating with the 'leaders of the community', granting the Gnanodaya Yogam an importance unwarranted by its actual standing among Tiyyas. Kottieth Ramunni was concerned to show that the Jagannatha temple represented the horizon of Tiyya religious belief and that religious processions from the other shrines/ temples were just trying to stir up trouble. It would kill two birds with one stone. The Jagannatha temple would not have to vie with the local shrines for a congregation and the Sri Gnanodaya Yogam could be recognised as the mouth-piece of the local Tiyya community.

The conflict between the Tiyyas and the Mappilas, in and around the towns of Tellicherry and Cannanore, was not translated into 'communal' terms at this point, i.e. Hindu *vs* Muslim. There were two major reasons for this. First, the Tiyya elites had very consciously defined themselves as a community apart, centred on their own circuits of worship, rather than as 'Hindus'. Secondly, their adherents too were beginning to dissociate themselves from the broadly Hindu religious networks in the rural hinterland which they saw as entrenching their caste inferiority. Though the Tiyyas attempted to constitute themselves as a religious community, they did not draw upon a broader religious identity. Moreover, this was largely a contest between prosperous Mappila and Tiyya elites in the small towns of Tellicherry and Cannanore. While Nayar tharavadus in the interior were concerned by the threat to their authority as Tiyya tenants moved to an alternative circuit of worship, they had more pragmatic concerns as well. They had symbiotic relations with the more prominent Mappila merchants on the coast, who helped them market their lucrative pepper crop.[40] Thus, both Nayar and Mappila elites had too many other loyalties and concerns on their hands to actually want to promote or provide any focus for conflict between 'Hindus' and 'Muslims'. In south Malabar where there had been a longer history of conflict between Mappilas and Nayars (both as Hindus and Muslims and as landlords and tenants), such processions often assumed a violent character. On 2 March 1915, the Palliyarakkal temple near Calicut was burnt down by Mappilas taking a festival procession to Konthanary mosque one-and-a-half miles east of Calicut.[41]

[40] *Local Self Government Dept. G.O.1745 (L and M) dated 17 April 1928* (KS).
[41] Report of town second class Magistrate, Calicut, 4 March 1915, *DR Magisterial 544/M.15 dated 26 March 1915* (KRA).

The impact of excise administration

There were other pressures at work which indirectly influenced the efforts to build a community of Tiyyas around the new temples. The stepping up of attempts by the state to tax the native liquor industry severely affected the traditional occupation of toddy tapping, of a significant minority among the Tiyyas.[42] From the late nineteenth century, Fort St George had begun to tax the native liquor industry in an effort to raise more revenue. The informal administration provided by the speculators and contractors began to be brought under the control of an excise bureaucracy.[43] From the very beginning, Malabar consistently recorded the highest number of offenders against excise laws in the Madras Presidency.[44] Attempts to curb infringements, by making land-owners and village officials responsible for excise crime on their properties, or in the villages under their control, were never entirely successful. The ubiquitous palm tree could have been tapped by anyone for private pleasure or profit. As excise officials observed, 'every man can ... have his own beer tap in his own back garden'.[45]

A brief description of the toddy tapping business and its administration will show how it naturally engendered symbiotic networks of illegality which would confound the efforts of any government to evolve a fool-proof management. The government auctioned toddy shops which were bought by Nayar, Tiyya or Mappila traders who received a supply of toddy from contractors. These contractors in turn, got their supplies either from trees under their control or from the coconut gardens of Nayar and Tiyya tenants and landowners. Toddy tapping was done solely by Tiyyas who sold toddy directly to the contractors, or to the shops, if it had been tapped illegally. The government got its revenue from the tax on palm trees and from the rental of arrack and toddy shops. However, there were many loopholes, the most important being the abundance of palms which meant that people could tap it for their own use leaving someone else to pay the tax.[46] Toddy drawn for the government distilleries at Nellikuppam was untaxed and there was always the likelihood that contractors would channel some away for public consumption. This was prevented to some extent by making the contractor responsible for the tree tax.

---

[42] In 1911, almost a fifth of working Tiyya males were entered in the Census as toddy drawers. *Census of India, 1911, XII, Madras, part 1,* table XVI.

[43] The pressure on the state to raise more money and the difficulty of constantly increasing assessment on the land, made the taxation of the native liquor industry an attractive alternative. Revenue from excise increased from Rs. 60 lakhs in 1882-83 to Rs. 5.4 crores in 1920. See Washbrook, *The emergence of provincial politics,* 50-2.

[44] *Report on the Administration of Abkari Revenue of the Madras Presidency* (henceforth *RARMP*), 1899-1900, 44, Appendix E-109.

[45] *RARMP*, 1920-21, 15.

[46] *RARMP*, 1916-17, 10.

However, they had a vested interest in the illicit tapping of trees because they could then get toddy at cheaper rates which could be distilled and sold for a profit. Tappers could also set up distilling units with supplies from illicit tapping, and this could be done with the connivance of the owner of a coconut garden who wanted to make some money on the side. Reciprocal relations of law breaking existed between Nayar or Tiyya landowners and tenants and Tiyya tappers. Loyalties spanned castes and economic groups, and were cemented over drink in toddy shops and unauthorised stills dotting the countryside. It is significant that among the 'offenders' brought to trial, a large number were from the 'upper classes on whose account the lower classes usually smuggle'.[47] Networks, now defined by the state as illegal, were too profitable to be given up.

The administration had to finally face the fact that it could not control illicit tapping and distillation both of which were enmeshed in local relations. By 1900, any attempt at local control was given up and a pragmatic and ultimately harsh policy of taxation was initiated. Taxes on trees were increased every year by a third to a half, and every increase was faithfully followed by an increase in what had come to be called 'abkari crime'.[48] Between 1917 and 1927, taxes on toddy rose by 50 per cent, on country spirits by 93 per cent, and the vend fees for arrack and toddy went up by 172 per cent. In 1918, shop renters were almost driven to temperance by the taxation policy of the government. They went on strike and boycotted auctions saying that they 'desired to abandon use of fermented liquor'.[49] The severe taxation policy of the government affected relations in the countryside to a considerable extent. Landlords and village officials were made responsible for rooting out excise crime, which meant a vesting of further powers of coercion in the hands of Nayar tharavadus, already a part of the revenue administration. Conflicts between Nayar officials and Tiyya tappers impinged on notions of interdependence which had been emphasised in the context of shrine festivals. Toddy tappers were driven to extremes by excessive extractions – by the landlord, toddy shop owner, contractors and seemingly every excise official who encountered them on the roads. The *menokki*, excise official, became an object of universal hatred and Nayanar's satirical short story 'Who killed the *menokki*?' [1893] reflects the general attitude. A *menokki* went missing; the obvious assumption made by the police was that he had been killed by a tapper. After the tapper had been considerably harried it was discovered that the *menokki*, after a heavy meal, had

[47] *RARMP*, 1902-03, 17.
[48] *RARMP*, 1907-08, 1; *RARMP*, 1914-15, 1. In 1900, the newly appointed Abkari commissioner for Malabar observed pithily that 'the only proposals [I] have to make are that we should undo what has been done'. *Revenue R.Dis. 5 dated 9 March 1900* (KRA).
[49] *RARMP*, 1918, 17; *RARMP*, 1927, 13; *Mithavadi*, September 1918.

lain down to rest under a tree, been struck by lightning and presently died.[50] As toddy began to be taxed beyond profitability, shops decreased, tappers retreated and illicit tapping became the order of the day.

The taxation policy closed down shops and areas where Nayars, Tiyyas and Cherumas had shared their drunkenness. Tiyya tappers who were subject to the daily oppression of excise officials and the long-term demands of the state became increasingly unwilling to carry on an expensive occupation. In September 1918, Kottieth Krishnan, K. Chantan and a few others associated with the new Tiyya temples, founded the Kerala Labour Union for toddy tappers who had decided to give up their profession. The Jagannatha temple was to be the centre of rehabilitation activities, and the Union explored the possibility of setting up a business for dealing in jaggery made from sweet toddy.[51] The hardship of the tappers, the possibility of shifting within the profession of tapping to producing something free of governmental exaction or social opprobrium, and the desire of the Tiyya leaders to win adherents to their temples all came together.

Tapper and liquor baron alike were hit hard and the Tiyyas found their monopoly of the toddy industry slipping away from their grasp. As vend fees for toddy and the prices of both toddy and arrack rose, attendance fell at toddy shop auctions, and increasingly so in the decade of the twenties. Shops remained unsold or were sold for very low rentals. Non-cooperation activities and the picketing of toddy shops by Congress and Khilafat volunteers played their part. The excise department noted with bemusement the influence of even Buddhism on a few tappers who had given up their profession.[52] Illicit manufacture made up the shortfall in supply caused by the reduction in the number of shops but the toddy trade had changed dramatically by 1930. The excise policy directly exacerbated the rivalry between Tiyya and Mappila as the latter inexorably assumed control over the toddy trade. Prospering Tiyya elites were not willing to invest in a trade which was becoming increasingly unprofitable and, moreover, was tinged with the stigma of lowness.[53] This left the way open for Mappila financiers who had been increasingly discomfited by Tiyya encroachment in the spheres of commerce and credit. Mappila cartels began investing in the toddy trade and the earlier pattern of a large number of

---

[50] Petition of tappers to the Kerala Labour Union, *Mithavadi*, September 1918. V.K. Nayanar, '*Menokkiye konnathu aaranu?*' in *Kesari Nayanarude krithikal (The collected works of Kesari Nayanar)* (Calicut, 1987), 6-13.

[51] *Mithavadi*, September 1918.

[52] *RARMP*, 1920-21, 15; *RARMP*, 1921-22, 9; *RARMP*, 1923-24, 9.

[53] The example of the Murkkoth family provides a striking example of the change in attitudes over a generation. Murkkoth Ramunny was the foremost toddy magnate in Malabar at the end of the nineteenth century, controlling toddy shops in Chirakkal, Kottayam, Kurumbranad and Calicut. His son Murkkoth Kumaran, one-time editor of the *Mithavadi*, was at the forefront of the campaign to disassociate the Tiyyas from the toddy trade. MSS of Murkkoth Kumaran's autobiography, 5-6.

small shops was replaced by a comparatively small number of big shops controlled by Mappila financiers from the coast. By 1936 auction sales had become a farce with no competitive bidding, since local cartels controlled all the shops.[54]

For one section of reformers, temperance was born out of the attack on the religious culture of the shrines; they emphasised the low status of Tiyya tappers at shrine festivals and looked askance at unbridled tippling. The pressures on the toddy business, and the emergence of a new kind of drinking further fuelled their campaign. Prospective imbibers were being pushed towards toddy shops by the government policy of raising taxes on trees, licensing requirements for tapping and policing sources of informal supply.[55] The diatribes against liquor stemmed too, from the changed nature of drinking. The burgeoning of toddy shops and a shift towards secular, individual, drinking as opposed to religious, communal drinking stoked the reformers' wrath. Drinking out of a communal context, unchecked by one's peers, allowed for the emergence of a notion of alcoholism as apart from sanctioned drunkenness. The equation of the drinking of alcohol with alcoholism and therefore, moral turpitude, marked the temperance campaign. There were other influences. In the first decade of this century the government of Madras, in a short-lived campaign to promote abstemiousness, had introduced the subject of temperance in school syllabi. The consumption of alcohol came to be enmeshed in issues of morals, religion, hygiene and physiology.[56]

It has recently been argued that much of the puritanism of the nineteenth and twentieth century caste movements stemmed more from 'western' inspiration than from an indigenous revulsion.[57] While the influence of missionaries on morals in Malabar was minimal, many of those educated in English castigated the consumption of alcohol. Curiously, they tended to see the consumption of alcohol as a western fashion undermining the traditional social fabric. An educated Nayar, self confessedly 'fed on the strong food of western science and civilization' saw the new age ushering in 'the sorry spectacle of the son drinking with the father, the elder with the younger brother, the daughter with the mother, the wife with the husband' and so on.[58] Murkkoth Kumaran, Tiyya

[54] *RARMP*, 1935-36, 15.
[55] For a similar argument in the context of Gujarat see D. Hardiman, 'From custom to crime: the politics of drinking in colonial south Gujarat', Guha ed., *Subaltern studies*, IV (Delhi, 1985), 193-4.
[56] *RARMP*, 1915-16, 5.
[57] Lucy M. Carroll, 'The temperance movement in India: politics and social reform,' *Modern Asian Studies* 10, 3 (1976), 440-1, 446. Carroll convincingly argues that missionaries, purveying Victorian ideas of temperance, had a significant influence on the Kayastha reform movement in the United Provinces. See also, 'Caste, social change and the social scientist; a note on the ahistorical approach to Indian social history,' *Journal of Asian Studies* 35, 1 (1975), 63-84.
[58] Panikkar, *Malabar and its folk*, 266.

litterateur and social reformer, wrote a satirical novelette titled 'Ambu Nayar', in which the moral degeneration of the eponymous hero begins when he wins a lottery. With money in his grasp, this traditional, rural gentleman undergoes a process of 'westernisation' and depravation. He joins a 'club', drinks alcohol, gambles and even falls in 'love' with a young girl with whom he plans to elope![59] Amidst this mixture of motivations: the attack on low casteness; a desire for social mobility and economic well-being; the attempts at self definition of a new elite; the pressures on the profession of toddy tapping itself; it is difficult, and unwise, to privilege any one explanation. Temperance was to be given a wider political platform by the Congress, particularly with Bepan Chandra Pal's polemic against the British government for realising revenue by keeping the Indian masses in a state of inebriation.[60] Even as regards the influence of nationalism and the Congress there are far too many threads to be unravelled. In the case of K.P. Kesava Menon, founder of the nationalist newspaper, *Mathrubhumi* (1923), his attitude towards alcohol was influenced as much by Gandhi as his early activities with the Home Rule League with its Victorian stand on temperance.[61]

Congress, the Mappila rebellion and 'Hindu' identity

The Gnanodaya Yogam had tried to construct a limited community based on an identity of caste. Tiyyas who prayed together at the Jagannatha and Sundareswara would stay together. There had been no attempt to garner the adherence of the Pulayas, Panans, Nayadis and other untouchable castes. A separate community of equal Tiyyas aspired to enter society as equals.[62] In Malabar, the Congress would link the movement away from the shrines with the idea of equality in the theme of temple entry – Hindus would enter the portals of the temples as equals. Here again, the idea of a religious community of equals was maintained; it was both an expansion of the original idea as well as a limitation in that it did not conceive of a wider secular unity. Part of the reason for this narrow definition lay in the conjuncture of the Mappila rebellion of 1921 which forced the Congress to retreat into a Hindu idiom of politics.

[59] M. Kumaran, *Ambu Nayar* (Calicut, 1965 edn).
[60] Bepan Chandra, *The rise and growth of economic nationalism* (Delhi, 1966), 556-61.
[61] The League was set up in Malabar by Manjeri Rama Iyer, a close associate of Annie Besant, and its early activities consisted of temperance campaigns and prayer meetings for lower castes. Interview with C.T. Kuttikrishnan, Secretary, Theosophical Society, Calicut, March 1987.
[62] A similar idea can be found in the thought of the Ad Dharm movement among the untouchables of Punjab. Mangoo Ram, the founder, saw the untouchables as constituting a *qaum* – a distinct religious community which had existed from time immemorial. Juergensmeyer, *Religion as social vision*, 46-50.

From 1920, the political activity of local Congressmen began involving greater numbers. At the Political Conference held in Manjeri, for the first time a resolution was passed which called for the protection of the interests of tenants. The tenancy agitation was led largely by Nayars who came from prominent landholding families in and around Calicut.[63] In 1921, this fragile rapprochement of interests began to splinter as the triad of tenancy, Congress and Khilafat began pulling political activity in different directions. There had been a history of outbreaks among the Mappila peasantry in south Malabar all through the nineteenth century. Agrarian oppression had forged a Mappila identity centred on *maulvis*, mosques and martyr shrines.[64] Demands for security of tenure, and the holding of meetings throughout south Malabar by tenant associations, created a degree of political involvement among Hindu and Mappila cultivators. While Khilafat allowed for a temporary alliance between the local Congress and Mappila sentiment, it could not paper over the divisions between impoverished Mappila agricultural labourers and Hindu landowners.

The district authorities and police worsened matters by their insensitive handling of Mappila leaders which culminated in a raid on Mambram mosque in August 1921. Leaders like Ali Musaliar and, subsequently, Variyamkunnath Kunhamad Haji assumed nominal control over a largely decentred Mappila groundswell in Tirurangadi and Malappuram. They attempted to set up an 'Islamic state' in the taluks of Ernad and Walluvanad. Even though proclamations were issued calling upon Mappilas not to attack Hindus, the rebellion assumed a more random, localised and communal character with the arrest of the leaders.[65] There were rumours of forced conversions of Hindus and a steady stream of Hindu refugees flowed into Calicut and Trichur. The Congress busied itself with preparing refugee camps and disowning the Mappila rebels.[66] In the five months before Variyamkunnath Haji surrendered and martial law was lifted in February 1922, the image of the Mappila had undergone a radical transformation. Stories of fanaticism, violence and conversions established themselves in the minds of a badly frightened Hindu population. As an early Congressman wrote in his autobiography, the 'ghost of Ernad' was to haunt all attempts in the twenties to widen the range of political activity in Malabar.[67]

[63] See Radhakrishnan, *Peasant struggles, land reforms and social change*, Malabar, 1836-1982 (New Delhi, 1989), 75-9; P.K. Karunakara Menon, *History of the freedom movement in Kerala* (Trivandrum, 1972), II, 66-82.
[64] Conrad Wood, 'The first Moplah rebellion against British rule in Malabar', *Modern Asian Studies* 10, 4 (1970), 543-56; Dale, *Islamic society on the south Asian frontier*, ch. 5. Dale tends towards a teleology which sees the Mappila Rebellion of 1921 as the apocalyptic finale of a process, which began in 1498, of the creation of a beleagured Mappila identity.
[65] Dale, *Islamic society on the south Asian frontier*, 209-17.
[66] See K. Madhavan Nayar, *Malabar kalapam (The ferment in Malabar)* (Calicut, 1987 edn) for a contemporary account by a Congressman.
[67] M. Sankaran, *Ente jivitha katha*, 226.

For the next decade, there was a retreat from secular political activity and an increasingly introspective Hindu style began to develop in Malabar. In northern India there was a resurgence of *shuddhi* activity by the Arya Samaj which tried to reclaim converts to Hinduism and purify it of untouchability. This new effort was, in part, directly inspired by the Mappila rebellion and led to the 'reappearance of communalism' as ulamas and Muslim sects responded to the challenge of a militant Hinduism.[68] On the whole, in Malabar there was more an attempt to 'create' a Hindu identity rather than to assert an existing one. The Arya Samaj began its activities in Palghat from 1922 and Pandit Rishi Ram came down from Punjab to reclaim lapsed Hindus. Rishi Ram created a furore in Palghat by taking some Ezhavas and Arya Samaj converts from lower castes into the Brahmin settlement in Kalpathy. The Brahmins cast aside their otherworldliness and beat up several processionists. This led to the formation of the Malabar branch of the Rantar Tablig-e-Islam which asked the 'Ezhava brothers' to embrace Islam as the Arya Samaj had been unable to help them.[69]

Temple entry for Hindus – the Vaikkam *satyagraha*

The Indian National Congress had always recognised the problem of untouchability, the extreme manifestation of caste hierarchy, out of the corner of its eye. It was only in 1920 that untouchability came to be defined in a particular sense as a 'reproach to Hinduism'.[70] Religious heads were requested to help in reforming Hinduism so that it could be purged of this egregious accretion. The redefinition of untouchability as a religious problem informed Congress activity in Malabar, as well as its attempts to tackle the differences and inequality between castes. The possibility of unifying the diverse caste movements under the umbrella of the Congress seemed possible only if Hinduism could be purified by the abolition of untouchability and everyone could enter it as equals. Ostensibly there was a constituency here, since the Tiyya temples had excluded untouchables and lower castes from their ambit. In a pamphlet called *Svatantryayuddham* [*Freedom struggle*], a Nayar Congressman rebuked the Tiyyas for not behaving as equals with Pulayas, Panans and Nayadis and not allowing them into Jagannatha or Sundareswara.[71] In the retreat from secular political activity after the Mappila rebellion, the role of arbiter between castes presented the Malabar Congressmen with a programme.

[68] Gail Minault, *The Khilafat movement: religious symbolism and political mobilisation in India* (New York, 1982), 193-201.
[69] Achuthan, *C. Krishnan*, 150. *Revenue R. Dis. 9525/25 dated 21 April 1926* (KRA).
[70] E. Zelliott, 'Congress and the untouchables, 1915-50' in R. Sisson and S. Wolpert eds., *Congress and Indian nationalism: the pre-independence phase* (Berkeley, CA, 1988), 185.
[71] C.K. Nambiar, *Svatantryayuddham* (*The war of liberation*) (Tellicherry, 1924).

Meanwhile in Travancore, the Ezhavas continued their agitation for acceptance in society. In 1919, a meeting of nearly 5,000 Ezhavas called for admission into all temples managed by the state. [72] T.K. Madhavan, a close associate of Narayana Guru carried this objective to the national realm. He introduced a resolution at the Kakinada session of the Congress in 1923, which stated that temple entry was the birthright of all Hindus. The assumption seemed to be that if all castes were allowed to enter temples which restricted entry to upper castes, then Hinduism could be purged of inequality. The way to caste equality seemingly lay through the portals of a temple. After the disaster of the Khilafat alliance, the Nayar leaders of the Congress needed a programme which could at the same time involve large numbers of people as well as subsume caste movements into a more general Hindu identity. In 1924, K. Kelappan Nayar convened an anti-untouchability committee within the K.P.C.C. and toured Travancore with a party of Congressmen from Malabar. It was decided that the Congress would fight for the rights of Ezhavas and lower castes to use the roads around Vaikkam temple. On 30 March 1924, K.P. Kesava Menon and T.K. Madhavan, accompanied by Nayar, Pulaya and Ezhava volunteers, attempted to walk on the roads near the temple and were arrested. The next day, three more Congress leaders including K. Kelappan (who by now had eschewed his caste surname) from Malabar were apprehended by the police. In the meanwhile, Gandhi had been following events with great interest and had sent goodwill telegrams to the organisers. However, there was a shift in his attitude with the arrest of all the Nayar Congress leaders. George Joseph (1887-1938), a Syrian Christian and one-time editor of *Young India*, assumed charge of the *satyagraha*. Gandhi immediately wrote to Joseph, specifying that the Vaikkam *satyagraha* was a Hindu affair and he 'should let the Hindus do the work'. Gandhi clarified that the Congress resolution at Nagpur had called upon only the 'Hindu members' to remove the curse of untouchability. [73]

Gandhi defined the Vaikkam *satyagraha* as a 'socio-religious movement. It (has) no immediate or ulterior political motive behind it ... It was directed purely against an age long, intolerable sacerdotal prejudice.' [74] Considering the particular colouring given to the *satyagraha*, it was not surprising that caste organisations of the higher castes, like the Nair Service Society, the Kshatriya Mahasabha, the Kerala Hindu Sabha and the Yogakshema Sabha of the Nambudiris expressed their wholehearted support. The SNDP was the lone *avarna* organisation to back the struggle, and rumours were rife that Narayana Guru had advocated more muscular methods to gain entry to the roads and that

[72] Karunakara Menon, *History of the freedom movement in Kerala*, II, 116.
[73] Gandhi to George Joseph, 6 April 1924, *Collected works of Mahatma Gandhi* (henceforth *CWMG*) (Ahmedabad, 1972), XXIII, 391.
[74] *CWMG*, XXIII, 441-2.

he had distanced himself from the activities of the SNDP.[75] In April 1924, a *jatha* of Akalis arrived from Amritsar to set up free food kitchens for the volunteers, amidst rumours that they were representatives of Sikh 'fanatics' who had created trouble in the Punjab with the Gurudwara reform movement.[76] Gandhi immediately called for the closure of the free kitchens and argued that help from outside was not necessary. He claimed, moreover, that the people of Travancore did not need charity. It was obvious that Gandhi viewed the Akali presence as the potential source of a conflagration. In an article in *Young India*, in language unwarranted by local circumstances, he stated 'that the proposed Sikh free kitchen I can only regard as a menace to the frightened Hindus of Vaikom'.[77] Gandhi's intercession, circumscribing involvement and removing the political edge of the movement, meant that temple entry petered out into an issue which was finally decided in the Legislative Council. A resolution to allow Ezhavas to use roads near the temples was defeated by one vote. The *satyagraha* continued fitfully till November 1925, when the Travancore government made diversionary lanes and managed to further defuse the situation.[78]

What were the consequences of the Vaikkam *satyagraha* for Malabar? For one it bolstered the spirits of a demoralised Congress which was able to recoup itself after the shock of the Mappila Rebellion of 1921. Equally, it gently moved them towards the *cul-de-sac* of Hindu politics and of seeing the problem of caste and untouchability as a purely religious issue; temple entry and caste equality meshed into a unit. Nevertheless, it was a programme with which the Congress in Malabar could attempt to bring all the castes into one consolidated movement. A pamphlet by a Nayar Congressman described the Vaikkam *satyagraha* as the achievement of 'Ezhava volunteers with the civilised classes as their leaders'.[79] Moreover, it gave the Nayars ammunition to gain entry for themselves into temples where Nambudiris denied them entry. As the pamphleteer went on to observe, 'to continue to feign respect for these crafty sacred thread wearers' was foolish so long as 'they kept God for themselves'.[80] Both Tiyya elites and tenants stayed aloof from such movements and saw themselves

[75] Karunakara Menon, *History of the freedom movement in Kerala*, II, 118, 125; R. Jeffrey, 'Travancore: status, class and the growth of radical politics, 1860-1940, the temple entry movement', in R. Jeffrey, ed., *People, princes and paramount power: society and politics in the Indian princely states* (Delhi, 1978), 156.
[76] Karunakara Menon, *History of the freedom movement in Kerala*, II, 121. The agitation in Nabha, the stream of *jathas* to Jaito, the involvement of the Congress, the arrest of Nehru and the opening of fire by the state authorities on a peaceful *jatha* in February 1924 were still fresh in the public memory. See Khushwant Singh, *A history of the Sikhs 1839-1964*, II (Princeton, NJ, 1966), ch. 13.
[77] 'Vaikom satyagraha', *Young India*, 1 May 1924, *CWMG*, XXIII, 516.
[78] Jeffrey, 'Travancore', 153-7.
[79] Nambiar, *Svatantryayuddam*.
[80] *Ibid.*

as 'an independent community owing allegiance to no religion'. Tiyya tappers and labourers continued to stay away from shrine festivals where they were expected to play a subordinate role, and in 1930 they conspicuously avoided the Kalaripadikkal festival.[81] While the Nayar Congressmen found it difficult to win the allegiance of Tiyyas, they were to be more successful in their efforts among the castes dependent on their tharavadus, especially the Pulayas and Cherumas.

Cleanliness and caste equality

Gandhi's definition of the issue of untouchability as one of differential cleanliness laid emphasis on the fact that upper caste Hindus had to inculcate habits of purity among their less fortunate brethren. This provided Nayars from dominant tharavadus in the interior with their own programme. Gandhi's advocacy of a simple and pure lifestyle seemed to have influenced many Nayars from dominant households. A.C. Kannan Nayar, the head of the Echikanam household in Hosdrug, 'came under the sway of Gandhism' in 1920 after reading a pamphlet on Gandhi. He began wearing *khadi* six years later on 6 April 1926, but it was only in 1927 that he actually began campaigning on behalf of the Congress, after being a member of the Swaraj party for a short while in 1925.[82] An identification with Gandhi did not necessarily mean an affinity with the Congress, and often involved only the aspiration to non-violence, temperance and a simple life, quite at variance with the lifestyles of Nayar country gentry.[83] This allowed them to attempt to build bridges between their tharavadus and dependent cultivators and labourers; relations which had been undermined to a certain extent by the movement away from the shrines. In the process, relations between castes were redefined conceiving cleanliness as that which distinguished 'high' from 'low'. The opposition between clean and unclean emerged as a major theme in the programme of Nayar Congressmen in Malabar, and this was to continue well into the next decade.

Initially, reform was attempted among those castes dependent on tharavadus as labourers or as ritual functionaries. A.C. Kannan Nayar, Congressman and landlord, enthusiastically recorded in his diary how he had organised the woodworkers and washermen dependent on his tharavadu and tried to incul-

---

[81] *Mathrubhumi*, 30 December 1930, 20 May 1932.
[82] *Diaries of A.C. Kannan Nayar*, 20 December 1925, 6 April 1926, 24 October 1927 (NMML).
[83] A pamphlet written in 1920 depicted the transformation wrought on a typical martial, hard-drinking, hot-tempered Nayar with the introduction of a *charkha* into his home. He gave up his favourite pastime of hunting, threw his gun into the household pond and devoted himself to spinning meditatively on the *charkha*. C. Padmavathi Amma, *Chakramahima (The saga of the charkha)* (Calicut, 1920).

cate habits of cleanliness and temperance in them.[84] A younger generation within the Nayar tharavadus drawn to the Congress organised their literally captive audience of Cheruma and Pulaya labourers into temperance leagues.[85] These Adi Dravida *sanghs* also called for the eschewing of animal sacrifice in religious ritual. In many cases, the adoption of purer lifestyles and religious practices by Pulayas and Cherumas had little to do with any crusade for social mobility, and stemmed more from the threat of the use of force by their superiors. It was a choice between purity or punishment. However, there were other influences at work as well, for nothing is as worthy of imitation as success and the Tiyyas were the success story of north Malabar. A pamphlet published in 1917, by a literate Cheruma, bemoaned the fact that more and more of his caste people were showing a tendency to adopt ballads and songs of their higher caste neighbours, the Tiyyas.[86] Tiyyas continued to assert their new-found sense of community and status not only in the exclusion of Pulayas and Cherumas from their temples, but also in an increasing tendency to impose sanctions on castes lower to them. These castes were caught between the pincers of Tiyya disapproval and Nayar enthusiasm for organising them. In villages along the coast, there were frequent attacks and, in 1929, there were several incidents of Pulayas being beaten up by Tiyyas for venturing on to public roads.[87]

In the wake of the Vaikkam *satyagraha*, Nayar Congressmen presented a transcendent alternative of admission into Hinduism in their new found role as arbiters of conflict. There were several facets to this activity, since equality had to be wrought on several fronts. It was a curious situation that Gandhi and the Congress had created. Untouchability had come to be characterised at the Nagpur session as a 'reproach to Hinduism' and by 1921 sanitation work was defined as 'honourable work'. If the unclean work that the sweepers did made them untouchable, then Congress workers would redeem that occupation by doing it as well thus expiating their sins as Hindus for having ostracised the untouchables.[88] The work was redeemed, but not the individual who had to be cleansed before being admitted into the Hindu fold.

Cleanliness was to keep surfacing in this period as a major theme in Congress activity – caste inequality was being defined initially as a matter of differential hygiene. Allied with this was the idea that if persons were to be

[84] *Diaries of A.C. Kannan Nayar*, 23 June 1929 and 7 July 1929 (NMML).
[85] Cheruma and Pulaya labourers were so closely bound up with the households for which they worked that the Commissioner for Labour had been worried about extending the work of his department to Malabar. He firmly believed that 'efforts to do anything to raise [*sic*] the Cherumas would cause trouble'. *Law (General) Dept. G.O.3543 dated 13 December 1924* (KS).
[86] Cheruman Chathan, *Pulapattu (Songs of the Pulayas)* (Calicut, 1917).
[87] *Mathrubhumi*, 10 and 12 December 1929.
[88] However, this was a curious redefinition as Zelliott points out. Gandhi's 'approach was to make *bhangi* [sweeper] work acceptable rather than remove the *bhangi* from sanitation work'. Zelliott, 'Congress and the untouchables', 186-8.

identified with the work they did, then a change of name would necessarily remove the stigma of their occupation. This was an idea taken up by several caste groups in this period: Tiyyas calling themselves *vaidyars* (*ayurvedic* doctors), Kammalars (artisans) calling themselves Vishvakarmas and even Nayars dropping their caste names as Kelappan did during the Vaikkam *satyagraha*.[89] Some Vaniyars (oil pressers) in north Malabar had begun to call themselves Nayars and, in Chirakkal, one was evicted for this reason.[90] For some it was not the casting-off a name, but the adoption of the physical appearance of a superior caste by which they demonstrated their self-esteem. Cheruma labourers who were recognisable by their shaved heads, or long, uncut hair began to sport *kudumis*: tying their hair up in a knot on the side of their head, like the Nayars did.[91] A meeting organised in 1929, by the north Malabar Congress committee, for the Adi Dravidas of Pazhayangadi showed the coming together of three concerns – cleanliness, nomenclature and Congress activity. One of the major resolutions was the adoption of the name of Adi Keraliyar for the untouchables. It provided both a change of name for removing the stigma of caste and endowed them with a historical validity as the first settlers in Kerala! However, the Congress insisted on holding a mirror up to the 'Adi Keraliyars' and stressed that the main reason for their low status was 'their lack of cleanliness'.[92]

What had hitherto been implicit and unquestioned about caste was brought into the open. Gandhi and the Congress had defined the problem of caste inequality in terms of an opposition between cleanliness and the lack of it, locating the whole issue not in terms of economic or social realities but a physical state. This introduction, at a historical moment, of the idea of cleanliness, as the central concept underlying inequality, allows us to understand in a more processual way the changing construction of the differences between castes. Dumont hypostatises the opposition between 'pure' and 'impure' as underlying the hierarchy of castes. It is possible to speculate that such notions gained wide currency and were disseminated in the process of the political redefinition of the basis of caste inequality by the Congress. Though uncleanliness as associated with the *bhangi's* profession had ritual connotations as well, since they removed human excrement, in Congress activity cleanliness became a secular metaphor for casteness. *Khadi*, conceived initially as a symbol of Indian self-reliance now came to assume a pivotal role in this context as the great leveller. Caste difference had been stressed earlier in the way people dressed. The advocacy of *khadi* implied that if everyone dressed

---

[89] *Mithavadi*, February 1915; P. Govindan, *Keraliya karmmala samaja vijnapanam* (*An advertisement for the artisans of Kerala*) (Calicut, 1922).
[90] Oral evidence of T. Narayanan Nair, *vakil*, High Court, Tellicherry, *MTCR, 1927-28*, II, 265.
[91] Innes, *Malabar Gazetteer*, 143.
[92] *Mathrubhumi*, 24 December 1929.

alike then difference could be eliminated. The wearing of clean, white, starched *khadi* emphasised cleanliness as well as the aspiration to sameness. A concern with cleanliness can be found in the early activities of missionaries as well as the efforts of the Home Rule League with its insistence on temperance and hygiene among the working classes. Missionary activity among the Pulayas in Travancore and the Shanars in Tinnevelly had stressed cleanliness in clothing and appearance among new converts. In the north, the attitude of the Congress towards cleanliness could have been conditioned by the proselytising Hinduism of the Shuddhi sabhas of the late nineteenth century and the Arya Samaj.[93] At this juncture, the association of cleanliness with casteness and the adoption of hygiene as a political programme was represented as a radical intervention by the Congress.

Once cleanliness had been introduced into the public arena as a concept it assumed the same force as an idea that socialism was to have in the next decade. At a meeting of the Adi Keraliyar in Kalliasseri (this time without the helping hand of the Congress) a resolution asserted that 'cleanliness is the *only* thing that distinguishes the upper castes from the Harijans' (emphasis mine).[94] Once the ostensible principle underlying differences was clarified, caste inequality was hoist on its own petard. Large sections of lower castes remained aloof from such activity because of the obvious dangers from conservatives, both among their equals and their superiors. In Kasergode, Congress activists from one of the dominant tharavadus invited a washerman clad in spotless *khadi* to drink water from the same well as they. The washerman was ostracised by his own community and had to pay a heavy fine for readmittance to his caste.[95]

Once the lower castes had been rendered clean – abstemious, bathed and given to daily prayer – then how were they to be admitted to society as equals? Many of the early Nayar Congressmen organised interdining with the castes dependent on their tharavadus.[96] However, these were localised activities and could not be reproduced on a larger scale because of the involvement of individuals in several circuits – that of their caste, relations with their landlord, and their locality. One way of uniting these isolated activities could have been to utilise religious fairs and fetivals to gain entry for lower castes to temples and

[93] See R. Jeffrey, *The decline of Nayar dominance: society and politics in Travancore, 1847-1908* (New York, 1976); R. Hardgrave, *The Nadars of Tamilnad: the political culture of a community in change*(Berkeley, CA, 1969); K.W. Jones, *Arya Dharma: Hindu consciousness in nineteenth century Punjab* (California, 1976), 202-5, 212-15 for the Shuddhi sabha activities of 'transformation of outcastes into clean caste Hindus'. For Congress and Home Rule League activity in Malabar see Kesava Menon, *Kazhinja kalam (Times past)* (Calicut, 1962).
[94] *Mathrubhumi*, 29 May 1934.
[95] *File on the oral history of Kasergode taluk* (A.K. Gopalan Centre, Trivandrum).
[96] *A.C. Kannan Nayar Diaries*; Sankaran, *Ente jivitha katha*.

shrines.[97] However, there were several obstacles to be overcome. There were temples which prohibited entry to Nayars, and private family temples which did not allow even lower sub-castes of Nayars a right to worship. Among the Nayars there were groups like the Samudayika Bahishkarana Sangham [Community boycott organisation] which attempted to work within the community to abolish animal sacrifice and the drinking of alcohol.[98] The perception of 'clean' and 'unclean' extended also to differences within the upper castes and did not mark an absolute divide between high and low. The association of alcohol and blood sacrifice with uncleanliness had assumed a potency over the past decade of caste activity. Therefore, the Nayar Congressmen had to set their own house in order, or fight for their own admittance to temples before they could take on the role of leaders.

Shrine festivals drew upon a limited community of worshippers within a well-defined geographical area. Moreover, the Nayar Congressmen were keen to dissociate themselves from the consumption of alcohol and blood sacrifices which accompanied worship at most shrines. In this, they were one with the Tiyya elites who advocated a withdrawal from the shrines, as well as those Tiyyas who were actually escaping from the entrenchment of their caste inferiority at shrine festivals. The rhetoric of cleanliness had to be synthesised with the larger issue of caste equality. Tiyya elites had partly solved the problem by standing as a separate, therefore equal community, by constructing their own temples. This meant that the Nayar Congressmen working with the notion of difference inherent in caste, and the idea of unity implicit in their nationalist message, were seemingly at an *impasse*. But all these strands, the movement away from shrines, the move towards cleanliness and its association with casteness, the possibility raised by the Vaikkam *satyagraha* of temple entry for all castes and, above all, the narrowing of Congress horizons into a Hindu introspection were rearranging themselves into a pattern. This pattern was that of a throng of clean, equal Hindus marching through the portals of a temple towards a nationalist unity. This was the new ideal, and the temple at Guruvayur was the Bastille to be stormed. Kelappan wrote to Nehru towards the end of 1931, 'Guruvayur temple is the last refuge of all caste arrogance and prejudice. Once untouchability is dislodged from there it will have no quarter outside.'[99]

[97] See G. Pandey, *The ascendancy of the Congress in Uttar Pradesh, 1926-34; a study in imperfect mobilisation* (Delhi, 1978), chs. 2 and 3 for similar activity in UP and the utilisation of the Kumbh Mela, for example, for Congress propaganda.

[98] N.E. Balaram, *Keralathile kammyunistu prasthanam (The communist movement in Kerala)* (Trivandrum, 1973), I, 50.

[99] K. Kelappan to J. Nehru, 23 October 1931. All India Congress Committee (henceforth AICC) File G/86, 1931 (NMML).

Conclusion

Throughout this period there had been a search for newer forms of community. Tiyya elites in the towns had attempted to create a separate and equal identity around urban temples, paralleling the communities of worship and sustenance around shrines in the countryside. Unlike their caste cousins across the border, the Nadars of Ramnad, the Tiyyas had not been overly concerned about entry into temples which denied them entry.[100] Some of the Tiyyas and lower castes remained within the shrine communities. Others did so while repudiating the reiteration of their perceived caste roles as festivals. A number moved out of this circuit altogether, motivated by equal mixtures of a desire for equality, economic advantage and the adoption of a different lifestyle and form of worship. The Congress enterprise in Malabar sought to remove caste difference, a hindrance in the attempt to create a unified Hindu identity. In practice, however, it developed as a limited imperative. Through ideas of cleanliness, hygiene, purity and abstinence, individuals were to be incorporated within a normative identity which equated an unclean physical state with the social condition of inequality. After the ephemeral unity of Khilafat and the Congress, both at the national as well as the regional level, it signified a retreat from attempts to build a community transcending religious difference. This would culminate in the attempt to gain entry into the temple at Guruvayur, and the limited, religious idiom of politics severely curtailed the enactment of civil disobedience in Malabar.

[100] As Hardgrave points out, the failure of the Nadars to gain access to Kamudi temple, as a result of a Madras High Court interdiction in 1897, meant that they moved from 'sacred' to 'secular' forms of achieving mobility. Hardgrave, *The Nadars of Tamilnad*, 108–29.

4   Civil disobedience and temple entry, 1930–1933

At the beginning of 1930, the Indian National Congress was at the crossroads. It faced the prospect of widening political differences between Hindus and Muslims, and the twin, contradictory pressures of one strong group rooting for complete independence and another reluctant to deprive itself of office by continuing a policy of non-cooperation. The Round Table Conference, early in the year, had not arrived at any concrete, viable resolution of India's political future. Amidst all the uncertainty and the prospect of organisational dissension, Gandhi appeared to be the one figure who could hold the centre together. Moreover, the launching of a controlled programme of civil disobedience seemed to present the possibility of restoring order within the ranks. At the same time it provided the Congress with a counter it could use to bargain with the colonial government.

The timing of civil disobedience was determined by national imperatives, but local Congress units showed remarkable flexibility in their response. For a span of three years from 1930, local political activity in Malabar seemed to mesh with the national campaign. The staples of nationalist activity – the manufacture of salt, the picketing of liquor shops and the propagation of *khadi* – were replicated, albeit with minor variations. Ostensibly, these were the motifs through which nationalist agitation could be most readily 'localised', since each was a reaction, to a greater or lesser degree, to colonial intrusion.[1] However, in comparison with other provinces like Gujarat, Bengal, UP and closer home, the Andhra region, civil disobedience activities in Malabar seem muted. There were no campaigns against payment of rent or revenue; no agitations among tenants or cultivators; nor indeed any trade union or worker militancy.[2] Moreover, there appeared to be no Congress organisation, apart from a few people who spoke in the name of the Congress. Questions like the relation between Congress strength and local militancy; radicalism on the

[1] See D.A. Low, 'Introduction' in D.A. Low ed., *Congress and the Raj: facets of the Indian struggle, 1917-47* (Delhi, 1977), 17-18.
[2] For regional studies see essays by B. Stoddart, D. Hardiman, G. Pandey in Low, *Congress and the Raj* and T. Sarkar, *Bengal, 1928-34: the politics of protest* (Delhi, 1987).

fringes of Congress control; and methods of mass mobilisation adopted by Congress workers appear incongruous in the context of Malabar.[3] A partial explanation for the lack of a wider political involvement may lie in two factors peculiar to Malabar. Civil disobedience elsewhere has been analysed against the backdrop of revenue resettlement operations and secondly, the impact of the Depression.[4] In Malabar, resettlement was completed only by 1934 and the pepper and coconut economy of north Malabar did not experience the crunch of the Depression till the mid thirties. But was it just a case of the dog that did not bark? Probably a more satisfying explanation would lie in the proposition that nationalism did not specifically address the problem of caste inequality at this juncture.

A Tiyya elite in the coastal towns had thrown down the gauntlet in the previous decade, by presenting the ideal of a community of equals around their new temples. This had, to an extent, disrupted relations between tharavadus and lower caste cultivators. Partly in response to this, Nayar Congressmen had resorted to a Gandhian programme of inculcating cleanliness and hygiene among the untouchable castes dependent on their tharavadus. While such activity held forth the promise of equality for the lower castes, it emphasised, at the same time, their subjection by the tharavadus. During the course of civil disobedience activity, Nayar Congressmen built up connections between their tharavadus and reasserted their influence in the villages. In north Malabar, Congress politics evolved as an exercise of caste authority and was perceived as the enforcement of nationalism by decree. Local conflicts predominated over national affiliations, as in the case of liquor picketing, where the toddy shops of Tiyyas were forcibly shut down by powerful tharavadus. The second phase of civil disobedience addressed itself directly, and wholly, to the exigent local issue of caste. Nayar Congressmen attempted to steal the thunder from the Tiyya movement by allying the ideal of a community of equals to the problem of caste inequality. They envisaged a unity of all castes around the temple at Guruvayur, and urged for the right of entry into the temple for lower castes. For a brief moment, nationalism was translated into an appealing local idiom. However, in the end, Tiyyas preferred their own temples and other lower castes remained suspicious of what appeared to be another attempt to emphasise the authority of the Nayars.

More crucial for the local perception of nationalism was the intervention by the Congress high command to severely curtail the possibilities opened up by the campaign for entry into the temple at Guruvayur. An issue like temple entry threatened to divide upper and lower castes into opposed camps, which was

---

[3] See Pandey, *The Congress in UP*, 7-8; Sarkar, *Bengal, 1928-34*, 3; D. Hardiman, *Peasant nationalists of Gujarat: Kheda district, 1917-34* (Delhi, 1981).
[4] See Pandey, *The Congress in UP*, 156-70; C.J. Baker, *The politics of south India, 1920-37* (Cambridge, 1976), 205-12.

something the national Congress could ill afford. In negotiating with the colonial government, as in the case of the Poona Pact of 1932, the Congress had to present itself as representing all castes. The 'local' issue of Guruvayur was 'nationalised', i.e. subordinated to the national imperative, thus depriving it of political content and restricting its appeal. Nationalism in Malabar would be circumscribed severely by its failure to address caste inequality.

Congress organisation in Malabar

On the eve of civil disobedience, the main characteristic of Congress organisation in Malabar was the lack of it. This was true of Congress organisation in both Tamilnadu and Andhra at the commencement of civil disobedience. However, in 1931 and 1932, falling agricultural prices and campaigns against government resettlement operations helped them to build up a coherent structure.[5] Though formal Congress units existed in Malabar, they were largely the remnants of the successful agitation for tenancy rights spearheaded by professional groups in the twenties and the ephemeral political conjuncture of Khilafat. The Kerala Pradesh Congress Committee (KPCC) had been formed in 1920, following the resolution at the Nagpur session of the All India Congress Committee which had called for the organisation of linguistic regional units. On the eve of civil disobedience, there were three Congress units in Malabar – the KPCC in Calicut, the district Congress committee in Palghat and the town committee of Cannanore.[6]

In the eastern villages, Nayar landlords like A.C. Kannan Nayar, attracted more by Gandhi than the Congress, devoted themselves to questions of cleanliness, hygiene and other issues which would not have caused a ripple on the surface of rural relations. For a younger generation of Nayars, the term 'Congress' indicated more a perception of affinity among themselves and a need for independent expression than an association with the national campaign against imperialism.[7] An instance of this was the setting up of the north Malabar *zilla* Congress committee. This was an informal association of younger Nayars from the dominant tharavadus rather than a link in a hierarchy of Congress organisations. It was founded in 1929 in Chirakkal, following

[5] Baker, *Politics of south India*, 253-4.
[6] Note by W.R. John on the Congress. *Madras Govt. Secret Files, Under-secretary's safe* (henceforth USS) *no. 718 dated 6 November 1931* (TNA).
[7] Both K.P.R. Gopalan (1910-) who would become one of the founders of the Communist party in Kerala and K.A. Keraleeyan (1907-1991), President of the All Malabar Peasant Union, began wearing *khadi* and associating with the Congress party as an act of rebellion against the heads of their respective households. Interviews at Kalliasseri and Calicut, February-March 1987.

incidents of attacks by Tiyyas on Pulayas who had ventured on to public roads. A 'conference' rallying Pulayas and other untouchable castes in the name of hygiene and abstinence had preceded the formation of this Congress unit.[8] Congress committees like these, in the eastern villages, attempted to redress the balance of power which had been disturbed by the setting up of the new Tiyya temples. They tried to undermine the increasing self confidence of the Tiyya tappers and cultivators by a reassertion of the connections between tharavadus and their dependent castes.

In the coastal towns, neither the Congress nor any other political party made much headway. Local elites managed to control the taluk boards and municipal councils on the strength of their regional influence alone. An alliance consisting of the pepper barons – the Kalliattu and Koodali tharavadus – and the Mappila merchant and exporter, A.K. Kunhi Moyan Haji, controlled the Chirakkal taluk board till its dissolution in 1930. By 1927, a third of the members of the Chirakkal taluk board were either the relations of Kalliattu Kammaran Nambiar or worked for him on his estates. One of the members was his trusted family physician.[9] Congress affiliation was strongest among Nayar lawyers and professional men in Calicut who had cut their teeth on the successful agitation for the Malabar Tenancy Act (passed in December 1930).[10] Within Calicut town, in contrast to the villages of Malabar, castes had begun to occupy particular quarters. Each such area was characterised by its own temples, caste organisations and libraries. The most notable of these spatial segregations was Chalappuram in Calicut which was the stronghold of the new breed of professional Nayars.[11] Congress activity, or rather, its presence, was confined to Chalappuram in Calicut and meetings were often held only on Sundays when the office bearers had time off from their legal practices. So far as the Mappilas were concerned, the Congress was seen, and rightly so, as a caste Hindu body dominated by the 'Chalappuram Gang' of lawyers.[12] E. Moithu Maulavi (1898-) who had been closely associated with the Khilafat movement in Malabar, found, on returning from jail, that his erstwhile Mappila associates in the Congress had begun to busy themselves with reform within their community.[13]

At this juncture, the Congress in the villages of Malabar was characterised by an ill-defined reformism. In the towns, there was either no organisation or,

[8] *Mathrubhumi*, 7, 12 and 20 December 1929.
[9] *Local Self Government Dept. G.O.1745 (L and M) dated 17 April 1928* (KS); *Local Self Government Dept. G.O. 2864 (L and M) dated 17 July 1930* (KS); Aaron, *Jeevithasmaranakal*, 95-6.
[10] See Radhakrishnan, *Peasant struggles, land reforms and social change*, 85-7.
[11] Aiyappan, *Iravas and culture change*, 33; E. Moithu Maulavi, *Maulaviyude katha (The Maulavi's story)* (Kottayam, 1981), 33.
[12] *AICC Files G-107/1930* (NMML).
[13] Moithu Maulavi, *Maulaviyude katha*, 107.

as in Calicut, one tinged with the anxiety that Congress activity would involve Hindu–Muslim conflict as in 1921. In March 1930, when the KPCC voted to participate in civil disobedience, K. Madhavan Nayar, the veteran of non-cooperation, resigned from the Congress. He did not want to be a part of the communal violence which he believed would ensue. Madhavan Nayar was persuaded to withdraw his resignation shortly afterwards 'in the interest of the national cause'.[14] Apart from the fear of a general conflagration there were real reasons fostering hesitancy. In 1930, it is difficult to speak of a Congress organisation. There were several individuals, for each of whom association with the Congress was one, and certainly not the most important, of many identities. K.P. Raman Menon, an office-holder in the KPCC was at the same time organising meetings of the Malabar Nayar Samajam and lobbying on behalf of tenants' associations for the speedy introduction of legislation.[15] Moreover, the KPCC, as an organisation, did not have any funds worth the name, even though individuals like Samuel Aaron, who were informally allied with the Congress, were quite wealthy. In a sense, the launching of any political programme would depend more on the willingness of wealthy well-wishers to subsidise it, than on directives from a high command. Finally, after Khilafat, there had been no one issue on which the Congress could organise. Tenancy agitation had been mainly resolved by the impending legislation of the Malabar Tenancy Act. This was in contrast to regions like Gujarat and coastal Andhra where the local Congress had managed to build a strong base among the peasantry by taking up the issues of revenue enhancements between 1925-30.[16]

The weakness of Congress organisation was to become evident within two months of the commencement of civil disobedience. The office bearers of the KPCC wrote despondently to headquarters that there were no village or district organisations any longer.[17] On 25 December 1930, the Kerala Congress was declared illegal, burying the last vestiges of organisation and control. Investigations by the AICC in 1931 revealed utter chaos. For two years between October 1929 and July 1931, there had been no receipt of membership fees; no accounts had been maintained; and there did not appear to be any evidence of correspondence between the provincial committee and subordinate committees, if any such existed.[18] In Malabar, it was a case of the local Congress not having its finger on the pulse of the countryside at all.

[14] *Mathrubhumi*, 1 April 1930.
[15] *Diaries of G. Sankaran Nayar*, 11 February 1931 (NMML).
[16] See essays by Hardiman and Stoddart in Low ed., *Congress and the Raj*, 59, 109-10.
[17] Report of K. Madhava Menon and A. Karunakara Menon, *AICC Files G107/1930* (NMML).
[18] Audit report, *AICC Files F 60/1931* (NMML).

Civil disobedience – the manufacture of salt

The salt *satyagraha* in Chirakkal *taluk* involved mainly those from prominent Nayar tharavadus and served to create a unity of purpose between them. Political activity was carried on amidst considerable restraint from the police who owed their jobs to the influential *satyagrahis* acting against the law. On 12 April 1930, K. Kelappan led a march of Congress volunteers from Calicut to Payyanur, traversing the villages of the interior, to manufacture salt. Prior to this K. Madhavan Nayar, the secretary of the KPCC, had toured north Malabar and established links with prominent tharavadus, like that of the Kalliattu Nambiar, to provide accommodation for the marchers. More important, the advance party approached Samuel Aaron, proprietor of the Aaron weaving mills and popularly known as the 'Birla of Malabar'. Aaron agreed to provide the funds necessary for the march, besides providing a field at Kokkanisseri where salt could be manufactured. Aaron also acted as a conduit for funds from other men of business in Tellicherry and Cannanore. In 1928, he had been elected a member of the Chirakkal *taluk* board supported by an informal lobby of businessmen.[19]

Fortified by the securing of finances, the marchers proceeded from Calicut to Payyanur through unfamiliar terrain, clad in white *khadi* and singing nationalist songs. They must have been watched by a bemused rural population who saw either strangers or the younger members of locally dominant tharavadus in an unfamiliar role; acknowledging the crowd with none of the arrogance of their elders. The police kept a respectful distance and in the countryside there was none of the violence that characterised their encounters with *satyagrahis* in the towns.[20] The chief reason may have been that the participation of village elites in processions elicited pragmatism from constables. Moyyarath Sankaran (1889-1948), writing of a procession he had organised from Badagara to Payyanur, mentions that the constables on duty came up to some of the participants to get their beat registers signed. When Kunhiraman Nayar, a young member of the Kalliattu household and Hariswaran Tirumumpu of the powerful Thazhekkat household were arrested, they refused to sign on the bail bond. Embarrassed police constables released them immediately.[21]

On 21 April, the main procession, led by Kelappan, reached Valapattanam and stayed at the house of T.V. Chathukutty Nayanar, the biggest landowner

[19] Aaron, *Jeevithasmaranakal*, 90-5, 139-40.
[20] The official history of the freedom movement in Kerala estimates the figures of those arrested and beaten by the police to be 1,730 between January and August 1932. All of these encounters were in the towns. Karunakara Menon, *History of the freedom movement in Kerala*, II, 261. No figures are available for the first phase of civil disobedience.
[21] Sankaran, *Ente jivitha katha*, 297; *Mathrubhumi*, 3 May 1930.

in the region.[22] The marchers reached Payyanur three days later and were accommodated in the house of Samuel Aaron. Salt pans were set up on Kokkanisseri field, and the manufactured salt was sold at Rs. 6 per *tola*. Naturally enough, only members of the locally powerful Nayar and Nambudiri families could afford to buy any of it.[23] Salt manufacture continued for a month and there were daily meetings at which the war council decided who would offer themselves for arrest on a particular day. Small groups of volunteers went into the interior, but their propaganda was restricted to winning over members of their own caste. They stayed in the houses of local landowners and village officials and rarely worked within the villages. By providing accommodation for the marchers at the houses of the locally powerful, the Congress had effectively restricted participation to either Nayars or Nambudiris, as those of lower caste would be denied entry into homes. In a sense, Congress activity in Payyanur often assumed the nature of a spectacle or performance. Local notables interacted with each other, manufactured salt and were arrested, while a curious rural population wondered what the fuss was all about. K.A. Keraleeyan remarked on how, for the rural populace, the name 'Congress' conjured up visions of people who, for reasons best known to themselves, subjected themselves to beating by the police.[24]

By mid June, the *satyagraha* in Payyanur began to fold up. The leadership of the KPCC blamed the failure of the salt *satyagraha* in the interior to the 'indifference of the rich and landed aristocracy', which meant that there was no one to provide leadership once the first few Congressmen were arrested.[25] It is quite evident that the KPCC did not envisage a broadening of the movement at this juncture to include lower castes as well. Besides, salt as such, never became an emotive issue and *satyagraha* was suspended at Calicut within a week since 'the amount of salt made was small'. In Payyanur too, salt-making activity waned, helped along by the reluctance, or wisdom, of the authorities who refused to make an issue of it. In a communiqué, the Collector of Malabar stated that he would not arrest any more *satyagrahis* since all they were doing was to boil water to which salt had been added.[26] Sometimes, fortuitously, Congress activities managed to break out of the charmed circle of upper caste involvement. When a *satyagraha* procession reached Kuniyan, they found a settlement of Tiyyas who had made a living by processing salt for the past twenty-five years. They had been inadvertently drawn into civil disobedience activity by the police, who made no distinction between mundane and idealistic motives. Most of the women of the community, who made the

[22] *Mathrubhumi*, 22 April 1930.
[23] Sankaran, *Ente jivitha katha*, 227, 249; *Mathrubhumi*, 26 April 1930; Kerala Congress Bulletin, 25 June 1930, *AICC Files G107/1930* (NMML).
[24] Interview, Calicut, 6 March 1987.
[25] *AICC Files G107/1930* (NMML).
[26] *Ibid.*, Report of K. Madhava Menon.

salt, were in jail and the marchers incorporated a few of the community in their procession.[27] Sometimes concerns of caste mobility were presented in the new vocabulary of the Congress. Members of the Mukkuva (fishing) community tried to align themselves with the Congress by stating that the making of salt would help in curing fish, while *khadi* nets (!) would reduce their dependence on merchants for nets and equipment.[28] These were serendipitous gains for the Kerala Congress and did not presage a lasting affiliation with their policies.

Congress activity reiterated existing bonds and widened networks of association between caste elites. Submitting a report on the activity of the Congress in Malabar, the president of the KPCC wrote that the volunteers offering themselves for processions and arrests were typically eighteen to twenty years of age and came from those sections of the 'landed aristocracy', described delicately as 'lacking in finance'. The report made a distinction between these declining tharavadus and the rich, 'landed aristocracy' which had stayed aloof from the movement. Of the seventy-nine volunteers arrested between 12 May and 15 June 1930, seventy-two belonged to the two upper castes. The leadership and organisation centred on a few individuals and with their arrests, 'no village organisation [existed] nor any District organisation'.[29]

In many cases, Congress mobilisation followed the genealogical map of Nayar tharavadus. A.K. Gopalan entered the civil disobedience campaign by recruiting other younger members of his tharavadu and approaching the various branches scattered throughout Chirakkal.[30] Not only did political activity follow familial connections, it also utilised the institutions set up by tharavadus. Many of the rural schools had been established by dominant tharavadus which employed their younger members as teachers. A.K. Gopalan recruited several of his students for picketing, and schools with radical teachers became recruiting grounds for political activity. Instituting proceedings against a certain Kunhambu Poduval, the head master of Vengara Labour School, for having participated in salt-making at Payyanur, the District Labour Officer warned that the 'schoolmaster [is] a potent influence in a village and on his conduct depends the behaviour of his students'.[31]

Many of the modes in which Congress activity was expressed were redolent of the power exercised by tharavadus over the sphere of their authority. On getting the news of Gandhi's arrest in April 1930, the dominant Nayar tharavadu in Payyanur called for the closing of the local bazaar. When volunteers were arrested at Calicut, T.V. Chathukutty Nayar ordered a *hartal* in Kokkanisseri bazaar and sent a suitcase full of his clothes to be publicly burnt

---

[27] *Mathrubhumi*, 1 May 1930.
[28] *Mathrubhumi*, 28 May 1930.
[29] Report of K. Madhava Menon and A. Karunakara Menon, *AICC Files G107/1930* (NMML).
[30] A.K. Gopalan, *In the cause of the people* (Delhi, 1973), 17.
[31] *Dept. of Labour R. Dis. 304/30 dated 29 October 1930* (KRA). All of Pothuval's brothers as well as the younger members of his wife's family participated in salt making at Payyanur.

in protest.[32] Even though the tharavadu-shrine complex had been eroded in the previous decade the authority of the dominant tharavadus in the eastern villages had not been dented. Even a mild adherent of the Congress like Kannan Nayar could conceive of inculcating nationalism by decree. He recorded in his diary that having received news of Bhagat Singh's death, he 'sent word' that *hartal* was to be observed in the area between Kottacheri and Puthiyakotta.[33] Noble imperatives of nationalism could very well be read as the arbitrary exercise of the prerogative of Nayar tharavadus. The previous decades had seen a growing estrangement between tharavadus and their dependents and adherents. Nationalism, or its manifestation in north Malabar, came at the end of a process both of greater interference by tharavadus in rural relations, as in the matter of implementing excise regulations, and withdrawal, as in the case of the shrine festivals.

Civil disobedience – campaign against alcohol

In the twenties, temperance activities and the propagation of personal cleanliness as panaceas for caste inequality had involved tharavadus more intimately with the lives of their dependents. However, such activity served as much to create affinities vertically between tharavadus and their labourers as horizontally between a like-minded generation of Nayars. The latter pursued the possibility of emerging as arbiters of the relations between castes in the countryside after Tiyya elites had thrown down the gauntlet in envisaging a new order. With the decline of enthusiasm for salt making, liquor picketing became the major activity carried on under the wide umbrella of the Congress. The campaign against alcohol united the disparate aims of a motley assortment of individuals. Those who were sympathetic to the Congress saw the drinking of alcohol as contributing directly to the coffers of an imperialist government, while undermining the health and morale of the populace. Yet others were influenced by 'Gandhian' values and, for them, temperance was part of the intellectual baggage of a simple, clean and pure life. A younger generation within the Nayar tharavadus were withdrawing from shared spaces of worship, at least partially, by the banning of alcohol and animal sacrifice at shrine festivals.[34] Tiyya elites attempted to distance themselves from a trade which, though lucrative, they were beginning to regard as demeaning. The increasing incursion of Mappilas into the toddy trade added a further dimension of conflict between the two communities. A large section of Tiyyas were moving away from the supply of

---

[32] *Mathrubhumi*, 7 May and 14 May May 1930.
[33] *Diaries of A.C. Kannan Nayar*, 24 March 1931.
[34] *Diaries of A.C. Kannan Nayar*, 6 March 1931.

toddy for reasons of economy and status. Tappers who bore the brunt of the government's exactions were drawn towards temperance to survive. Others detached themselves from the circuits of worship and dependence around tharavadus and shrines and their perceived roles as suppliers of toddy.

The Congress programme of liquor shop picketing fell on fertile soil and exacerbated existing tensions. It strengthened the hands of Nayars who were beginning to resent Tiyya resurgence in the coastal towns which, in turn, had sparked off a sense of incipient community within their caste fellows in the hinterland. The KPCC's programme involved a wholesale attack on the production and sale of toddy. Exhibitions exhorting temperance displayed posters which set up a series of oppositions. Wealth and poverty were the first set – the growing of coconut as a cash crop as opposed to 'destroying' the palm by tapping. Dependence and independence were contrasted – the tree could be used for its edible fruit and its marketable coconut fibre, rather than the products being eschewed for enriching the toddy contractor. Finally, there were the poles of health and sickness – 'miserable', 'poorly dressed' drinkers and 'happy', 'well-dressed' vendors of toddy.[35] In creating a distinction between the exploitative vendor and the seemingly hapless cultivators ('six trees will support a family for a year'), subtly, perhaps unintentionally, the KPCC was trying to create a rift between Tiyya vendor/contractor and Tiyya tapper/cultivator. Nayar Congressmen had presented themselves as impartial arbiters between the Tiyyas and the untouchables in the twenties. With the attack on liquor, as a part of civil disobedience, they were trying to carve out a constituency within the Tiyya community itself. It was like walking a tightrope. Nayar Congressmen tried to reconcile their role of policing excise infringements, as members of prominent tharavadus, with their new found role as saviours of the Tiyya community from itself.

Liquor picketing assumed great popularity, coming as it did on the heels of excessive taxation and the fact that many of the shops were being taken over by Mappilas along the coast. A majority of the 350 volunteers in jail by September 1930 were liquor shop picketers.[36] From the very beginning, Tiyyas participated in numbers in the picketing of liquor shops (an offhand estimate by K. Madhava Menon put the figure at 45 per cent of the total volunteers).[37] In the interior, as in Mattanur and Iritty, where Tiyyas still retained control over toddy shops, Mappilas participated in picketing Tiyyas shops though they remained suspicious of the motives of the Congress. In Mappila majority areas like Irikkur, there were disturbances at meetings organised by the Congress.[38]

The success of liquor picketing was determined, in the last instance, by the

[35] Temperance poster exhibition, *AICC Files G – 132* (NMML).
[36] *Mathrubhumi*, 22 July 1930.
[37] Movement in Kerala, 1930. *AICC Files G107/1930* (NMML).
[38] Gopalan, *In the cause of the people*, 26.

attitude and participation of rural elites. In the interior, the volunteers were mainly from locally dominant tharavadus. They were used to the exercise of authority and, in the words of A.K. Gopalan, 'treated labourers like labourers'.[39] In Hosdrug taluk, shops at Madikkai, Alayi and Erikkulam were shut down almost immediately because they were picketed by younger members of the powerful Eccikanam tharavadu.[40] Liquor picketing in the countryside was highly systematised and K. Madhavan and K.P.R. Gopalan, both belonging to powerful tharavadus in their respective regions, recalled how peaceful demonstrations during the day were followed by more muscular persuasion at night.[41] Some tharavadus and shrines remained beyond the pale of Congress persuasion and the temerity of Tiyya picketers. Shrines were not dependent on shops or vendors for the supply of toddy, and the festival at the Muthappan shrine in Parassinikadavu was celebrated with alcohol in the teeth of Congress opposition.[42]

Congress activity worked by decree. In Payyanur, the populace were asked to stay away, in particular, from one liquor and three toddy shops. By the beginning of 1931, picketing, backed by the full authority and force of the Nayar tharavadus, was beginning to produce results. A secret police report stated that all over Chirakkal 'liquor sellers [were] getting desperate'. In the towns too, a similar pattern emerged, possibly as a result of the growing influence of the Mappila lobby. Reporting on Congress activity in Tellicherry it was noted that local toddy sellers were 'summoned' to the town Congress committee and 'ordered' to stop sales.[43] Shops which did not give an undertaking that they would not bid in the annual sales in October 1930 were picketed. Fifty per cent of the shops were sold for lower rentals, and government excise revenue declined by 70 per cent.[44]

On the whole, the results of the picketing of liquor shops were quite at variance with the intentions of the local Congress. Both liquor shop picketers and earlier, the excise administration, had overlooked the basic fact of the free availability of toddy – it could have been had from any palm by cutting an incision in a spathe. Excessive taxation by the government had made the toddy trade uneconomic and hit the tapper severely. Picketing for reasons of nationalism, temperance or the exercise of authority further transformed the toddy industry. The business was driven into the interior, and shopkeepers

---

[39] Gopalan, *In the cause of the people*, 21.
[40] Madhavan, *Payaswiniyude teerattu*, 53.
[41] Interview with K.P.R. Gopalan, Kalliasseri, 28 February 1987; Interview with K. Madhavan, Kanhangad, 3 March 1987.
[42] *Mathrubhumi*, 24 May 1930.
[43] CID report to the District Magistrate, Malabar, 20 April 1931. *Madras Govt. Secret USS 718 dated 6 November 1931* (TNA).
[44] *AICC Files G107/1930* (NMML). At Tellicherry, only nine shops could be sold at the full price, and 120 had to be disposed of at a third of the price. *Mathrubhumi*, 3 August 1930.

converted their homes to liquor shops with the connivance of liquor and excise officials.[45] Illicit distillation increased, and tapping on an individual scale, both for personal consumption and local sale, rose. By 1937, the Abkari department faced the grim reality that 'excise crime' had become linked with the economic life of certain classes of people.[46] Moreover, distillation in the interior and constant picketing had phased out the small shopkeepers. Increasingly, financiers entered the market and the large number of independent small shops came to be controlled by a cartel from the coast. From 1935, bidding at auctions had become a thing of the past. The Madras government appears to have become suspicious that hooch kings out to secure a monopoly were behind picketing and the disruption of the licit liquor trade.[47] Finally, picketing struck the final blow at the idea of the toddy shop as the liminal space where castes drank together. Nayar and Tiyya elites had already abstracted themselves from the shared realm of shrine worship laced with alcohol. Increasingly, there were instances of Nayars being refused a drink at toddy shops because of the association of their caste with Congress picketing.

The previous decade had seen the decline of the monopoly of the Tiyyas over the toddy trade, due to excise pressures and the desire of certain groups for a purified community. Civil disobedience carried this trend even further and Mappila merchants gained control over the toddy trade. Here again Congress activity had moved along the faultlines of the local politics and, to an extent, resolved the conflict between the Mappilas and Tiyyas on the coast, and Nayars and Tiyyas in the interior, to the latters' disadvantage. The campaign against alcohol and liquor picketing had resonances within other communities. Congress activity sparked off, albeit belatedly, a movement for temperance among the Chaliyas (weavers) of north Malabar. They were drawn to temperance, curiously enough, because of the association of the Congress with *khadi*. As a community they were on the decline, faced with competition from factories, mills and cheap foreign imports.[48] The propagation of *khadi* presented a ray of hope and the community tried to align itself wholly behind the programme of the Congress. In Payyanur, the Chaliya Sabha imposed a fine on alcoholics to coincide with a march by Congress volunteers through the street they inhabited. Chaliya settlements in Puzhathi, Puthiyatheru, Azhicode and Chovva gave up alcohol *en masse*, and the sale of toddy in these areas declined remarkably. They soon became impatient with the slow rate of progress, and there were complaints particularly from Puzhathi, that *khadi* propagation did not seem to be improving their business.[49] In this case it was not so much

[45] Letter to Gandhi from Calicut, *Madras Govt Secret USS 718 dated 6 November 1930* (TNA).
[46] *RARMP*, 1937, 16.
[47] *RARMP*, 1936, 15. See Baker, *Politics of south India*, 214-15.
[48] Evidence of P.V. Gopalan, MLC, Calicut, 6 June 1926. *Report of the Unemployment Committee, 1927*, 321.
[49] *Mathrubhumi*, 6 June 1930 and 21 September 1930.

nationalism which had seemed attractive, but the perceived potential of the Congress to secure the economic well-being of the weaving community.

By March 1931, picketing lost itself in local byways, and what had started out as a replication of nationalist activity was transformed into attempts to settle old scores and assert local influence. In the early stages local elites had used their authority to shut down shops; now picketing became a free for all. The president of the Chirakkal taluk Congress committee was forced to advertise in the *Mathrubhumi* asking motley groups and individuals to try and register themselves with the KPCC before picketing using the name of the Congress.[50] Tree owners were asked by local 'Congress' bodies to refuse to allow their trees to be tapped for toddy, spathes were cut off from trees and shops were set on fire.[51] Liquor picketing lost its way in the conflicts between castes for status; the desire of groups to gain monopoly of the toddy business; and occasionally, the violence of the indigent.

Civil disobedience – *khadi* propagation

Khadi propagation provided an issue which held the promise of garnering wider loyalties. White, clean and carrying intimations of equality, it had united the efforts of Congress-minded Nayars and untouchables in the twenties. At the fourteenth annual meeting of the Nambudiri Yogakshema Sabha in May 1930, both Nambudiris and Ezhavas gathered wearing *khadi*.[52] For Nayar youths, the wearing of *khadi* caps became in itself a symbol of defiance, because it involved a departure from the traditional Nayar way of wearing the hair long and tied on the top of the head. When the *Mathrubhumi* was launched in 1923, it carried the slogan, '*khadi* – cure for poverty, friend of independence, sign of self respect'.[53]

Khadi fulfilled the needs both of indigenous industry as well as the stricken weavers. Factories in Malabar had been hit by a crisis of overproduction due to the indiscriminate introduction of improved looms in factories which hoped to compete with cheaper Japanese imports. In 1930, nearly all the factories were bogged down by arrears of unsold stock.[54] Previously, factories had produced sheets, towels, shirts and the like for export, while the weavers supplied articles of daily wear.[55] Increasingly, weavers were squeezed out by cheap imports, and the owners of factories used this conjuncture to capture the

[50] *Mathrubhumi*, 31 March 1931.
[51] *RARMP*, 1931-32, 18.
[52] *Mathrubhumi*, 17 May 1930.
[53] *Mathrubhumi*, 17 March 1923.
[54] *RDIMP*, 1930, 17.
[55] *Statistical appendix to the Malabar Gazetteer, 1933*, xxi.

market for clothing, and utilise the growing pool of unemployed and skilled labour.

Picketing of foreign cloth was concentrated in the towns of Calicut, Tellicherry and Cannanore. Simultaneously, the Swadeshi League, with the president of the KPCC at its head, established contacts with cloth merchants along the west coast.[56] Samuel Aaron, the owner of a spinning and weaving mill, saw the Swadeshi League more as a conduit for Indian made cloth rather than as an organ of Congress propaganda. He inaugurated a swadeshi shop in Cannanore which sold cloth made in his mills at Pappinisseri. Moreover, links were established with all the Swadeshi Leagues and branches, some of which, like the one at Karinnur, were then diverted to acting as retail outlets of the Aaron Mills.[57] In Tellicherry, the West Coast Cotton and Silk Mills began to manufacture khadi cloth, employing over a hundred women and children of weaving families. It was decided that cotton would be sent to the homes of poor and unemployed weavers to be made into thread.[58] Under cover of swadeshi and khadi, alliances were forged between mills, merchants, factories and their erstwhile opposition. This was part of the bargain struck between the Congress and Indian textile mills during the period of civil disobedience, by which the the sale of mill products was permitted by picketers.[59]

Factories, employing four to five weavers each, increasingly registered themselves as swadeshi mills. By 1931, there were forty-six of them in north Malabar alone whereas there had been only twenty-five the previous year.[60] Though weavers found employment, they were subject to these gimcrack establishments which were devoted to making a quick profit and abided by no regulations regarding safety or welfare.[61] There was occasional resentment; Aaron's mills were broken into and some of the buildings burned on a few occasions.[62] Attempts to form workers' unions foundered on the sands of the caution of the Congress. Early unionisers like U. Gopala Menon saw unions as akin to the caste associations of earlier decades. 'I believe what were at one time workers' organizations over the course of time became the castes of today'. Gopala Menon once sternly admonished a meeting of workers, telling them not to aspire to become janmis. Without a trace of irony, he added that 'Workers must not forget that the owner of property who does no work ... is one

[56] Kerala Congress Bullettin, 11 June, 1930. AICC Files G107/1930 (NMML).
[57] AICC Files P35/1932 (NMML)'; Mathrubhumi, 15 June 1930; Swarajya, 4 December 1930, extracted in Madras Govt. Secret USS 718 dated 6 November 1931 (TNA).
[58] AICC Files 83/1931 (NMML).
[59] See Pandey, The Congress in UP, 56.
[60] AICC Files 83/1931 (NMML).
[61] In 1931, there were only four factories registered under the Factories Act of 1911. Statistical appendix to the Malabar Gazetteer, xxi.
[62] Sankaran, Ente jivitha katha, 273.

who suffers more than the poor worker.'[63] Cloth merchants in the towns, though initially apprehensive about the shenanigans of the Congress, were soon converted to the cause of *khadi* by increased sales. In Calicut, all the Hindu and Muslim merchants sealed their bales of foreign cloth and a number of piece goods merchants signed a pledge to stop all imports till Diwali in October 1931. Calicut market was bright with Congress flags hanging from the shops of cloth merchants.[64] Cloth merchants were to remain staunch allies of the Congress; Shyamji Sundardass became President of KPCC in 1935. Of the eighty-eight delegates from Malabar to the Bombay session of the All India Congress Committee in 1934, more than a quarter were merchants or agents.[65]

Khadi propagation had little effect in the eastern villages except for some support from weavers who could find no employment in the factories. The success of the campaign against foreign cloth was again dependent on the influence of tharavadus who were inclined towards the Congress. So much of nationalist activity seemed to be continuations of their earlier exercises of authority that it was viewed with great mistrust. In Madikkai, Kannan Nayar organised a dramatic blaze of foreign cloth in the compound of the school managed by himself. The cloth was supplied by local Chitrapur Saraswat brahmins who were the sole dealers in foreign cloth in the area.[66] Travelling through the villages in the interior of north Malabar, in the wake of civil disobedience, A.K. Gopalan found that *khadi* was 'an object of ridicule' and cheap foreign cloth and a daily tot of toddy were preferred to Congress ideals.[67]

Civil disobedience – Congress and the Mappilas

It has been observed that Congress organisation in the twenties and thirties reached out to limited sections of Indian society and that too with a Hindu bias.[68] In the case of the KPCC's timidity in its dealings with the Mappila community, at one level it reflected the nationwide concern to prevent a repetition of the agitation of Khilafat. However, in this too there were local peculiarities. A report from the KPCC stated that the salt law had been broken all over Malabar except in the erstwhile 'rebel' areas. Only one Mappila, and

[63] *Mathrubhumi*, 16 September 1932.
[64] Note by Collector, Malabar, 21 April 1931. *Madras Govt. Secret USS 718 dated 6 November 1931* (TNA); *AICC Files G152/131* (NMML).
[65] *AICC Files 5/1934* (NMML).
[66] Interview with K. Madhavan, Kanhangad, 3 March 1987.
[67] Gopalan, *In the cause of the people*, 20, 25.
[68] Pandey has shown in the case of UP that the Congress was concerned to minimise propaganda and activity in areas with a high proportion of Muslims to avoid inflaming 'communal' passions. *The Congress in UP*, 22-34, 149.

that too from Palghat, was with Kelappan's march all the way from Calicut to Payyanur. The second march, which left from Palghat, was joined by Moithu Maulavi, Mohammad Abdur Rahman and N.P. Abu but they left for Payyanur by train so as not to incite trouble on the way! The procession on foot from Payyanur, heading for the Guruvayur *satyagraha* on 21 October 1931, stopped short of the 'rebel' area. The marchers took a train from Feroke to Tirur 'because of a rumour that the Mappilas would prevent them from moving into Ernad'.[69]

North Malabar had been untouched by the Mappila rebellion and the responses of Mappila youths and Congressmen alike were far more positive. The Young Men's Muslim Association had attempted to mitigate the legacy of 1921 and remove the bogey of the 'mad Mappila'. The salt marchers were greeted throughout their journey – at Alavil, Azhikode and Valapattanam – by crowds led by the YMMA shouting '*Hindu–Muslim maitri ki jai*' (long live friendship between Hindus and Muslims).[70] Young Mappilas took part in picketing the shops of Mappila merchants in Calicut, Cannanore and Tellicherry, to the considerable relief of Hindu Congressmen and government officials alike.[71] This younger generation forged links with one another through Congress activity and meetings organised by Mappila youths dealt more with questions of community reform. Meetings of the YMMA considered ways of reducing litigation within the community and the theological rifts between the various sects.[72]

Attitudes within the KPCC did not encourage an unequivocal attachment to the Congress on the part of the Mappilas. At the Badagara conference in May 1931, one of the hotly contested issues was on the nature of the upsurge a decade earlier. L.S. Prabhu, one of the Congress old guard, strongly argued that the events of 1921 had been of a purely communal nature, while Moithu Maulavi tried to press for redefining the Mappila rebellion as a peasant revolt. By September 1931, the KPCC had thawed sufficiently to pass a resolution for the release of the Mappilas arrested for their involvement in the rebellion.[73] However, mutual suspicion persisted between the communities, and the Guruvayur *satyagraha* in 1932 would mark the retreat of the Congress into sectional, Hindu concerns. The leadership of the KPCC was largely Hindu and predominantly Nayar. Besides, coming as they did from the landed families of south Malabar, and having had their fingers burnt in 1921, they saw the

---

[69] *AICC Files G107/1930* (NMML); Moithu Maulavi, *Maulaviyude katha*, 155-7; Madhavan, *Payaswiniyude teerattu*, 55.
[70] *Mathrubhumi*, 22 April 1930.
[71] D.M. Malabar to Chief Secretary, Government of Madras, 22 April 1931. *Madras Govt. Secret USS 718 dated 6 November 1931* (TNA).
[72] Moithu Maulavi, *Maulaviyude katha*, 168.
[73] Madhavan, *Payaswiniyude teerattu*, 52; *Fortnightly Report* (henceforth *FR*) for the second half of September 1931 (IOL).

Mappilas mainly as a threat to law, order and property. It would be a new generation of Hindu Congressmen and those coming from north Malabar who would work towards a *rapprochement* with the Mappilas.

Civil disobedience – issues of caste and community

Local horizons and local issues tempered nationalist aspirations and national issues were not so much localised as transformed. Concerns of caste mobility and community reform continued apace. Nationalists with revised memories tend to portray their involvement with matters of their community as an aberration, or at best, a minor detour from the high road of nationalism.[74] If we are not to see community activity as being phoenix-like – destroyed by the heat of nationalism and being reborn once the fire has died down – then we must recognise the concurrent temporality of community and nationalist efforts. Even as sections among the Nayars were participating in civil disobedience, the north Malabar Nayar Samajam was debating the abolition of matriliny and the removal of differences between the sub-castes of Nayars. While considering the declining fortunes of several Nayar tharavadus, a tentative proposal wondered whether the adoption of temperance and *khadi* would help alleviate their poverty.[75] Participation in Congress as well as community reform activity did not appear as a contradiction. The Samudayika Bahishkarana Sangh (Community Boycott Association) was set up by K.P. Gopalan, a Tiyya Congressman, to encourage interdining between Tiyyas and castes lower to them and to boycott those who held to caste prejudices.[76] Among the organisations of untouchables there was declining enthusiasm for temperance leagues and other mild pastimes of earlier Nayar reformers. Even as picketing and *khadi* propagation were going on around them, they began to agitate for the grant of wastelands for cultivation and free access to public places, aligning themselves on occasion with maverick 'Congress' workers.[77]

In Malabar, the working of nationalism strengthened a sense of identity among Nayar elites. Large numbers of Nayars, and not only those from powerful tharavadus, had been involved in Congress marches and activity. This had altered the self-perception of a community beleaguered by Tiyya and

---

[74] For representative statements see Vishnu Bharateeyan, *Adimakal engane udamagalayi*, 25; Moithu Maulavi, *Maulaviyude katha*, 107, for a 'return' to community activity in a nationalist trough and Gopalan, *In the cause of the people*, for a 'giving up' of community activity for nationalism. Gopalan, however, presents his political career as a linear progression towards communism.

[75] *Mathrubhumi*, 10 February 1931.

[76] *Mathrubhumi*, 13 December 1930.

[77] *Mathrubhumi*, 10 December 1930 and 21 May 1931.

Mappila prosperity as well as a sensation of their own declining fortunes. Of the 450 arrested for civil disobedience by December 1930, over 40 per cent were Nayars. The numbers may have been even higher as some volunteers dropped their surnames which makes it difficult to distinguish their castes from the lists of names in the newspapers.[78] Many of the Nayar organisations saw their community as the prospective leaders of the Hindus. In May 1932, the All Kerala Nayar Samajam stated that 'All those who have been resident in Kerala for over a generation, speak Malayalam and observe Onam and Thiruvathira (festivals) should be allowed to become Nayars.'[79] Its president, Rama Varma Tampan, saw a dissolution of caste, religion and community in the all-embracing category of Nayarhood. He stated, in no uncertain terms, that the whole world should become Nayar because the word 'Nayar' was the 'epitome of humanity itself'. This was a significant shift as during the agitation of Nayar professionals and lawyers in south Malabar during the twenties, the larger category evoked had been only that of the *kanakkar* or tenants.[80] In June 1932, the north Malabar Nayar Samajam came up with a similar call to all Nayars and indeed to all Malayalis. It was proposed that on account of their progressive views, the Nayars should 'lead the other depressed communities in the creation of a new age'.[81]

The next phase of civil disobedience would be absorbed into the *satyagraha* at Guruvayur temple; in a sense the logical culmination of the attempt to enter Vaikkam a decade ago. What began as a movement led by the Nayars for the entry of lower castes into Guruvayur ultimately became a Nayar campaign for their own caste. The cause of the untouchables and lower castes was subsumed in the narrow concerns of the Nayar leaders and, later, the wider imperatives of the Congress high command. In a sense, the message of nationalism and that of the leaders of the Nayar associations seemed similar. In May 1932, Rama Varma Tampan had stated with righteous chauvinism that 'it is only fit that the smaller communities should dissolve and become part of a larger community'.[82] If he had in mind only the more limited community of Nayars, the Guruvayur *satyagraha* would attempt to create a larger Hindu community.

The Guruvayur *satyagraha* – the first phase

The signing of the Gandhi–Irwin Pact on 4 March 1931 was followed by a cessation of Congress activity. In the lull that ensued, many of the activists

[78] *Mathrubhumi*, 18 December 1930.
[79] *Mathrubhumi*, 11 May 1932.
[80] *Ibid*. See Radhakrishnan, *Peasant struggles, land reforms and social change*, 75-89.
[81] *Mathrubhumi*, 1 June 1932
[82] *Mathrubhumi*, 11 May 1932.

gained breathing space to think about the direction future activity should take. It had become clear that Congress efforts had failed to win the support of any group, let alone their allegiance. Though several fragmented and temporary alliances had been forged – with Tiyyas over toddy shop picketing, Chaliyas over the propagation of *khadi*, between Congress and mill owners – the Congress had not managed to create a unity above particular interests.

The individuals constituting the Kerala Congress came to recognise the fact that Vaikkam had set into motion a process which had neither lost its edge nor been subsumed by nationalist politics. In the previous decade, Nayar Congressmen had attempted to present themselves as honest brokers between a resurgent Tiyya community and untouchables. However, Pulayas and Cherumas had been granted entry into Srikanteswara temple in 1930 and the Sundareswara temple was planning to open its doors soon.[83] The Tiyya leaders had widened their political ambit and neatly hijacked Congress strategy, having presented themselves as alternative rallying points. Temple entry was made into a Presidency-wide issue and in March 1930, a massive meeting of Nadars, Billavas and Tiyyas was held calling for entry into temples for all castes. This became a constant slogan at meetings of the SNDP in Malabar.[84]

Tiyyas worshipping at Jagannatha and Sundareswara continued to see themselves as a community apart, rather than as Hindus. Efforts to establish links with the SNDP by the Hindu Mahasabha were spectacularly unsuccessful. Madan Mohan Malaviya was jeered at in an SNDP meeting and in response to his call of '*Ramachandra ki jai*', the entire audience responded with a cry of '*Ravana ki jai*'.[85] All this did not augur well for the Congress, since many of their number had moved away from caste activity, and were out of touch with the militant mood among the untouchable and Tiyya lobbies. An article by Kelappan, on the necessity of temple entry, gives an indication both of the distance of the Congress leaders from the temper of the times as well as the continuance of their earlier paternalism towards untouchable castes in the interior. He stressed that, 'It is because they are unclean and do not worship God that temple entry is a necessity for them. Will they understand us if we speak of an all pervasive, ubiquitous God.'[86] It was to be less a question of understanding than of disinterest when the Guruvayur *satyagraha* got underway.

Kelappan, K. Madhavanar, L.S. Prabhu and others had been incarcerated in Vellore jail, following their infringement of salt laws. They had thought seriously about the question of how lower castes could be incorporated with the

[83] *Mathrubhumi*, 25 January and 1 June 1930.
[84] *Mathrubhumi*, 20 March and 4 June 1930.
[85] *Mathrubhumi*, 1 June 1930. The *Mathrubhumi* continued to indulge in wishful thinking when it maintained that 'ninety nine out of a hundred Tiyyas are believers in Puranic Hinduism and devotees of Narayana Guru'.
[86] *Mathrubhumi*, 15 October 1931.

Congress and arrived at the decision that fighting for temple entry at Curuvayur would achieve this objective while at the same time tackling the question of caste inequality.[87] This was seen as being both a revitalisation of Hinduism as well as the purging of inequality from the religion. Kelappan encapsulated the programme of the Congress in the second phase of civil disobedience when he thundered in a public speech, 'A twentieth century version of Hinduism is an immediate necessity'.[88]

Between the third and the fifth of May 1931, the fifth all-Kerala political conference met at Badagara and passed a resolution for temple entry to be inaugurated as the Congress programme. The reaction of the putative beneficiaries was not overly enthusiastic. A Tiyya conference stated, much to the dissatisfaction of the *Mathrubhumi* (edited by Nayar Congressmen), that if the Congress satisfied other demands of the Tiyyas they might consider joining the Congress.[89]

The Guruvayur temple was situated in Ponnani taluk in south Malabar and drew upon worshippers largely from that region. By mooting for entry into the temple at Guruvayur, the Congress was trying to create a focal point for all Hindus in Malabar. In a sense, it was similar to the conception of Jagannatha and Sundareswara, but while these were the focus of a limited Tiyya community, Guruvayur envisaged a wider community of equal Hindus. The temple could be approached from all sides but entry was restricted to upper castes alone after a certain point on each side. This was more a matter of custom than anything else, since Tiyyas came to pluck coconuts from the garden around the temple and tank. During the *Ekadasi* festival, members of all castes used to enter the temple and the 'fiction was maintained that nothing of the sort happened'.[90]

The Congress represented the Guruvayur *satyagraha* as a fight for entry into temples for all castes. There were other conflicts beneath the surface which were to emerge and transform the character of the campaign. One aspect of this conflict was exemplified by the fact that Nayars were prohibited from approaching the *sanctum sanctorum* or ringing the temple bells hung in front of it. The right to ring the bells was no trivial matter. Mannath Padmanabhan, the founder of the Nayar Service Society in Travancore, had long emphasised that this was a fundamental privilege denied to the Nayars by the Nambudiris in the attempt to stress the former's status as *sudras*.[91] The theme of Brahmin overlordship had been a minor, but significant issue in the attempts at forming Nayar organisations at the beginning of the century. At a meeting of the

[87] Swami Anandateertha, 'Short note on temple entry in Kerala', quoted by A.M.A. Ayrookuzhiel, *Swami Anandateertha: untouchability, Gandhian solution on trial* (Delhi, 1987), 31.
[88] *Mathrubhumi*, 16 August 1931.
[89] *Mathrubhumi*, 12 May 1931.
[90] Note by J.A. Thorne of the Revenue Department. *Madras Govt. Secret USS 813 dated 6 February 1933* (TNA).
[91] Vishnu Bharateeyan, *Adimakal engane udamakalayi*, 25.

Keraliya Nayar Samajam in 1914, one of the resolutions stressed the need to have priests from their own castemen, as Nambudiris would 'only perpetuate the slavery of the Nayars'.[92] An article in the *Malayala Manorama* had stated the issue more forcefully: 'Social laws are tied up with religious laws. If we have to complete the transformation of society, the reformation of religion is necessary. We need to set up our own temples to escape Brahmin overlordship'.[93]

The upper echelons of Nayars, and that too in south Malabar, had more intimate connections with Nambudiris because of the establishment of relations between younger Nambudiris and women of the Nayar tharavadus. This had come to be questioned both by a younger generation of Nambudiris who were prevented, by custom, from marrying within their own community, and Nayars who were arguing for reforms within their own community.[94] Anti-Brahmin feeling was prevalent, in a stronger form, towards the Tamil Brahmins, known by the derogatory term *pattar*, a high concentration of whom were to be found in Palghat. Ritually, they occupied a higher status than the Nayars and served as priests and ritual officiants in temples where the Nayars were prohibited from ringing the bells or approaching the inner shrine. Very often, Nayar tharavadus with declining fortunes, unable to 'attract' relations with Nambudiri men, entered into a symbiotic swapping of status for wealth with *pattars*. While it was undeniable that a relation established with a Tamil Brahmin was a conduit to wealth, *pattars* came to be reviled by sections of Nayars for their seeming eagerness to batten off declining Nayar tharavadus.[95] This element of conflict was to assume a major role in the Guruvayur *satyagraha*.

Extensive plans were laid before the *satyagraha* was to commence. Kelappan and other Congressmen toured north Malabar for a week in early October 1931 to arouse enthusiasm. A.K. Gopalan and Keraleeyan organised a meeting at Kandoth, near Payyanur, to press for the right of Tiyyas and untouchables to venture on to the public road. A procession – *jatha* – led by Keraleeyan was attacked by 'conservatives' and the Malabar District Board immediately announced that the road was to be declared open to members of all castes.[96] This provided much-needed publicity, but when the first batch of volunteers set out under T. Subramaniam Tirumumpu in October 1931, from Cannanore for

---

[92] *Mithavadi*, May 1914.

[93] *Mithavadi*, June 1914.

[94] See Arunima, 'Colonialism and the transformation of matriliny', ch. 4.

[95] In a south Malabar village studied by Aiyappan in 1940, the 'Nayar aristocracy' had been reduced to comparative poverty on account of reckless borrowing from *pattar* usurers over the previous decade. Aiyappan, *Iravas and culture change*, 26. See Sankaran, *Ente jivitha katha*, 17-18 for an insight into relations between declining Nayar families and Tamil Brahmins in Kurumbranad.

[96] *Hindu*, 21 October 1931; Gopalan, *In the cause of the people*, 29. The *jatha* of Akalis to the Vaikkam *satyagraha* had left a deep impact on the political scene and the Punjabi word became a part of the political vocabulary of Malayalis.

Payyanur there were only 'a few Adi-Dravidas' in the group.[97] On 1 November 1931, the temple management put up barriers as the Congress workers approached in three batches. The volunteers, of whom a majority were Nayars, had woken up early in the morning, had a bath, applied sandalwood paste on their foreheads, covered their torsos in towels and then proceeded for *satyagraha*.[98] The *satyagrahis* were playing according to the rules here; though they were political activists they were approaching the temple as devotees. Besides, they were serving as exemplars of the pure ritual of worship at temples as opposed to the informal, and occasionally bacchanalian worship at shrines. If Hinduism had to be cleansed of inequality, it could be only through the entry of clean castes; clean in both body and spirit. As Kelappan had stated earlier, it was precisely because the Pulayas and Cherumas were 'unclean' that 'temple entry [was] a necessity for them'.[99] The Guruvayur temple became the focus of attention in Ponnani taluk. Every evening, the *satyagrahis* would sit outside the temple and organise prayer meetings and readings from the Hindu scriptures.[100] Devotees who came to pray at the temple used to attend these meetings instead and offerings were given to the *satyagrahis*. Outside the closed world of the temple, a proselytising, open, all embracing Hinduism was being created. Though there were attempts to relate the *satyagraha* to the national struggle, the content was distinctly in keeping with the Hindu identity that was in the process of formation.

In January 1932, the end of the political truce declared by the Gandhi–Irwin Pact in January 1932 led to the dissolution of Congress committees all over Malabar. The KPCC, the south Malabar district Congress committee and the taluk committees of Ernad and Kurumbranad were declared illegal.[101] There was no central organisation to provide any direction and the activities of the Congress became nothing more than an aggregate of the activities of individual volunteers at Guruvayur. A major compulsion towards fragmentation came from the directives of the Congress high command itself. When L.S. Prabhu, a veteran Congressman, was appointed Dictator to oversee Congress activities in Malabar, Gandhi wrote to him advocating caution regarding temple entry, defining it as an 'act of repentance on the part of the high caste Hindus'. He particularly emphasised that the political status of the anti-untouchability programme 'may be said to be unimportant'.[102] As at Vaikkam, it was important for Gandhi that the Hindu community should not be split into hostile camps. Having forgone the attempt at a broader definition of the Guruvayur

---

[97] *Hindu*, 21 October 1931.
[98] Madhavan, *Payaswiniyude teerattu*, 55.
[99] *Mathrubhumi*, 15 October 1931.
[100] *Hindu*, 2 November 1931; Bharateeyan, *Adimakal engane udamakalayi*, 55.
[101] Fort St George notifications 149, 152, 168, 203, *L/P and J 290/1932* (IOL); *Public (General) Dept. G.O. (Ms) 8 dated 5 January 1932* (KS).
[102] *Mathrubhumi*, 10 January 1932.

satyagraha as a movement involving all communities, it was becoming quite clear by February 1932, three months after its inauguration, that limited, local objectives were surfacing. The District Magistrate wrote with a sigh of relief that the 'movement [was] now directed against the management of the temple and in no way against the British Government'.[103]

The high point of the movement was reached in late December when a few untouchables bathed in the western pond of the temple. Scandalised 'savarna' Hindus petitioned the Governor saying that the movement was the work of Tiyyas, Pulayas, Cherumas and Nayadis: 'the illiterate, uncivilized, and unscrupulous'.[104] Peaceful *satyagraha* was soon abandoned, and A.K. Gopalan attempted to enter the temple and reach the *sanctum*. He was beaten up severely by Nayar retainers in the temple.[105] Krishna Pillai's statement, at this juncture, of Nayar machismo as against the effeteness of the Nambudiris, and those Nayars dependent on them, became a symbol of the *satyagraha*. 'Let the bold Nayar ring the bell and let the cringing Nayar living on crumbs beat on his back.'[106] Pillai too entered the temple and rang the temple bells in defiance of the sanctions against Nayars doing so. Bell ringing soon became a regular feature and every morning Nayars would enter through the eastern gate reserved for Brahmins and ring the temple bells. Once inside they demanded to be fed alongside the *pattars*.[107] Kelappan had to issue frequent statements that political activity was not directed against any particular community. Mannath Padmanabhan, the representative of the Nayars from Travancore did not help matters by referring, in public speeches, to the 'pattars from Pandinad' (a derogatory reference to Madras) who did not know their place and asking Nayars what they proposed to do about it.[108] What had started out as a campaign on behalf of the lower castes and untouchables, in the name of nationalism, had resolved itself into a conflict between the Nayars against the Nambudiris and Tamil Brahmins. Temple entry could have been knitted into a wider social programme but now it became an end to be pursued in exclusion to all else.

Even as the *satyagraha* gathered momentum, it became clear that Tiyyas intended to stay away from attempts to draw them into Hindu temples. At a meeting of the south Malabar Tiyya Sangham held in November, there was strong opposition to the Guruvayur campaign. Resolutions were adopted asking the Tiyyas to keep their 'self respect' and purify their own practices. Another meeting proposed that the community as a whole should 'blacklist' all

---

[103] District Magistrate, Malabar to Chief Secretary, Madras, 15 February 1932. *Madras Govt. Secret USS 813 dated 6 February 1933* (TNA).
[104] *Ibid.*, Memorial for Savarna Hindus of Kerala, 30 December 1931.
[105] Gopalan, *In the cause of the people*, 45.
[106] T.V. Krishnan, *Kerala's first Communist* (Communist Party publication, 1971), 21.
[107] *Mathrubhumi*, 9 and 10 April 1932.
[108] *Mathrubhumi*, 1 January 1932; *Mathrubhumi*, 2 June 1932.

temples.[109] Interestingly enough, Tiyya reformers and Congressmen were beginning to speak the language of purity. The meeting of the Tiyya Sangham stressed the need to adopt 'higher' worship at their own temples and to eschew animal sacrifice and low practices. Nevertheless, the need to distance themselves from Hinduism was an oft-reiterated theme. At a meeting in May 1932, C. Krishnan announced emphatically that 'as long as we remain within Hinduism, we give Brahmins the right to categorise us'.[110]

There were other ramifications, as the notions of purity of ritual, cleanliness, casteness and the sense of a Hindu community of equals fostered by the initial enthusiasm of the *satyagraha* found expression. In Cochin, the Legislative Assembly passed a resolution banning indecent activities at the Kodungallur shrine. In April 1932, several people were arrested for singing obscene songs at the temple festival which had been a byword for bacchanalian activity in the previous decades.[111] If the Jagannatha and Sundareswara temples had managed to dent the flow of Rabelaisian pilgrims to Kottiyur in the previous decade, the ripples of nationalism circumscribed Kodungallur. Puritanism, though, never managed to complete its triumphal march. The failure of the new Tiyya temples to admit untouchables, and the hesitancy of the Congress in investing temple entry with any overtly political content, meant that circuits of worship in the countryside continued as usual. The initial burst of enthusiasm for reform on the part of the Nayar Congressmen had been diverted towards Guruvayur. In Edakkad, the annual festival complete with cock sacrifice and alcohol went ahead in 1932 despite protests from young Congressmen.[112] Only the previous year, under great pressure, the managers had decided to eschew 'low' rituals. Untouchables in Kuruva, near Cannanore, continued to organise *teyyattams* at their shrines complete with toddy and the letting of blood.[113]

Though the entry of lower castes into temples was introduced into the political idiom of Malabar, it could not attain the status of a general programme of action. In Malabar, the right of managing and superintending temples had not been taken over by the colonial administration, and dominant families continued to control temples as private domains. In this context, the opening of temples to general entry quickly became a question of intransigence or benevolence on the part of the managers of individual temples; an issue in which neither the law nor state could be appealed to. In December 1931, Tiruvangad temple near Tellicherry considered throwing open its doors. By March 1932, with the growing sectarian nature of the Guruvayur *satyagraha*,

[109] *Mathrubhumi*, 4 and 6 November 1931.
[110] Report on the south Malabar Tiyya meeting. *Mathrubhumi*, 20 May 1932.
[111] *Mathrubhumi*, 12 April 1932.
[112] The petition to the temple authorities stated with some dislike that those who wished to impede the traditional performance of the festival 'had been in jail several times'. Obviously, Congress activity did not possess the same aura for everyone! *Mathrubhumi*, 28 April 1932.
[113] *Mathrubhumi*, 11 October 1935 and 4 January 1936.

the Sundareswara temple announced the imminent admission of untouchables into its precincts.[114] It was not until the agitation at Guruvayur had been checked that the matter of temple entry ascended to the Legislative Council. The Zamorin of Calicut, who had been vested with the power of 'superior and superintending trustee' of the Guruvayur temple, remained adamant in his refusal to throw open the temple to all castes.[115] In June 1932, the High Court of Madras decided that though certain castes were allowed on festival days to use the roads around the temple, 'no general right of way could be inferred therefrom'. In rationalising his procedural decision, Justice Ramesam observed that 'rights created by custom, especially religious custom, have to be respected, *even if not reasonable from a wider point of view*'.[116]

The Guruvayur *satyagraha* – the second phase

A combination of Congress caution in awarding a political status to the temple entry campaign; the particular interests of the leaders of the *satyagraha*; and the operation of the law had restricted the influence of the campaign to an increasingly small circle. Worse was yet to come. Just as in 1923, Vaikkam had been 'nationalised' and its political implications annulled, in 1932, Guruvayur became the victim of national politics. The situation emerged into a blaze of national publicity and Kelappan had his finest moment as the man who could have wrested temple entry for the untouchables. In the end, Guruvayur became an incident which threatened the national affiliation of untouchables with the Congress. The grand imperatives of the Poona Pact between Ambedkar and Gandhi necessitated its relation to the sidelines.

At the Round Table Conference, Gandhi had spoken of resisting the introduction of a separate electorate for untouchables with his life. His closest aides, particularly Vallabhai Patel, had warned that this would be an ill-advised move as it could spark off 'imitative fasts'. In August 1932, the Communal Award granted separate constituencies to the untouchables and Gandhi wrote to the British Prime Minister about his decision to start a fast from 20 September 1932, unless this decision was revoked. The conception of the fast involved a moral edge as well, as Gandhi hoped to 'sting(ing) the conscience of caste Hindus into right action'.[117] Meanwhile in the face of the Zamorin's

---

[114] *Mathrubhumi*, 26 December 1931 and 22 March 1932.
[115] See High court decision in *Zamorin of Calicut* v. *Mallisseri Krishnan Nambudiripad* quoted in Moore, *Malabar law and custom*, 273-4.
[116] Emphasis added. *Criminal Revision Case 291 of 1932. H.C. Madras 14 June 1932* (KRA).
[117] Judith M. Brown, *Gandhi and civil disobedience: the Mahatma in Indian politics, 1928-34* (Cambridge, 1977), 313-15.

intransigence in refusing to allow entry to untouchables, Kelappan decided to embark on a fast to impress the need for temple entry for all castes. It was a brief moment when the possibility arose of the Guruvayur *satyagraha* acquiring an appeal transcending Nayar-Nambudiri conflict and the disinterest of the lower castes. The date Kelappan chose – 21 September – was inopportune, for Gandhi had embarked on his fast a day earlier. In a letter both condescending and stern, and echoing Patel's sentiments, Gandhi wrote, 'I believe that your fast is in imitation of my fast and does not arise from an inner inspiration. If this is true, then as I am commander-in-chief regarding matters like fasts ... you must give up your fast.'[118]

On the national front, Gandhi's fast put upon Ambedkar the moral burden of capitulating on his demand for separate electorates for untouchables. Ambedkar gave in, but drove a hard bargain in the Poona Pact which was signed on 24 September 1932. The idea of separate electorates for untouchables was given up in return for a guarantee of more seats in the provincial legislatures.[119] A day later, at a Hindu leader's conference in Bombay presided over by Madan Mohan Malaviya, a resolution drafted by Gandhi was passed stating that every effort would be made to remove social disabilities by 'legitimate and peaceful means'.[120] On 26 September, two days after the Pact had been signed, the Cabinet accepted the proposals and Gandhi broke off his fast. Now that the dangers of dissension at a national level had been sorted out, Kelappan's continuing fast seemed an aberration presenting the possibility of the further expression of discontent.

The Zamorin of Calicut wrote to Gandhi, imploring in the latter's own idiom that temple entry 'would wound orthodox conscience and such wounding would amount to coercion'.[121] Kelappan refused to accept this as sufficient grounds for giving up the fast and stated with righteous passion that 'the question of wounding the hearts and self respect of thousands of depressed brethren is more real and important than the alleged wounding of the orthodox conscience'.[122] He insisted that the giving up of the fast would mean a setback for the movement. Gandhi continued to put pressure on him to withdraw his decision employing the curious argument that the 'immediate prospective result must not affect the decision on pure ethics'.[123] In the face of this per-

---

[118] *Mathrubhumi*, 27 September 1932.
[119] Ambedkar received a further guarantee of 18 per cent of the general seats for British India in the federal assembly. See Brown, *Gandhi and civil disobedience*, 319-21.
[120] See *CWMG*, LI, 139.
[121] *Ibid.*, 150-1.
[122] *Ibid.* Gandhi also appealed to the procedural point that Kelappan had not given sufficient notice of his decision to fast, prompting a terse rejoinder that ten months was ample time. Telegram to Kelappan, 29 September 1932.
[123] Telegram to Kelappan, 1 October 1932, *CWMG*, LI, 162.

sistence Kelappan went off his fast on 2 October, eleven days after he had begun it, and without having gained his objective.

The Guruvayur *satyagraha* had been successfully 'nationalised' and made to conform to the necessities of national politics. In Malabar, Gandhi's intervention hobbled a significant movement towards a politics which could have embraced lower castes and untouchables. In regions like Andhra, Gandhi's espousal of the cause of the untouchables had made little difference to local Congress politics, since the dominant landholders would have none of this unwanted radicalism.[124] In December 1932, Gandhi made it quite clear that Kelappan's fast had threatened to put a spanner in the works just as the compromise of the Poona Pact was being arrived at.[125] In the course of time, the local specificity and imperatives of Guruvayur became blurred, as it slowly assumed the form of an adjunct of a national programme. This was evident by the end of 1932, when Gandhi wrote to the Viceroy on the introduction of the Removal of the Depressed Classes Religious Disabilities Bill in the Madras Legislative Council. He represented the bill as a response 'to the movement that set in as *a direct result of* [the] Yeravada Pact' (emphasis mine).[126] By January 1933, Gandhi had come to see Guruvayur as nothing more than an 'offshoot of the withdrawal of the Cabinet decision'.[127]

What of temple entry itself? It continued to be seen within the paradigm of the 'purification of Hinduism' and the 'conversion even of the most orthodox' effectively limiting the political potential as well as the participation of anyone other than the upper castes.[128] The untouchables were to be the admiring audience in this show of self sacrifice and high ideals arranged for them. Gandhi emphasised that Guruvayur was a test case and it was to be treated as such; the 'cry of general entry into all temples was not to be raised'.[129] The political aspect of untouchability had been 'settled' by the Poona Pact; only the religious aspect remained. This necessarily meant that those who were not Hindus could not 'interfere' with what was now defined as a 'deeply religious movement'.[130] By 1933, the issue of temple entry was excised from the ideology of Congress politics and Gandhi was emphatic that those who emphasised a connection were 'wholly mistaken'.[131]

[124] Stoddart, 'The politics of coastal Andhra' in D.A. Low, ed., *Congress and the Raj*, 124.
[125] 'Mr. Kelappan's fast over the opening of Guruvayur temple was actually going on whilst the Pact was emerging and I asked him to suspend it ...', Statement on untouchability XIII, 30 December 1932. *CWMG*, LII, 307.
[126] Telegram to the P.S. of Viceroy, 30 December 1932. *CWMG*, LII, 309.
[127] Letter to Parmananda K. Kapadia, 8 January 1933. *CWMG*, LI, 399.
[128] Letter to Kelappan, 15 October 1932; Statement on Untouchability III, 7 November 1932; Interview with P.N. Rajbhoj, 11 November 1932, *CWMG*, LI, 242, 368, 404; Statement on Untouchability IX, 26 November 1932, *CWMG*, LII, 72.
[129] Letter to U. Gopala Menon, 15 November 1932, *CWMG*, LII, 438.
[130] Letter to K. Kelappan, 23 November 1932; Interview with API, 2 January 1933, *CWMG*, LII, 44, 344.
[131] Letter to M.V. Parameswaran Chettiar, 25 February 1933, *CWMG*, LIII, 412.

After the suspension of Kelappan's fast, Gandhi had proposed a postponement of any fast for three months in which time a referendum could be organised on the issue of temple entry in Guruvayur. But it was made very clear that the fast would have to be put off if the referendum showed that the majority were still against allowing untouchables into the temple. When the referendum was finally held in December 1932, 77 per cent of the voters were in favour of allowing temple entry.[132] Now that the teeth of the agitation had been drawn, the issue of temple entry, as in the case of Vaikkam a decade ago, retreated into the debating chambers of the Legislative Council. In 1932, the Removal of the Depressed Classes Religious Disabilities Bill was introduced in the Madras Legislative Council. It proposed that if fifty voters were to write to the trustees of the temple to put the motion of universal entry to a vote, and if a majority voted in favour of temple entry, then that decision would be binding on the authorities concerned. Gandhi sent a telegram to the Viceroy of India saying that the 'bill proposes no innovation in Hindu belief'; it was merely trying to restore *status quo ante* the advent of the British.[133] As an anti-imperialist stance this was exemplary; it saw caste inequality as buttressed by the British. However, it dangerously hid the fact that caste was inbuilt in Hinduism; a point that the Tiyya movement had constantly stressed. Gandhi stated that the 'law as it stands makes impossible the operation of *the Hindu mind* on certain religious customs and usages and the measures are designed to release the Hindu mind from those fetters' (emphasis mine). This assumed not only that there was one unified, Hindu opinion but that this was opposed to the idea of caste. The Government of Madras dithered on procedural grounds. It stated that trustees of temples should carry out the intentions of the founder. If the 'circle of beneficiaries', i.e. entrants into temples, was widened it would be a breach of trust. It would create 'rights against positive religious injunctions' and 'generally reduce Hindu temples into secular institutions'.[134] Moreover, if legislation was really needed it could await the vote of the reformed legislature under the terms of the new constitution of 1935.

Even as late as 1938, Gandhi was insistent that 'the whole of the movement is one of the conversion of the Sanatani heart. You cannot force the pace'.[135] Gandhi's policy of making haste slowly eventually produced results. In August 1939, the Madras Hindu Temple Entry Disabilities Removal Act was passed.[136]

---

[132] Letter to P.N. Rajbhoj, 8 December 1932, *CWMG*, LII, 147. Of the 27,465 individuals canvassed for their opinion, 15,568 voted to allow entry into temples for all castes, while only 2,583 voted against. *Mathrubhumi*, 27 December 1932.
[133] *Home Political F50/1.33 Poll. and K.W. dated 29 November 1933* (NAI). See also *Home Political 5/46/32* (NAI).
[134] Note on Temple Entry Bill. *Home Political 50/2/33* (NAI).
[135] M.K. Gandhi to M.C. Rajah, 5 October 1938. *M.C. Rajah Papers* (NMML).
[136] The Act restricted itself to temples with an annual income of over Rs. 5000 and if 50 Hindu voters were to request entry, then 'notwishtranding any law, custom or usage to the contrary,

And, a decade later, the Madras Temple Entry Authorisation (Amendment) Act enabled all classes of Hindus to have right of entry even into temples constructed for the benefit of particular sections of the Hindu community.[137]

Conclusion

It has recently been argued that the period 1930-34 'witnessed a vigorous propagation of the ideology of nationalism' in Malabar.[138] However, this is true only if we concentrate on the *form* of Congress activity, without analysing its *content* and, more important, its *consequences*. Civil disobedience in Malabar had moved along the local faultlines of power, resolving itself, in a large part, into the activities of younger members of dominant tharavadus. The enactment of nationalism by decree and the assertion of authority by tharavadus meant an erosion of rural community. Congress activity served not so much to create wider unities as to exacerbate existing conflicts between Tiyyas and Nayars in the interior and Tiyyas and Mappilas on the coast. The rhetoric of a community of equal Hindus around the temple at Guruvayur came at an opportune juncture. The entry of untouchables into temples and, therefore, into a Hinduism cleansed of inequality, could presumably be followed by the entry of equal Hindus into the realm of the nation. This intimation of equality was dashed at one level in the petty conflicts for status between Nayars against Brahmins. At another level the possibility of forcing entry for all castes into Guruvayur was subordinated to the national imperatives of the Poona Pact. The theme of this phase of political activity had been that temple entry would resolve the problem of caste inequality.

From the mid thirties there would be an attempt to create wider, secular identities with a strong sense of opposition to the imperatives and programmes of the nationalist Congress. The assumption behind political activity would be that the removal of economic inequality would obliterate caste. A transient Hindu identity would be replaced by the search for the secular unity of workers and peasants. Krishna Pillai, one of the founders of the Communist party of Kerala was to write in 1934, 'Tiyya, Nayar, *pattar*, Mappila and Christian – one must forget these differences and assert that "I am an agricultural worker, I am a mill worker and my success is the success of each worker belonging to my

trustees could throw open the temple'. *Home Political 24/11/38* (NAI); *Home Political 50/1/38* (NAI).
[137] *ARMP*, 1949, 7.
[138] K. Gopalankutty, 'Mobilisation against the state and not against the landlords: the civil disobedience movement in Malabar', *The Indian Economic and Social History Review*, 26, 4 (1989), 459-80.

class".[139] This vision too would be confounded by the realities of multiple divisions within rural society which would not allow for more than a conjunctural unity.

[139] Krishna Pillai, *'Mathathinalla chorinanu poruthendathu' (One must fight not for religion but for food), Mathrubhumi*, 1 April 1934.

5   The transformation of rural politics, 1934–1940

The commencement of civil disobedience had been determined by national imperatives. Its suspension too, in 1933, was called for by the Congress high command. In July 1933, in spite of Gandhi's ostensible reluctance to impose a national programme, he ordered Congress organisations to disband and advocated social uplift through the 'constructive programme' of *khadi* and sanitation.[1] Coming as it did on the heels of the abandoning of confrontation, Gandhi's oscillation between dithering and dictating aroused anger in the provinces. The pressure on local politics to conform to national commands spawned a desire in the provinces to combat 'the irresponsible and arrogant dictatorship enthroned in the Congress by Gandhi'.[2] In Malabar equally forthright opinions were expressed. Krishna Pillai, one of the founders of the Kerala Congress Socialist Party, wrote in July 1934 that 'the ability of Gandhi to lead India on the path of mass organisation is now at an end. Gandhi is scared to lead mass activity along the right path.'[3] The search for an alternative national programme took two divergent roads. Congressmen weary of conflict proposed a return to electoral politics, and the Swarajya Party was revived in 1934. A younger radical group drafted the constitution for a socialist party which was to act as the 'basis for coordinating the activities of all socialists in the Congress with a view to radicalise it'.[4] In May 1934, the Congress Socialist Party was established.

Both at the national and provincial level, Congress socialist political activity seemed to function as the conscience of the Congress. Particularly in Bihar and Andhra, socialists were involved in expanding the frontiers of Congress influence by organising the peasantry. Congress socialism has been studied from diverse perspectives. These assess the ideals of the socialists ranging from opportunism to radical nationalism and their motives extending

[1] See Brown, *Gandhi and civil disobedience*, 330, 342-5.
[2] Swami Govindanand to Sambamurti, November 1933, quoted by B.R. Tomlinson, *The Indian National Congress and the Raj, 1929-42: the penultimate phase* (London, 1976), 37.
[3] *Mathrubhumi*, 11 July 1934.
[4] See Z.M. Masani, 'Radical nationalism in India, 1930-42: the role of the all-India Congress Socialist Party' (unpublished DPhil dissertation, University of Oxford, 1976), 50-1.

from individual grievance to transcendent ideology: 'ultra-nationalist opposition'; 'ginger group' within the Congress; 'a bundle of disgruntled elements'; the epithets vary.[5] In the context of Malabar, it will be argued that 'Congress Socialism' represented a local reaction *against* nationalism, in view of the subordination of local politics to the exigencies of the national party. First Vaikkam, then Guruvayur, had been relegated to the backwaters of Hindu religious reform, and the Congress had refused to politicise the issue of caste. Congressmen in Malabar continued to follow the national constructive programme which tried to ameliorate rather than transform caste subordination. The Harijan Seva Sangh, which united the activities of the Congress in Malabar, had as its creed that, 'The habit of personal cleanliness is the chief pride of the caste Hindus and the chief ingredient of resulting untouchability'.[6]

From 1935, the socialists in Malabar worked within the confines of the locality, and their highly successful rural mobilisation made little attempt to ally itself with wider concerns of province and nation or, indeed, of the Congress. Socialist leaders, in their attempt to gain control over the Congress organisation may have adopted the stance of being the radical conscience of nationalism. A statement of intent by the nascent socialist group read, 'Our immediate programme is to encourage the Congress to use its limitless influence to organise industrial and agricultural labour, to encourage the political struggle of the citizens of the native states; and to unite the struggles of the oppressed with the Indian national struggle'.[7] However, peasant unions ploughed local furrows and addressed immediate concerns of subordination and excesses of authority. Wider political unities – a community of Tiyyas, or a community of equal Hindus – gave way to the inwardness of the resolution of inequality within the villages. Elsewhere, as in Bihar, rural radicalism and nationalism continued to maintain close links. It has been argued that Swami Sahajanand and the Kisan Sabha prevented the escalation of rural conflicts derived partly from their 'acceptance of the primacy of the national struggle'.[8]

The onset of the Depression lent an urgent edge to the search for a new idiom of politics which would tackle, head on, the problem of caste inequality. Buoyant prices had kept afloat a class of independent small cultivators and the profits from cash crops had subsidised the imports of rice into the region. A crash in prices combined with the decline of international demand precipitated

[5] Masani, 'Radical nationalism in India', 84-5; Tomlinson, *The Indian National Congress*, 51; Pandey, *The Congress in UP*, 72. In Kerala, they have been recently credited with 'transforming' the Congress into a body 'engaged in militant anti-imperialist and anti-feudal agitations'. K. Gopalankutty, 'The task of transforming the Congress: Malabar, 1934-40', *Studies in History* 5, 2, n.s. (1989), 177.
[6] Annual report of the HSS for the years 1933-34 and 1934-35. *AICC Files G-14/1934-5* (NMML).
[7] *Mathrubhumi*, 11 July 1934.
[8] See S.J. Henningham, *Peasant movements in colonial India: north Bihar, 1917-1942* (Canberra, Australia, 1982), 149.

a crisis of food at one level, and undermined the position of the small cultivator at another. There was an enforced shift towards subsistence cultivation, underscoring the dependence of cultivators on dominant tharavadus for land, credit and grain. Meanwhile, the authority of the tharavadus was subverted by legislation which ensured security of tenure for tenants and, more crucially, allowed for the partition of tharavadu property. The partition of tharavadus, in a period of economic depression, cast adrift their branches in the countryside, leaving many among them with prestige but out of pocket. Initial socialist activity consisted of efforts by a new generation of the rural elite to renegotiate rural community by curtailing the excesses of authority exercised by tharavadus. The resentment of the dependent and the fissures within the elite came together in the moves towards the formation of peasant unions.

The activities of unions were initially circumscribed by the cautious attitude of a reforming elite which sought to go thus far and no further. There were attempts to build community by collective activity in *jathas*, formation of volunteer unions and tapping into the culture of the reading rooms in the villages. However, the experience of collective activity and expression led to a significant erosion of erstwhile rural authority on the one hand and deference on the other. The decade was to end in pitched battles between peasant unions and the police who had underpinned the authority of the powerful tharavadus. The moderate overtures of Gandhian reformers were superseded by an assertion of rights.

The impact of the Depression

The boom in the prices of cash crops in the twenties was matched by the enthusiastic response of cultivators. The resurvey of Malabar in 1936 revealed the extent of expansion of cultivation in the previous decade. Between 1900 and 1930, almost two *lakh* acres of land had been brought under pepper and coconut with a sudden spurt in the late twenties when the prices of pepper and coconut had peaked. Between 1920 and 1929 there was a fall in the production of pepper in the Dutch East Indies, with a shortfall of supply by 15,000 tons in 1927-28. Malabar filled the gap in supply and prices touched their zenith in 1928.[9] Cultivation of pepper soared from 1926, and in the north east of Chirakkal and Kottayam, rich forest land was leased out by dominant tharavadus, like the Kalliattu and Koodali. In the interior, entrepreneurial cultivators opened up hitherto unsurveyed land along the foothills and plunged into the

---

[9] *Revenue R.Dis 3431/36 dated 2 April 1936* (KRA); Thomas and Sastry, *Commodity prices in south India*, 48.

forests.[10] The intrusion on areas hitherto cultivated by tribal groups was offset by informal alliances of credit and dependence on dominant tharavadus. In Kurumbranad, and along the coast, many cultivators incurred debts in order to acquire land and become small landowners. They were confident of paying off loans, with the proceeds from the soaring profits of coconut and pepper.[11]

Then came the unexpected crash in the prices of these crops which had created fortunes overnight. In 1928, 1,000 coconuts had sold for Rs. 49-2-10 and a *bharam* of pepper for Rs. 534-6-0. By January 1931, prices fell to Rs. 27 per 1,000 coconuts and Rs. 146-0-0 for a *bharam* of pepper. As Baker has observed, the weakening of international demand was felt earliest in the market for primary 'temperate' products grown in both industrial countries and elsewhere. 'Tropical' products like pepper felt the slump only by the middle of the decade. This was aggravated in Malabar by the optimistic expansion of cultivation till almost 1933.[12] The peak prices of 1928 had led to manic cultivation of pepper and even old gardens had been renovated. Thus, the crash in prices coincided with the unloading of a mammoth crop on the market.[13] As heavy crops of pepper built up in Malabar, and exports declined, sales came to depend on the limited Indian market and the abnormal demand from Italy, which was the only European country to continue buying from Malabar. It was not until 1936 that foreign demand finally ceased. The collapse of speculative buying of Malabar pepper in London; the invasion of Abyssinia by Italy which led to a cessation of demand from that quarter; and the import, by the speculators, of lower-priced pepper from Singapore and the East Indies to Bombay in 1935-36 meant that the market was in the doldrums. Pepper cultivators used to swings in prices continued to expand cultivation till 1933, little realising that this was a more severe and long-term crisis.[14] The random cultivation of pepper on homesteads and along the foothills in the north and north east of Chirakkal and Kottayam had been unable to face the more systematic and economic cultivation on plantations in the East Indies. Similarly, individual coconut gardens of small farmers could not stand up to the competition from Ceylon whose coconut plantations were able to place the commodity on the market at a lower price.[15] Ceylon, which used to export

[10] Letter from A.R. MacEwen, Special settlement officer, 25 March 1927. *Revenue Dept. G.O. 1609 dated 19 August 1927* (KS).
[11] *Revenue DR 617/35 dated 4 April 1935* (KRA).
[12] *Revenue Dept. G.O. 493 dated 4 March 1931* (KS). (1 *bharam* = 20 *maunds* = 82.28 lbs). See C.J. Baker, *An Indian rural economy 1880-1955: the Tamilnad countryside* (Delhi, 1984), 117-18.
[13] Pepper crops in 1931 were a quarter above the average production and prices fell from Rs. 80 per cwt to Rs. 30 per cwt. *RDIMP*, 1931, 21.
[14] *Revenue Dept. G.O. 493 dated 4 March 1931* (KS); *RDIMP*, 1936, 38; *DR 3215/32 dated 3 March 1933* (KRA). Director of Industries and Commerce to Secretary, Development, 2 July 1941. *Revenue Dept. G.O. 2259 dated 6 August 1943* (KS).
[15] Thomas and Sastry, *Commodity prices in south India*, 18.

coconuts to Holland, Spain, Denmark and Italy began dumping coconuts on Malabar from 1932 as European demand fell by almost 80 per cent.[16]

Forests had been part of the expanding economy and in the post-war years the timber industry down river at Baliapatam and Calicut had received a boost. The limited deforestation undertaken by the expansion of pepper in the foothills was coupled with tharavadus granting *kuttikanam* (rights of cutting trees) to contractors and private individuals. Forests were no longer remunerative assets with the falling prices of pepper and the decline in the demand for timber.[17] Large tracts were still on lease to entrepreneurial cultivators who hung on grimly to their plots. Pepper was given up in preference to the cultivation of hill rice to mitigate their dependence on the tharavadus for grain at a time of scarcity. Cultivators still needed green manure which had to be foraged from the private forests owned by individual families. Since the owners of the forest could not realise rent from the pathetic amount of grain produced, they resorted to curtailing customary rights of collecting manure and firewood and making these conditional on payment of levies. Traditional rights of pasturage and use of forests were to be eroded throughout this decade as tharavadus tried to realise money as well as assert their rights of ownership in the face of fugitive cultivation. The incorporation of village elites into excise administration and the involvement of the tharavadus with the enforcing of Congress activity during the period of civil disobedience had introduced strains in rural relations. Now with attempts to appropriate as private what had been customarily shared, the tharavadus were further abstracting themselves from traditional networks of obligation.

Another sphere of the erosion of the rural community was in the inability of tharavadus to provide credit at a time when all other sources of credit seemed to be drying up. The survey report of Chirakkal taluk in 1931, prior to resettlement, had stated baldly that money was scarce and it 'was impossible to raise loans'.[18] With the crash in the prices of pepper, the merchants on the coast were less forthcoming with advances. Banks had been willing to lend money on the security of pepper crops but with the produce now of doubtful value, they too were reluctant. Previously, cultivators had access to credit from a variety of sources including self-help lotteries organised amongst themselves.[19] Now, they were becoming dependent on the tharavadus for cash advances and lands in order to grow subsistence. The latter, far from being in

---

[16] *Mathrubhumi*, 11 January 1936. Exports to Kerala as a whole, previously only 9.25 per cent of Ceylon's trade had risen, by 1935, to 34-39 per cent. *Revenue Dept. G.O. 2654 (Ms) dated 24 September 1938* (KS).

[17] Evidence of V.K. Menon, MPBEC, IV, 530-1; *RDIMP*, 1930-31, 21; *Ibid.*, 1932-33, 21; *Ibid.*, 1934-35, 30; *Ibid.*, 1935-36, 36; *Ibid.*, 1937-38, 51.

[18] *Revenue Dept. G.O. 493 dated 4 March 1931* (KRA).

[19] Moore, *Malabar law and custom*, 230; Oral evidence of V.K. Menon, MPBEC, 1930-31, IV, 533.

a position to lend, were themselves in need of money. With the onset of the Depression, dominant tharavadus increasingly began to exact 'feudal levies' from their tenants over and above the rent.[20] These levies involved an extra share of the crop during the harvest, gifts and tokens of dependence in recognition of a landowner's authority. Moreover, rents were once again being collected in kind as the tharavadus attempted to build up their grain stockpile. Previously levies could have been extracted only from those immediately dependent on a tharavadu – service castes and the agricultural labourers. As more groups began to rely on the tharavadu as a safety net for land, credit, manure, rights of pasturage and in the last instance, grain, there was an attempt to extract extra levies from wider sections of the agrarian population.

Many recent works have seen the Depression as a watershed in the reconstitution of rural relations of power, a period in which the dominance of rural magnates was undermined.[21] As Baker puts it, the bedrock of the south Indian rural magnates' authority was the control exercised over the liquidity of the local economy; credit was one of the most important bonds of social control. With the onset of the Depression, the ability of the magnate to provide credit to his clients is undermined, and so, therefore is his standing as a patron. One of the major weaknesses in this approach is that it does not even consider realms of interaction between superior and inferior other than that of credit. A magnate who is out of pocket is out of power. Networks of reciprocity, obligation, deference, worship and labour bound the landlord and labourer. It is significant that in Malabar not only did the rural elite try to work out new ways of negotiating power, but a whole new class of dependents sought to refashion erstwhile modes of behaviour and notions of obligation. Rural society was not torn apart but reconstituted; allowing for a greater bargaining between its constituents in which initially, the socialists, and then, the communists played a mediating role. This chapter will look at the process by which the dominant as well as the declining sections among the rural elite adapted. The final chapter moves towards the denouement with the tharavadus bolstered by the state and calling the shots.

The collapse of many of the small factories set up in the twenties by prospering tharavadus and tenants riding the pepper boom, and dwindling credit facilities in the towns for petty trade removed the foothold that many of

---

[20] The Malabar Tenancy Committee of 1940 had taken special note of the burgeoning of 'feudal levies' in the preceding years. *MTCR, 1940*, I, 52.

[21] C.J. Baker, 'Debt and the Depression in Madras', in C.J. Dewey and A.G. Hopkins eds., *The imperial impact: studies in the economic history of Africa and India* (London, 1978), 238; Baker, *Politics of south India* and *An Indian rural economy*; Bose, *Agrarian Bengal*. For an important earlier statement, in the context of Burma, about the decisive impact on agrarian society of the breakdown of credit during the Depression see M. Adas, *The Burma delta: economic development and social change on an Asian frontier, 1852-1941* (Madison, WI, 1974).

the poorer cultivators had gained in the towns.[22] Sundareswara and Jagannatha temples had managed to build a fragile unity between town and countryside as Tiyya elites knitted the provision of credit and employment with building a community of worship. If rural communities were coming to be based more on sustenance, the newborn, fragile, temple community in the towns was becoming centred on the more intangible association of worship. In the summer of 1936, fractures became evident in the nascent community around the Tiyya temples, as rival groups volleyed for legitimacy as the representatives of the Tiyyas. The older generation of leaders of the Gnanodaya Yogam continued to be obsessed by the local and community concerns of the previous decade. A younger generation of professional Tiyyas was forced to establish wider connections with other groups rather than stand as a community apart. First, there was the slump in the price of coconuts, the crop which had underwritten the success of the Tiyya tenants in the first two decades of this century. Secondly, the Mappila mercantile community continued to prosper; their monopoly over the rice trade, and the fact that the mills at Bombay and Karachi continued to take coconut oil from Malabar, allowed them to ride the Depression.[23] Their relative prosperity manifested itself partly in the mushrooming of *srambis* in Cannanore and Tellicherry.

The inability, or reluctance of caste organisations in Travancore and Malabar to make the transition from cultural politics to an engagement with the state precipitated a crisis of sorts. C. Krishnan, one of the older generation which had resisted classification as Hindus, and had emphasised that the Tiyyas were a community apart, now converted to Buddhism. Sahodaran Ayyappan, the Pulaya leader from Travancore, who had briefly flirted with socialism, followed suit. Tiyyas and Ezhavas were wooed by Christians, Muslims, Sikhs and the maverick ideologue E.V. Ramaswamy Naicker who advocated the formation of a Self-Respect movement. Some Ezhava leaders advocated Christianity: C.V. Kunjuraman negotiated with the Anglican Bishop of Kottayam. Others like C.K. Kuttan 'converted' to Hinduism.[24] In the summer of 1936, Travancore was besieged by *jathas* of Sikhs from Amritsar, one of them led by Master Tara Singh himself, and *maulvis* who said that circumcision could be dispensed with if speedy conversion was desired. By June, the Shiromani Gurdwara Prabandhak Committee was considering the setting up of *gurdwaras* all over Travancore and Malabar.[25]

---

[22] *Papers relating to the Industrial Conference, Ooty, September, 1908*, 22; Evidence of G.F. Baker, Henke's Tile Works, Feroke, *Indian Industrial Commission, 1916-18*, III, 358-60; *RDIMP*, 1926-27, 21; *Ibid*, 1927-28, 24; *Ibid.*, 1931-32, 17; *Ibid.*, 1935-6, 37.

[23] While foreign trade at Tellicherry port fell from a value of Rs. 116.82 *lakhs* in 1927-28 to 24.07 *lakhs* in 1934-35, trade along the coast remained steady. There was a fall from 52.29 *lakhs* to 41.71 *lakhs* in the same period. *RSTMP*, 1927-28 and 1934-35.

[24] C.K. Pullapilly, 'The Ishavas of Kerala and their historic struggle for acceptance in the Hindu society', *Journal of Asian and African Studies*, 11 (1976), 24-46.

[25] *Hindu*, 20 March, 21 April, 12-14 May, 8 June 1936.

The crisis was resolved in a similar way in both Malabar and Travancore. As Tiyya elites began losing out in local conflict the community turned to the province and the promise of electoral representation held out by the Government of India Act, 1935. In 1936, the Malabar Tiyya Association, representing the younger generation allied with the Congress and appeals were made to all Tiyyas to register as voters.[26] In Travancore, the Ezhava middle classes joined the Travancore State Congress in opposition to the Maharaja till 1938.[27] In north Malabar an amalgam of economic pressures, the aspiration to a wider politics, and the failure of the attempt to stand as a community apart forced a section among the Tiyyas to adopt militant Hindu stances. In March 1936, P. Madhavan, a Tiyya lawyer and Member of the Legislative Council, spoke about the growth in the number of *srambis* which were 'infringing on the ancient rights of Hindus'.[28] The nature of the conflicts between Tiyya and Mappila religious processions became overtly 'communal' in this decade. In 1934, the Gnanodaya Yogam had managed a temporary truce with Mappila leaders but by 1936 it was clear that a 'younger generation of Tiyyas [were] bent on disregarding [the] pact of 1934'. Local authorities were forced to ban processions of any kind in 1936 to prevent escalation of conflict.[29] Among the Mappilas too, there was a transition to a politics engaging with the state from their earlier stance of cultural regeneration through organisations such as the Young Men's Muslim Association (1926) and the Muslim Majlis (1930). K.M. Seethi Saheb, an erstwhile member of the Cochin Legislative Assembly, moved to Tellicherry and established the newspaper *Chandrika* in 1934. This was to become the mouthpiece of the Muslim League set up by the Mappila merchant Abdul Sattar Sait who was elected to the Central Legislative Assembly in 1934 on the Muslim League ticket.[30]

The impact of legislation on tharavadus

Meanwhile, the conjuncture of two pieces of legislation, one dealing with tenancy and the other with reform of the Nayar tharavadus, had contradictory

---

[26] *Hindu*, 6, 8, 9 June 1986.

[27] Jeffrey, 'Travancore'. Jeffrey's overly simple analysis is constructed in terms of a teleological movement away from the politics of caste and religion towards the 'secular' politics of Congress.

[28] *Mathrubhumi*, 7 March 1936.

[29] *RAPMP*, 1934, 14; *Revenue DR 5691/36 dated 12 May 1936* (KRA); *Home Dept.(C) G.O. 393 dated 1 May 1936* (KS); *Revenue DR 2776/ dated 16 March 1936* (KRA); *Revenue DR 3584 dated 16 March 1936* (KRA); *Home Dept. G.O. 34 (Confdl.) dated 30 April 1936* (KS).

[30] R.E. Miller, *The Mappila Muslims of Kerala: a study in Islamic trends* (Madras, 1976).

effects. The first legally strengthened the position of the tenants at a time when they were becoming economically dependent on landowners for land, credit and grain. The second weakened the unity of the tharavadus, undermining their authority in the countryside, just as economic forces had indirectly enhanced the possibility of an exercise of their authority.

The tenancy movement in south Malabar had retreated from the public arena, after the attempt to knit tenancy and Khilafat agitation in 1921 had produced a monster the conservative Frankensteins felt they could not control. Between 1924 to 1930, the tenants' lobby spearheaded by the indefatigable G. Sankaran Nayar, the Secretary of the Malabar Tenants' Association, worked its way through the bureaucratic maze at Fort St George. G. Sankaran Nayar's diaries reveal how much the passing of the Act had to do with lobbying behind the scenes and ensuring that files passed through pro-legislation bureaucrats. The entry for 20 October 1930 states that the Tenancy file was routed through K.R. Menon who recommended unconditional assent to the bill. Sir Frank Noyce, the Revenue Member, intended it to have gone to a British official who would have blocked the file. Sankaran Nayar noted with evident satisfaction, 'There we have been able to outwit him [Noyce]'.[31]

The lobbying of the tenants associations of south Malabar bore fruit with the passing of the Malabar Tenancy Act which came into force on 1 December 1930. The Tenancy Act of 1930 ensured fixity of tenure to the cultivator on wetlands, freedom from eviction for *kanam* tenants, and reduced the fee payable at the time of renewal of the *kanam* tenure. It was a piece of legislation skewed largely in the interests of south Malabar, neglecting the coconut cultivators on garden lands (the *kuzhikanakkaran*), the pepper cultivators and those practising fugitive cultivation in the north. The tenant cultivator on garden lands was not given fixity of tenure, but only the right to renewal of the lease. In an era of depressed prices, even this would have to be negotiated as landholders were keen to divert land towards less risky endeavours. The interests of the tenants' lobby in south Malabar and the government's over-weening desire to prevent a repetition of the uprising of 1921 dovetailed neatly in the Act. However, the MTA, 1930 created a niche for tenancy legislation at a time when rights over land were beginning to be contested in north Malabar. In the latter half of the decade, the extension of the provisions of the Act to various groups and regions, was to form a major theme of rural agitation.

While tenants benefited from the passing of the Act, the position of the breed of small landowners which had arisen in the previous decade was severely affected. With the granting of freedom from eviction, fewer tenants were inclined to joint registration for the purposes of the payment of revenue, and

---

[31] *Diaries of G. Sankaran Nayar* (NMML).

were content to let the landlords foot the revenue bill.[32] The Collector was flooded with petitions from landholders for joint registration, none of which could be affected because the contracts had ended, and the tenants now had fixity of tenure under the Act. Quite a few of the small landowners had derived income from amounts received on renewal of tenures and the granting of overleases. The MTA, 1930, by reducing the one and curtailing the other, left them dependent solely on uncertain rents and the usufruct from lands directly in their possession. By 1934, the administration had begun to worry that 'the *janmis* [were] losing a good deal of their influence and control of their tenants'.[33] Even as the extraction of rent proved difficult from now ensconced tenants, landowners still had to bear revenue obligations. Notwithstanding the fall in the prices of cash crops, the resettlement of Malabar, between 1930-33, contemplated the enhancement of revenue by 18.75 per cent in the cases of garden and wetlands. Revenue remission was considered only in 1934 and that too for only so long as the prices of pepper and paddy were still falling.[34] In 1937, the Agricultural Debt Relief Act of the Congress ministry wiped out the arrears of rent payable in areas under the MTA, 1930.[35] This, coupled with the depression in prices meant that the smaller landlords derived no profit from produce while prospects of rent from their tenants gradually receded.

In the previous decade those who had managed to acquire land had leased out a major portion to tenant cultivators and were now at the latter's mercy for the payment of rent and revenue. Many of the small landlords who had risen on the boom in prices fell back to earth. A detailed economic survey of Kurumbranad taluk in 1935 found that many 'intermediate' landholders were 'groaning under the weight of debts' which they had incurred in order to buy land. With the slump in prices and the consequent inability to repay loans, land changed hands rapidly.[36] Many moved from being tenant to landowner and back again in the course of a decade. A few tried to maintain their status as landholders even in the face of non-payment of rent by increasingly recalcitrant tenants. The settlement officer remarked in sheer exasperation that it was 'mere

---

[32] In 1920, the Malabar Land Registration Act laid down that tenants were not legally liable for land revenue unless they were jointly registered with the landlord. The latter were not keen to create a record of rights for the tenant and very few joint registrations had actually taken place. *Revenue Dept. G.O. 488 dated 25 Februaaary 1935* (IOL); *Revenue Dept. G.O. 630 dated 8 March 1938* (IOL).

[33] Note of T.B. Russell, Collector to Secretary to Commissioners (Land revenue and settlement), 25 January 1933, *Revenue R.Dis. 6351/32 dated June 9 1934* (KRA); Note of Collector, 30 January 1942, *Revenue DR 1369-41 dated 11 March 1942* (KRA).

[34] *Revenue R.Dis. 1620/33 dated 31 March 1933* (KRA); *Madras Revenue Dept. G.O. 272 dated 9 February 1934* (KS); *Revenue R. Dis. 3431/36 dated 2 April 1936* (KRA).

[35] B.V. Narayanaswamy Naidu and P. Vaidyanathan, *The Madras agricultural debt relief act: a study* (Annamalai, 1939), 10-11.

[36] Indebtedness of cultivation enquiry by Special Officer, Chorode, Kurumbranad, *Revenue DR 619/35 dated 4 April 1935* (KRA).

pride of possession that [made] them hold on to their old liabilities when they are getting little or nothing from the land'.[37] In those troubled times the dignity of being a landowner was an intangible, but real consolation for those whose fortunes had risen and fallen so dramatically. Even as these *parvenus* were being levelled by economic forces, many of the larger tharavadus were taking back the land for the purchase of which they had advanced loans. A major part of the transactions were cases of the purchase of debtors' land by creditors. In north Malabar the average value of the sale document was Rs. 153, showing both the decline in the value of the land as well as how small the plots of the new landowners of the previous decade had been.[38] The smaller landowners were in more of a fix – the want of funds to file suits to recover rents, the decline in income from usufruct, their inability to get back the home farm lands leased out at the end of the last decade and, ultimately, their dependence on the dominant tharavadu of the region.

While smaller landowners were in dire straits, the dominant Nayar tharavadus became the focus of succour in their roles of landowners, creditors and granaries in the countryside. At the same time, they were being riven by internal conflicts. What had begun in the late nineteenth century as a movement for marriage reform among the Nayars, supported by a vocal, largely urban professional elite, had ramified by the early twentieth century into a movement drawing upon Nayars of all classes for reform of the tharavadus.[39] Even when the Marriage Commission had been appointed in 1890, it was clear that the question of marriage would naturally raise issues of individual property and the vesting of inheritance in a family unit other than the matrilineal tharavadu.[40] By the early twentieth century, these two themes of marriage and property came together. That a nuclear family of man, wife and children was more 'natural' was an emergent theme, and R.M. Palat's Marriage Bill of 1931 tried to guarantee the 'right of succession to the property of the deceased husband and father'.[41] In 1931, the Matriliny Bill, which would become law in 1933, stated that the matrilineal tharavadu was 'no longer the focus' of Nayar lives, and that the 'social stream [was] flowing along more natural channels'.[42] It called for recognition of marriage, the right of 'free divorce', the 'enforcement of monogamy' and, crucially, the rights of individuals to claim their share of the tharavadu property by allowing for partitioning of the tharavadu. Between 1890 and 1933, notions of marriage, family and property underwent a rapid

---

[37] *Revenue R.Dis. 3431/36 dated 2 April 1936* (KRA).
[38] *Report on the administration of the Registration Department of the Madras Presidency (ARDMP)*, 1930-33, 4, 7.
[39] See Arunima, 'Colonialism and the transformation of matriliny', ch. 6.
[40] *Report of the Malabar Marriage Commission, 1890* (Madras, 1891), I, 3.
[41] *Law (General) Dept. G.O.89 dated 28 February 1931* (KS).
[42] Marumakkathayam Bill of V.P. Narayanan Nambiar (Bill no. 13 of 1931) in the Madras Legislative Council, *Law (Legislative) Dept. G.O.892 dated 21 August 1931* (KS).

transformation. The Act of 1933 put the legislative seal on a process of partitioning of the matrilineal tharavadu, in response to moral, economic and internal pressures.

In north Malabar, the process of expansion of cultivation was tied up with the establishment of branches of the tharavadu as pioneering outposts. The crash in the prices of pepper meant that many of the younger members could call for partition but without the resources to sustain a branch. The parent tharavadu in most cases controlled the wetlands as well as the granary, making the establishment of a branch, in most cases, an empty gesture of independence. Many of these branches lacked the clout to negotiate with unruly, wily tenants and encroaching cultivators and were forced to resort to diplomacy rather than force. Links had to be forged not only to play off one faction or competing tenant against another, but also to amass ballast for withstanding the pressure of the parent tharavadu. At a time when dominant tharavadus were withholding customary rights and instituting new levies, allies were not hard to come by. Socialist organisation in this period would rely to a large extent on the relations forged between younger members of dominant tharavadus and cultivators. In the previous decade, younger members had already begun to reach out to their dependent labourers organising them under a broadly Gandhian philosophy of cleanliness and temperance. Now there was a new vocabulary and ideology, new pressures arising within the tharavadu and from a depressed economy, and a political idiom that would be less quietist and more militant.

Primarily, it was a question of who could lay a claim to individual plots of land. Conflict was not restricted to the parent tharavadus and their branches alone. At the immediate level, it was more a question of whether it was the cultivator or the landowning tharavadus who could more forcefully assert their respective claims to the land. Very often, these matters were settled in the procedure most familiar to the dominant tharavadus; recalcitrant occupants were murdered and the land taken over.[43] Previously, tharavadus had presented a united front in such strong-arm methods, now they were literally houses divided against themselves. Politic tenants were able to play off one faction or branch of a tharavadu against another and internal conflicts between nephews, uncles and overseers were translated into local conflicts and vice versa. In the course of the Depression and under the influence of legislation, the community of tharavadu and cultivators had come to be stripped down to its bare essentials – control over land, forest and granaries. Control over resources was to be the premise on which the community rested, not a shared participation in festivals or worship nor the perception of sharing in dearth and prosperity. Now there was dearth and those who could dispense their obligations were divided against themselves, each trying to create their own sphere of influence. Unity within the dominant tharavadus and a buoyant economy had marked both

[43] *RAPMP*, 1936.

the strength of the community and the independence of the constituents of the rural community. Divided tharavadus and a depressed economy would signal a weakened sense of community and the dependence of the cultivator, but in an era of uncertain power exercised by those who had been dominant.

The formation of peasant unions

In the period 1934-40, peasant unions were organised in the eastern villages of north Malabar by the activists of the Kerala Congress Socialist Party (KCSP), which had been founded in October 1934. Political activity was not restricted to the criticism of the inequalities in the agrarian structure or calls for the reform of the pattern of landholding. It attempted a wholesale change in the attitudes of people; a transformation of rural structures of deference and authority. Rural political activity was largely initiated by a socialist leadership drawn from prominent Nayar tharavadus in north Malabar. Quite often, they came from the branches bereft of resources by the enactment of the partition bill. Moreover, many of these branches had an as yet undefined sphere of influence, and both the exercise of authority as well as the gathering of support had to be negotiated. They attempted to build an alternative order which could reemphasise a sense of community, but which would be shorn of the accretion of emphases of traditional authority.

The younger members of dominant tharavadus were to play a prominent part in this attempt at renegotiation.[44] They were the products of the new intellectual climate which attempted to transcend the inequality of caste, but paradoxically, they were able to work among and organise cultivators and labourers, precisely because they commanded respect as members of the rural elite. Here one must disagree with Jeffrey's unsubstantiated proposition that the partition of the matrilineal households created a generation of deracinated Nayars.[45] In the aftermath of Depression and the partition of the dominant tharavadus, the

---

[44] A.K. Gopalan (1904-77), who eventually became a communist MP and leader of the opposition in Parliament after the first general elections in 1951, was a member of the Ayillyath tharavadu in Chirakkal, which had originally been a Nayar 'ruling family'. Gopalan, *In the cause of the people*, 1; K.A. Keraleeyan (1910-), President of the All Malabar Peasant Union in the late thirties and early forties belonged to a tharavadu related to Ayillyath by marriage. Interview, Calicut, March 1987. K.P.R. Gopalan (1906-), played a prominent part in the Protest Day Celebrations in 1940, and was sentenced to death. He was reprieved after the personal intervention of Gandhi. The post of *adhikari* in Kalliasseri was traditionally held by the *karanavan* of his household. Interview, Kalliasseri, February-March 1987.

[45] R. Jeffrey, 'Matriliny, Marxism and the birth of the Communist Party in Kerala, 1930-1940', *Journal of Asian Studies*, 38, 1 (1978), 77-98. He further states that an 'ideological void' was created by the decline of matriliny. However, it is not made clear how matriliny functioned at the level of ideology, if it did at all in any coherent sense.

younger members were trying to bolster their vestigial status by acting in conjunction with their erstwhile dependents. Individuals like A.K. Gopalan and Keraleeyan could play the role of arbitrators between cultivators and labourers and their masters. Coming as they did from the same social class (and in most cases, caste) as the dominant landholders, they were able to intercede for their constituency on equal terms. But, they were regarded with initial suspicion by the potential beneficiaries as belonging to a stratum which had exercised dominance over them.[46] An example of this is the case of Subramaniam Thirumumpu, who came from the powerful Nambudiri family of Thazhekkat. He had been active in social reform in north Malabar prior to civil disobedience. Even after his entry into the organisation of peasant unions, there continued to be a mixture of awe and resentment towards him among his colleagues as well as his erstwhile dependents.[47] There was the inevitable conflict between leading and yet aspiring to remain *primus inter pares*, which led to piquant situations. When organisers were sent to villages, the KCSP leadership emphasised that they must, as a matter of strategy, ask for rice gruel to drink. This was intended to emphasise that though the peasant organisers were of higher caste they were not concerned with laws of caste pollution. Such strategies occasionally misfired, causing doubts about the caste of the leaders and therefore the degree of respect to be accorded them. Cultivators usually gave their equals toddy, reserving gruel for charity to the lowest castes.

Early political activity was to be coloured by the caution of a reformed rural elite which wished to go thus far and no further. They were willing to campaign against feudal exactions and caste oppression which they now depicted as arising out of the relation between 'landlords' and 'cultivators'. However, there was a significant departure from the earlier restrictive vocabulary. Instead of the limited imaginings of caste or a Hindu nationalism an appeal was made to the all-encompassing and vague category of cultivators. A characteristic statement was made in 1934 by Krishna Pillai, one of the founders of the KCSP: 'land all over India must be deemed to belong to cultivators by a proclamation'.[48] Though there was the occasional attempt to specify rural categories, this remained at the level of theorising by the leadership. At a meeting in Ponnani, E.M.S. Nambudiripad stated that agricultural labourers were to be organised separately because they earned a 'wage'. Needless to say such distinctions were not adhered to in the process of actual organisation.[49] The lack of specificity meant, in effect, a reaching out to landlord, tenant and agricultural labourer.

With the KCSP's decision to work within the Congress to radicalise it by

[46] Madhavan, *Payaswiniyude teerattu*, 94, 96.
[47] Interviews with K.A. Keraleeyan, Calicut and T.C. Narayanan Nambiar, Narath, February-March 1987.
[48] *Mathrubhumi*, 1 February 1934.
[49] *Mathrubhumi*, 26 May 1937.

'organising agricultural labour', political activity in Malabar acquired another dimension. In December 1934, a sub-committee was formed within the KPCC comprised of Krishna Pillai, Chandroth Kunhiraman Nayar and K.P. Gopalan. It was to conduct agitations for reduction of revenue and rural indebtedness and resolutions were passed to this effect.[50] The announcement of this programme precipitated a split in the Congress. K. Kelappan, K. Madhava Menon, M.P. Govinda Menon and K. Raman Menon broke away and formed the Congress Right which remained faithful to Harijan welfare and the propagation of *khadi*. They belonged to an older generation of Congressmen (both Raman Menon and Madhava Menon were born in 1896, while Kelappan was born in 1889) and were, with the exception of Kelappan, professionals and lawyers from south Malabar. At a meeting in September 1935, a set of more radical proposals was put before the KPCC including the abolition of land revenue, exempting 'small cultivators' from income tax and vesting proprietary right over land in the actual cultivator.[51] Nevertheless, there was to be a broad divergence between resolutions adopted in the heated atmosphere of the KPCC meetings and actual practice in the countryside.

Vishnu Bharateeyan, Keraleeyan and eleven others in the *desam* of Kolacheri made the first attempts to form a peasant union in 1935. Bharateeyan was a Nambisan (a caste of temple officials below the Nambudiris in the putative hierarchy of castes) and came from one of the prominent tharavadus of Kolacheri which had fallen on hard times. Bharateeyan, in keeping with his background, was a man of religious demeanour, much given to peppering his speeches on class exploitation with references from the *Bhagavad Gita* and the Puranas. This is significant in that becoming a socialist/communist did not necessarily mean an abandoning of a previous identity or intellectual baggage.[52] Initial attempts at organisation were met with polite, respectful avoidance of confrontation, despite the fact that the dominant Nambudiri landowner in the region, who held over 95 per cent of the lands, gave none of his tenants any proof of their tenure. It was a lucky break which allowed the KCSP to intervene. The Nambudiri wrested the crop of his overseer without paying him any compensation. Bharateeyan interceded on his behalf and instituted a civil suit which prompted the payment of the requisite compensation. News of this spread to other villages and the KCSP was able to establish a union in Kolacheri.[53] Early attempts at organisation depended on the possibility of being able to take advantage of fissures in the structures of authority, as for example, bad blood between overseers and landlords. Very often, overseers acted as the link between activists and agricultural labourers.[54]

[50] Proceedings of KPCC meeting, 29 December 1934. *AICC Files P-15/1934-36* (NMML).
[51] Meeting of KPCC, 29 September 1935, *AICC Files P-15/1934-36* (NMML).
[52] Interview with Keraleeyan, Calicut, March 1987.
[53] Vishnu Bharateeyan, *Adimakal engane udamakalayi*, 82-7.
[54] Interview with K.P.R. Gopalan, Kalliasseri, March 1987.

Political activity in the countryside reflected a continuation of the endeavours for caste equality of the previous decades. The first all-Malabar peasant meeting was held at Parassinikadavu on 1 November 1936 and processions (*jathas*) of peasant unions came in from Cannanore and its neighbouring villages. Bharateeyan encapsulated unconsciously the progression of the themes of political activity in Malabar over the past three decades when he stated in his opening speech, 'There are only two castes, two religions and two classes – the haves and the have nots'.[55] Two major resolutions were adopted at this meeting. One was the need to abolish customs and speech usages which emphasised the status of lower caste labourers.[56] This marked a major shift from the objectives of caste associations and the activities of Gandhian Congressmen which had stressed self-help and self-betterment over the need to question inequality. The other resolution dealt with the need to combat the accretion of feudal levies which tharavadus had begun to extract from their labourers and dependents. A study of the demands made by peasant unions between 1937 and 1939 demonstrates the nature of political activity in the initial stage – thus far and no further. A peasant union was formed in Alavil in July 1937. At its first meeting it was resolved that the four *paisa* levy for every *seer* of paddy collected by the landlord, the raja of Chirakkal, should be opposed.[57] A procession of labourers led by A.V. Kunhambu, whose family held extensive lands in adjacent Karivellur, went to meet the raja. Kunhambu refused to discuss the matter with the overseer of the raja's estates and insisted that the direct relationship between the palace and the peasants was being interfered with.[58] It is significant that traditional relations of authority were not being questioned, only their corruption was. However, it is equally important that now the unions determined what was fair and were resolved to stick by it. They demanded that the system of undermeasuring their payments of rent at the rate of eleven *seers* as nine and three-quarter *seers*, should be stopped. The raja offered a compromise of ten *seers* but this was rejected and the union insisted on the correct measurement of grain.[59]

At a meeting presided over by Keraleeyan, again directed at the raja of Chirakkal, 'feudal levies' added on to the rent were opposed. So was the new practice of requiring a year's rent in advance from prospective cultivators on wetlands.[60] A procession of 2,000 peasants approached the Kurumathur Nambudiripad and demanded the abolition of *akrama pirivukal* (irregular exactions) and the commissions which were to be paid to overseers who collected the rent. One of the major demands concerned the granting of

[55] Vishnu Bharateeyan, *Adimakal engane udamakalayi*, 86.
[56] *Ibid.*, 89.
[57] *Mathrubhumi*, 29 July 1937.
[58] Kurup, *Kunhambuvinte katha* (*The life of A.V. Kunhambu*), Kottayam, 1982.
[59] *Mathrubhumi*, 29 July 1937.
[60] *Prabhatham*, 10 October 1938.

permission to collect firewood from the forests of the Nambudiripad. He was informed that the annual rent would be paid only after the union had met and considered the issue.[61] Another procession of 4,000 peasants marched to the Kalliattu Thazhatheveettil tharavadu in Kalliattu *amsam* and demanded the appointment of unbiased overseers, the correct measurement of grain rents and the abolition of unpaid labour.[62] Other demands raised at various meetings related to the prevention of the buying and selling of labourers along with leased lands and the termination of the practice of demanding seeds as part of the rent. In November 1938, 7,000 peasants went in a procession to Karakkatidathil Nayanar and demanded an end to trade in serf labour.[63]

The demands were diverse in scope and included in their ambit the bonded labourer, the free agricultural labourer, the tenant cultivator, the cultivator on wetlands as well as the small landowner. There were several common threads; the most important being the distinction made between *akrama* and *krama pirivukal*. An inchoate sense of a moral economy emerges from this opposition between regular and irregular exactions. There were no threats of rents being withheld, at worst there was a delay in payment. At this stage, political activity is comparable with the struggle in Bihar over *bakasht* lands led by the Kisan Sabha and the left. Henningham characterises it as an attempt to 'work within the *zamindari* system, either to reestablish rights which had previously existed, or else to take advantage of rights under the law which had existed over the years'.[64] E.M.S. Nambudiripad was at pains to clear any misunderstanding and wrote to the Governor of Madras that no-rent campaigns were not part of the programme of peasant unions.[65] Nor were there any demands for the redistribution of land. Despite the limited nature of union activity, rumours were rife that an 'Ernad type uprising', i.e. along the lines of the Mappila rebellion, was being contemplated. Unions stated that cultivators and agricultural labourers would pay a legitimate rent and no more; none of the accretions of demand following the crisis of the Depression would be countenanced. This was particularly evident in the undermeasuring of grain rents as in the collection of *nuri* (a handful of grain set aside for the landlord every time a certain number of measures was reached) or *vasi* (one and three-quarter measures for every measure). The most blatant of these feudal levies was the collection of the *chillara purappadu*, literally, miscellaneous levies at the time of festivals.[66]

The revoking of customary rights by dominant tharavadus, like the collection of firewood and manure from forests, became a major focus of opposition.

[61] *Prabhatham*, 31 October 1938.
[62] *Ibid.*
[63] *Prabhatham*, 14 November 1938.
[64] Henningham, *Peasant movements in colonial India*, 167.
[65] Governor's report, 10 March 1942. *Public and Judicial Files 117-C-3* (IOL); Narayanan Nair, *Aranuttandugalilude (Through half a century)*, Kottayam, 1973, 179.
[66] *MTCR, 1940*, I, 52.

Customary rights like fugitive cultivation on wasteland were steadily transformed into leases, and rents were collected in cash. Several *jathas* to the
tharavadus of the extreme north and north east of Chirakkal took up the issue
of the collection of green leaves for use as manure. One *jatha* managed to
successfully wrest rights to collect green leaves from the forests of the
Thazhekkat tharavadu.[67] With the crash in the prices of cash crops, many
cultivators began to encroach upon the forests to grow hill rice and onto
uncultivated wasteland for other subsistence crops like horsegram and
blackgram. Cultivation on inferior land was arduous and required ploughing
and cross ploughing up to fifty times to pulverise the soil. Green leaves were
scattered, ploughed in and left to decay.[68] The demands of the peasant unions
for wasteland were intimately linked with the question of sustaining customary
rights to use of forests and reflected the spread of cultivation to more inferior
land. The bigger landowners retaliated by prohibiting *punam* cultivation on
their wastelands and hills. If they did give land on leases they demanded the
settlement of rent in advance of the crop. Customary loans given to cultivators
waned as there was increasing uncertainty that these, let alone the rents, would
be paid.[69]

Landholders desirous of profits preferred to lease forests to planters or even
to cut down trees than allow the cultivation of unremunerative crops. In 1939,
the Collector of Malabar lamented the fact that any long-range policy of forest
conservation was 'utterly out of the question'. Either trees were being cut down
indiscriminately to 'defray current expenses' or random cultivation was being
allowed which meant that forests were being encroached upon in an unsystematic
and destructive fashion.[70] The activities of peasant unions too contributed to
deforestation in a minor way. In November 1938, a meeting of 2,000 men
approached a landlord to claim the customary right of collection of firewood.
When they were refused, several trees were cut down in protest.[71] This steady
intrusion on the forests had two consequences. First, it brought the new breed
of cultivators into competition with the tribal groups practising slash-and-burn
cultivation of hill rice. Secondly, it brought to light the existence of bonded
labour – both tribal and untouchable caste – in what had been remote fastnesses
penetrated only by the overseers of dominant tharavadus like Kalliattu and
Vengayil. In 1939, a delegation of the All India Students' Federation visiting
north east Chirakkal had to inform the tribal inhabitants that it was the British
and not the Vengayil Nayanar who ruled the country.[72] Here again, the

[67] Kurup, *Kunhambuvinte katha*, 134-5.
[68] *RDAMP*, 1927, 75; *Revenue DR 8153/34 dated 24 January 1934* (KRA).
[69] FR for the first half of February 1939, *L/P and J/5/199* (IOL).
[70] Reply of the Collector to the enquiry of the Malabar tenancy commission. *R.Dis. 7962/39
     dated 3 October 1939* (KRA).
[71] Sessions Case 22/1938, *Home Dept. G.O.3903 (Confdl.) dated 18 July 1939* (KS).
[72] *Prabhatham*, 9 January 1939.

demands of the peasant unions were objecting to what was *akrama* when they called for the abolition of bonded labour. The competition developing between the tribal groups and cultivators desperate for land was not entirely to the former's disadvantage. In the peasant unions they acquired an ally against their exploitation as unpaid labour by the tharavadus. In Kalliattu, tribal groups like the Mavilar, Kuruchiyar and Vettuvar formed uneasy alliances with peasant unions who were motivated as much by profit as by altruism. Having incorporated potential opposition they were then able to twist the arms of the owners of the forests into leasing land for *punam* cultivation and even fix the rent in some cases. At Eleri, the landlord was forced to lease land at the rent fixed by the union of six bushels per acre.[73]

The undermining of deference

Rural political activity could not remain long within the confines of *akrama* and *krama* envisaged by the KCSP organisers. Increasingly, it began to undermine relations of social deference. Unions burgeoned all over north Malabar; some of them acted as informal protection squads and intervened in cases of eviction or demands of feudal levies. Yet others tried to create their own sphere of influence and functioned, in many ways, as erstwhile caste councils had done. The formation of unions had as much to do with ties of region, kinship and caste as the presence of any particular class interest. The Chittariparamba peasant union in Chirakkal consisted of small landowners, tenants, tenant cultivators and agricultural labourers who had in common the fact that they were from the same *desam*.[74] Besides, the propensity for union activity to escalate into violence often meant that the interests of their constituents could frequently be at odds.

In August 1938, a peasant's conference was held at Blathur, in Kalliattu *amsam*, attended by 7,000 members of peasant unions. Bharateeyan wrote of the conference that the atmosphere was so heated that no resolutions could be passed unanimously. A meeting was held near the dominant tharavadu of the area with ten representatives each from neighbouring villages. The landlord was told that he could no longer attack the wives and daughters of his labourers with impunity. He would be called by his name, Anantan Nambiyar, in future and no honorifics would be suffixed in addressing him. Moreover, peasants would not move out of the way when he passed them on the road and neither

[73] Madhavan, *Payaswiniyude teerattu*, 99; *Prabhatham*, 14 November 1938.
[74] Evidence of K. Kunhiraman, representative, Chittariparamba Karshaka Sangham. *MTCR, 1940*, II, 250.

would they stand up when he went by.[75] It was a radical change from earlier
relations in the countryside; people who had stepped off the road when upper
caste landlords used the road were now bearding them in their houses. In
Panniyur, peasant union members forced the landlord, Iswaran Nambudiripad,
to give receipts for loans and the interest paid on them as well as forgo feudal
levies.[76] As a poem published by the Chirakkal taluk peasant union punned,
'For long the landlord has taken *vasi* [feudal levy]/Reducing peasants to
poverty/Now by forming unions/We shall show our *vasi* [obstinacy]'.[77]

Changes were steadily becoming evident in attitudes, behaviour and even
attire. Lower castes and untouchables began wearing waistcloths which reached
below the knee and headcloths were not taken off in the presence of superiors.
Reporting for the *Prabhatham* on the changes in the countryside, P. Narayanan
Nayar wrote that following the formation of the peasant unions more peasants
in the countryside had begun wearing shirts and sporting moustaches. These
were privileges that had hitherto been reserved for the Nayars.[78] Moreover,
words were undergoing ideological redefinition. The word *janmi* had previously referred to larger owners of land.[79] It was endowed with a pejorative
inflection by association with large landowners and absentee landlords and, by
extension, with the system of 'feudalism'. As Krishna Pillai asserted in one of
his speeches, '*janmisampradayam* [the rule of *janmis* i.e. feudalism] is responsible for the oppression of cultivators. In no civilised country does it exist
any longer.'[80]

The experience of going in *jathas* was vitally important in engendering a
sense of rebellion against existing norms. In conception, the *jathas* were
similar to the religious processions to Kottiyur and Kodungallur. Landowners,
tenants, cultivators and agricultural labourers marched together and the sheer
numbers, ranging from 4,000 to 7,000, ensured anonymity as well as a sense
of community. Both these factors influenced the fact that many of the *jathas*
adopted confrontational stances against tharavadus and landowners till then
regarded as ineffably superior. These processions were similar to the pilgrimages
to Kottiyur in another respect: their potential for disorder. At Kurumathur, the
dominant Nambudiri landowner was kept awake all night by the banging of
coconut shells by the members of a mammoth *jatha*, until he acceded to their
demands.[81] *Jathas* came to represent the strength of the 'people' as against

[75] Vishnu Bharateeyan, *Adimakal engane udamakalayi*, 127-8.
[76] *Prabhatham*, 28 November 1938.
[77] *Krishikarude pattu* (*Songs of the cultivators*) (Chirakkal taluk karshaka sangham, 1938).
[78] *Prabhatham*, 9 January 1939. See also E.K. Nayanar, *My struggles: an autobiography* (Delhi, 1982), 10.
[79] Gundert, *Malayalam English nighandu*, 395.
[80] *Mathrubhumi*, 8 March 1936.
[81] Nayanar, *My struggles*, 10; Interview with K.P.R. Gopalan, Kalliasseri, March 1987. In another case, 15,000 members of a *jatha* kept the Kalliattu *janmi* awake all night shouting protests against his atrocities. *Prabhatham*, 14 November 1938.

'authority' by the end of the decade and very often they entered into pitched battles with the police. Initially *jathas* had been emblematic of the concerns of the KCSP leadership, derived as it was from the dominant tharavadus and deeply desirous of order. They had been led by KCSP organisers like Keraleeyan, A.K. Gopalan or Chandroth Kunhiraman Nayar who came from prominent Nayar tharavadus in Chirakkal. When the processions reached their destination, it had been customary for the members of the unions to wait outside while the leaders went and negotiated with their own kind. This had as much to do with the reluctance of both KCSP organisers and besieged landlords to entertain radical demands raised by the rude and illiterate as with the operation of caste rules. Household buildings were constructed in such a fashion as to allow each caste entry only till a particular point, as for example, Pulaya labourers being allowed only till the gate house or *padippura*. To allow members of the *jatha*, a motley assortment of castes, to enter the compound of a household, let alone the inner rooms, was unthinkable. Though in the initial stages, the potential of processions was curtailed by the predilections of leadership and caste, the experience of collective strength built up by the *jathas* allowed peasant activity to move out of the confines of KCSP control.

Many peasant unions began to resort to the methods which had been adopted by caste councils in an earlier period to punish errant members and bring the recalcitrant to heel. Now, significantly, the weapon was turned against those who had wielded it earlier. Those landlords who refused to do away with feudal levies were subjected to *vannathimattu*, or the denial of the services of the washerwoman.[82] At Patichal, the organisers of the peasant union approached teachers of the local board school and tried to enlist them in their position as local notables and makers of opinion. One of the teachers refused to have anything to do with the union. When the teacher's mother died, the union forbade the services of washerwomen, leaving the house under the shroud of pollution.[83] The use of these ritual punishments is important since they worked within notions of community. The threat of pollution mattered because it meant the possibility of ostracism; those punished would be cast out. But there was an important difference. That the erstwhile dependents and service castes of the tharavadus were now working against them shows the extent of the decline of the community centred on the tharavadu. The effects of the Depression as well as partitions had left most tharavadus with very few resources to command allegiance. In Kayyur, the trustees of the local shrine kept the ornaments of the deities under their control and appropriated the donations made during daily prayers and festivals. Peasant unions objected to this practice and many of the ritual performers, Vannans and Malayans, dependent on the shrine joined the

[82] *Prabhatham*, 28 November and 26 December 1938; *RAPMP*, 1938, 15.
[83] *CC5/39, Court of the Joint Magistrate, Tellicherry* (Tellicherry Court Record Room) (henceforth TCRR).

unions, with the growing inability of the tharavadus to sustain worship or those responsible for it.[84]

Unions had managed to create enclaves of power in *desams* and in the process enforced a degree of discipline among their members as well. At Iritty, a resolution that demanded that peasants be allowed to ask for reduction of rent independently of the union was promptly quelled.[85] More often, unions directly under the control of the KCSP organisers were the ones loath to enter into overt confrontational situations. In Kodaliprom, when the village revenue officer collected a commission exceeding the rent by 25 per cent, Bharateeyan drafted a letter of complaint to the *tahsildar* of Chirakkal taluk. The revenue officer was suspended and the need for social ostracism or more direct conflict was avoided.[86] However, the experience of collective strength gained in *jathas* and the imposition of social strictures on superiors meant that the activities of unions could not be contained by the predilections of the KCSP. Unions on their own initiative worked largely within the notion of a moral economy while redefining its rules. When P. Kammaran and his brother refused to join the peasant union at Urathur, his family was blacklisted and the entire village refused to speak to them or to allow them entry into homes. In another instance, a Nambudiri landlord of Kankole was forced to bring in labourers and bullocks from another *desam* since the local union forbade anyone within the village from working for him.[87] Furthermore, individuals could now appeal to unions outside their own *desam* to arbitrate conflicts. In Manipuzha, the Nambudiri landowner had sixty-two acres of wasteland which had been assessed as 'unoccupied dry' and was therefore not subject to payment of revenue. With the increase in demand for cultivable land, the landlord was keen to evict his tenant, Chandu, and give it all out on lease. Chandu was equally keen to acquire at least part of the land on improving tenure and approached his paternal uncle who was the president of the peasant union in nearby Alakkad.[88] He in turn approached A.V. Kunhambu, whose Akhila Bharat Yuvak Sangham (All India youth organisation) had gained a foothold in northern Chirakkal. Volunteers of the ABYS went and occupied the field of Manipuzha Nambudiri. The police had to be called in to evict the squatters.[89]

The experience of collective action and independent enterprise soon freed union activity from the constraints imposed by the KCSP leaders. Unions mushroomed all over north Malabar, organised around specific issues, and at

[84] K.K.N. Kurup, *The Kayyur riot: a terrorist episode in the national movement in Kerala* (Calicut, 1978), 40.

[85] *CC 93/38, Court of the Joint Magistrate, Tellicherry* (TCRR); *Home Dept. G.O. 3903 (Confdl.) dated 18 July 1939* (KS).

[86] Vishnu Bharateeyan, *Adimakal engane udamakalayi*, 23.

[87] CC 524/39, II class Magistrate, Taliparamba, *Home Dept. G.O.3903 (Confdl.) dated 18 July 1939* (KS); *CC106/38, Court of the Joint Magistrate, Tellicherry* (TCRR).

[88] Sessions case 22/1938, *Home Dept. G.O.3903 (Confdl.) dated 18 July 1939* (KS).

[89] Kurup, *Kunhambuvinte katha*, 132.

times they acted as a local counter force against a tharavadu's authority. Most of them owed nothing more than a formal allegiance to the KCSP leadership who now needed an issue which would garner the support of wider groups as well as allow them to exert a degree of control over diverse initiatives. Union activity did not reflect solely the 'rise of class based peasant movements' as Karat argues.[90] Unions were divided by caste and region, and very often affiliation with a union was purely temporary, in order to sort out individual grievances.

The attempt at moderation – amendment of the Tenancy Act

With the growing tendency of peasant initiatives to move beyond the control of the KCSP, there was considerable alarm among the leadership. The Akhila Bharat Yuvak Sangham, the brainchild of A.V. Kunhambu, provided particular cause for anxiety as it had managed to gain an ascendancy in the *desams* of Peralam, Kodakkat, Kuttamath and Peelicode where large tracts of wasteland and forest were available. Keraleeyan, a relative of Kunhambu was sent to gauge the strength of the ABYS in Karivellur and other regions. Finally, Krishna Pillai himself approached Kunhambu in 1939 and, as a senior activist, advised him that the ABYS should not emerge as an alternative to the communist party. Kunhambu agreed to dissolve his units and transferred the organisation's sole possession – a table – to the office of the socialist party.[91]

However, not all groups were going to respond in a similar fashion. As yet, the KCSP had only managed to ride the wave of the agitation for wastelands. Challenges to rural authority had gone on apace, and remained outside the ambit of socialist leadership. Jeffrey characterises the agitation as one appealing to the 'middle peasant' on the grounds that reducing revenue, ending feudal exactions and the like were 'clearly middle peasant demands'. He tends to ignore the undermining of deference in the countryside as well as the struggle for wasteland which clearly had a long prior history.[92] The attack on deference appealed to peasants all along the scale, ranging from labourer to the landowner reduced to tenant by the Depression. Demands for wasteland came as much from the 'poor peasant' as the 'middle peasant'. Moreover, at this stage, tenant cultivators and small landowners were still not in the realm of controlled political activity. The issue of extending the provisions of the MTA, 1930

---

[90] See P. Karat, 'The peasant movement in Malabar, 1934-40', *Social Scientist*, 50 (1976), 30-44 and 'Organised struggles of the Malabar peasantry, 1934-40', *Social Scientist*, 56 (1977), 3-17.

[91] Kurup, *Kunhambuvinte katha*, 122, 134-5.

[92] R. Jeffrey, 'Peasant movements and the Communist Party in Kerala, 1937-60' in D.B. Miller ed., *Peasants and politics: grass roots reaction to change in India* (London, 1979), 139.

seemed to provide a possible focus. Tenant cultivators on garden lands (*kuzhikanakkar*) had not been provided with security of tenure under the Act. At this juncture, with the crash in the prices of cash crops, their position was even more tenuous. *Kuzhikanakkar* had begun to withhold rent in parts of north Malabar, and the tenant's associations which had been set up prior to the passing of the Act were now beginning to come to life.[93]

The KCSP began to organise rallies demanding the extension of the provisions of the MTA to north Malabar and the amendment of certain clauses. They did not make any fundamental critique of the Act and remained firmly within the niche created by the government for future legislation. In Bihar, *kisan sabhas* and the provincial Congress committees mobilised peasants around the proposed Tenancy bill in 1938. As in Malabar, the demands of the peasant leaders concerned those who already held land on tenures: cutting rent demand by half and the stopping of evictions for non-payment of rent.[94] Fair rent was to be fixed at half the net produce and this provision was to be extended to garden lands as well. The system of paying renewal fees at the end of the period of tenure was to be ended as was the requirement that cultivators on wetlands pay a year's rent in advance. The expansion of cultivation to the margins was reflected in the demand for the extension of the provisions of the Act to *punam* and pepper cultivators.[95] In order to publicise the proposed amendments, the Malabar Tenancy Bill amendment day was observed on 6 November 1938 and peasant unions allied with the KCSP in north Malabar held meetings specifically addressing this issue.[96]

Activity concerned with the MTA climaxed on 18 December when two *jathas* from the peasant unions of north and south Malabar marched to Calicut to present their charter to the Collector. The Collector could not meet the *jatha* due to unavoidable circumstances.[97] Concurrently, the second all Malabar peasants conference was held at Chevayur. Here A.K. Gopalan countered the 'allegations' directed against peasant unions and portrayed them as working within the confines of legality. This was important both to garner the support of the tenantry who were alarmed by the initiatives of the landless, and to convince the Congress government that the KCSP had the movement in its control. The tension created by the attempts of the KCSP leadership to swamp the initiatives of the unions was reflected in a strongly worded resolution. This threatened non-payment of rent and the imposition of social boycott in the countryside if the government did not consider altering the MTA.[98] Keeping

---

[93] FR for the first half of November 1938, *L/P and J/5/198* (IOL); Oral evidence of T. Chathu, schoolmaster, Badagara. *MTCR, 1927-28*, II, 352-3.

[94] Tomlinson, *The Indian National Congress and the Raj*, 97-9.

[95] K. Keraleeyan, 'Required changes in the Malabar Tenancy Act', *Prabhatham*, 24 October 1938.

[96] *Prabhatham*, 14 November 1938.

[97] *Prabhatham*, 31 October 1938.

[98] *Prabhatham*, 26 December 1938.

in mind the increasing unrest in north Malabar, T. Prakasam, the Revenue Minister, toured the area and later announced the setting up of a Malabar Tenancy Committee. For the first time, a third of the respondents to the enquiries of a Tenancy Commission were peasant associations.[99] A.V. Kunhambu wrote later that gathering information for the commission had provided many KCSP organisers and peasant unions with a better insight into agrarian problems and helped them to understand better what had been mere slogans like 'death to feudalism'.[100] As the concerns of the tenants, shifting cultivators, and those reclaiming wasteland came together around the specific issue of amendment of the MTA, union membership received a boost. In 1939, under the broad umbrella of the All Malabar Peasant Union (AMPU), there were 180 unions in north Malabar alone with a membership approaching 20,000.[101]

The search for an alternative culture

The Guruvayur *satyagraha* in 1932-33 had come to a halt in the cul-de-sac of imagining a wider Hindu unity, and at the same time resolved itself into a matter concerning Nayars alone. In the search for a secular culture which would help transcend particular identities of caste and religion, the socialists tried to exploit a factor unique to Malabar – a literate populace. Literacy was to be the premise of the new socialist culture based on reading rooms, and in this the KCSP tapped into a rich vein. A ritual form like the *teyyattam* provides us with an insight into the realisation by the lower castes of knowledge as power. The texts of the *teyyattam*, composed by Malayans and Vannans, spoke of the injustices committed against lower castes by arrogant Nayars. During the performance, the dancer, possessed by the spirit of the dead, spoke his mind to the Nayar or Nambudiri chastising him for errors of omission and commission. It was not only the fact of being possessed, but the knowledge of the performer which allowed the reversal of customary roles. Legends associated with the *teyyattam* speak of Malayans who managed to marry into brahmin families, or learn the arts of the upper castes by virtue of their knowledge which allowed the 'disguise' of their low status.[102]

The lower caste movements of the early decades had emphasised the link between power and knowledge. Literacy as providing a 'disguise' for status

---

[99] *MTCR, 1940*, I, 2. Of the 459 replies received, 145 were from peasant associations. Eighty-three of these were from Chirakkal and Kottayam.
[100] Kurup, *Kunhambuvinte katha*, 227.
[101] Balaram, *Keralathile kammyunistu prasthanam*, I, 83-4.
[102] A well-known Malayalam proverb has it that Saraswati, the goddess of learning, resided on the tongue of the Malayan. Chanthera, *Kaliyattam*, 33, 36, 115.

and as a strategy against the oppression of the upper castes was an inherent idea. The Keraliya Karmmala Samajam (Kerala Artisans Association), had stated as early as 1911, 'to establish the foundations of the world ... two things are necessary – education and wealth'.[103] Meetings of the Araya Mahajana Sabha (Fishermen's Congress) had asserted in 1920 that their salvation 'depended on education and education alone'. It is significant that untouchable movements even elsewhere in India saw the basic polarity in society as being between 'knowledge and ignorance' rather than a Dumontian opposition of purity and pollution. The Ad Dharm movement in Punjab had as one of its slogans 'Education leads us to where the truth resides'.[104] Education was seen as the panacea for poverty and inequality and that which guaranteed the security of future generations. Conservatives were beginning to fear that with the younger generation of 'cobblers, carpenters' and others increasingly going in for elementary education instead of learning their hereditary trade, 'special classes of people would become utterly extinct'.[105] In 1938, one of the pamphlets published by the Chirakkal taluk peasant union spoke of debts and pauperisation among agricultural labourers. However, their ultimate sorrow lay in the fact that, 'Though we struggle/Are we able to dress our children even in rags/And put a slate and pencil in their hands'.[106]

The desire for education was fuelled by the increasing opportunities provided by a hierarchy of elementary, secondary and high schools. These displaced, to some extent, the informal education imparted in the villages and the village schools.[107] By 1931, there were 1,004 elementary schools for boys and 317 for girls, which made Malabar the district with the highest school-going population in the Presidency.[108] In 1922, the local *cheri* schools of the lower castes were amalgamated with the schools managed by the District Board. Free and compulsory education was introduced by the Tellicherry, Chirakkal, Kottayam and Kurumbranad taluk boards. As a result, the number of untouchables in schools not specifically meant for them increased considerably. This trend was strengthened by a decision of the government of Madras that a school was to be treated as 'inaccessible' and liable to loss of recognition if no pupil belonging to the 'depressed classes' was found on its

---

[103] P. Govindan, *Keraliya karmmala samaja vijnapanam* (*An advertisement for the artisans of Kerala*) (Calicut, 1912), ii.
[104] *Hindu*, 29 June 1920. See Juergensmeyer, *Religion as social vision*, 119-20.
[105] Evidence of V.V. Parameswara Ayyar, Palghat, *Report of the unemployment commission, 1927*, 251.
[106] *Prabhatham*, 19 December 1938.
[107] Aiyappan, *Iravas and culture change*, 127.
[108] In 1933, there were 18,000 pupils attending secondary school; the largest number in the Presidency. By 1936, the percentage of school-goers to the population was 17.2 for males and 9.6 for females. *Report on the working of the Local Boards in the Madras Presidency*, 1931, annexures D and E; *Report on Public Instruction in the Madras Presidency* (henceforth *MPIR*), 1937, 3-4.

| | 1901 | | | |
| | Literate | | Percentage in population | |
	MALES	FEMALES	MALES	FEMALES
Chirakkal	28347	4463	18.3	2.7
Kottayam	23605	4644	23.0	4.3
Kurumbranad	33852	5267	20.0	3.2

| | 1931 | | | |
| | Literate | | Percentage in population | |
	MALES	FEMALES	MALES	FEMALES
Chirakkal	55882	16447	29.4	7.9
Kottayam	43387	15196	34.8	10.9
Kurumbranad	50780	9987	25.2	4.8

(Statistics from K.N. Krishnaswami and T.G. Rutherford, *Statistical appendix for Malabar district*, 1933 xxxvii).

rolls.[109] Between 1901 and 1931, the rise in the numbers of literate was phenomenal.

The growing number of schools and the rise in literacy found expression in the number of reading rooms that were established both in the countryside and in the towns. Each caste, in its attempts to organise associations, built reading rooms alongside their own temples to allow their caste fellows access to both knowledge and god. There were twenty-eight registered reading rooms with 2,802 members in 1924; the number had risen by 1932 to fifty with 6,635 members.[110] These ranged from buildings made of brick to sheds made of mud with straw roofs, stocking the daily newspapers and sometimes with a library as well. The names of the reading rooms reflected three successive historical currents. Those set up by caste associations had names which indicated their purpose – the Gnanaprakashini (Light of Knowledge) and the Vidyabhivardini (Promoter of Knowledge) at Kadirur were among the oldest. Then there were those set up by early Congressmen who named them after national figures like Motilal Nehru (Taliparamba) and Sri Harsha (Kalliasseri). Others reflected a national aspiration like the one established by Bharateeyan at Naniyur, which was called Bharatiya Mandiram (Temple to India). In later years, the commu-

[109] *MPIR*, 1922-23, 5-6, 31; *Law (Education) G.O.1446 dated 14 July 1935* (KS).
[110] *MPIR*, 1924, 93; *MPIR*, 1932, 178. After 1932, no more statistics for reading rooms are recorded in the reports.

nists named reading rooms after 'martyrs', i.e. those who had died in encounters with the police. One such reading room (now a library as well) was the Abu-Chathukutty, named after two *beedi* workers who were shot in demonstrations in 1940.

Activists of the KCSP tapped this source and the reading rooms were stocked first with newspapers like the *Mathrubhumi,* and later the *Prabhatham* as well.[111] Early Congress workers had treated the distribution and sale of the *Mathrubhumi* as an essential part of nationalist activity. This was continued as part of the compulsory manual labour programme for Congress workers in 1935-36 in which they were required to sell at least 1 rupee worth of books or pamphlets of national importance.[112] The *Prabhatham* was launched in 1936 with E.M.S. Nambudiripad as the editor but was closed down within six months. This was on account of the high security demanded by the Madras Government, in order to curtail the *Prabhatham*'s report on peasant and worker radicalism. It resumed publication in 1938, was conceived of as a newspaper which would inform as well as act as a centrepiece of discussion. In 1933, the *Mathrubhumi* introduced a section called 'worker's world', but the *Prabhatham* tried to cater mainly for workers and peasants. It was a new world populated only by the working masses and the exploiting classes. There was a page devoted to news about agricultural labourers in the interior and the mill workers and municipal employees in the towns. The formation of unions, resolutions adopted at meetings, reports of conditions in factories, the existence of bonded labour in the foothills and the progress of strikes received extensive coverage. Another regular feature was devoted to the peasantry and spoke about the avalanche of unions in the years following the formation of the Congress ministry in 1937, the processions against oppressive landlords and detailed criticism of the Malabar Tenancy Act of 1930.

One of the novelties in the organisation of the reading rooms was the communal drinking of tea, as one person read the newspapers and the others listened. Using literacy figures to determine the influence of a newspaper can be misleading, if only because newspapers were nearly always read communally. Tea and coffee lubricated discussions on the veracity of the news and of political questions, and a new culture emerged around the reading rooms. It was premised on sobriety and knowledge rather than the drunken companionship transcending consciousness which characterised the toddy shops. The importance of tea and coffee lay in the fact that they were recently introduced beverages and did not fit into any taboos regarding what could be shared between castes. Tea shops and reading rooms all over Malabar provided a

---

[111] There is only one surviving volume of the *Prabhatham*, with a few issues from 1938 and 1939, and it is held in the library of the State Council of the Communist Party of India, in Trivandrum.

[112] *AICC Files P-15/1934-36* (NMML).

common place for people to meet and to drink together regardless of caste. This was significant in the context of the decline of charity in the aftermath of the Depression. One of the repercussions was the demise of wayside endowments like the *vazhiambalam* and the *tannir pandal* where the poorer wayfarer could get rice gruel and water.[113]

Through the reading rooms, newspapers and tea shops a whole new world was imagined, and discussions built up a collective memory of organisation, strikes and campaigns against landlords as well as victories of reduced working hours, more wages and less rent. Each of the earlier attempts to construct a community of equals had promoted singular and limited identities and purveyed these through their newspapers. The *Mithavadi* had spoken about both the problems as well as the achievements of the Tiyyas and the world had been refracted through the lens of caste prospects. Though the *Mathrubhumi* tried to widen its sweep, it was essentially a Congress newspaper and, by the end of the decade, it had come to be seen as an organ of the right wing in the KPCC. To an extent, the *Prabhatham* continued with this particularist tradition, by speaking for 'workers' and 'peasants' alone, but there was a significant departure. For the first time, there was a newspaper which catered for the newly literate and semi-literate and drew upon traditions of collective activity. Moreover, an instrumental edge was given to these efforts as literacy was linked with political awareness.[114]

What did socialism mean both to the socialist leaders as well as the workers and peasants who frequented the reading rooms? K.P. Gopalan observed with characteristic candour: 'we had socialist aims without knowing anything about Socialism'.[115] Articles published in the *Mathrubhumi* on Capitalism and Labour were remarkable more for their polemical fervour than for an exposition of socialist ideas. 'Ignorance is the fundament of capitalism. Anger is its armour, cruelty its weapon.' 'The synonyms of capitalism are treachery, oppression, deception, selfishness and contempt.'[116] Words underwent redefinition; *muthalali*, which had meant owner of property, now came to mean capitalist with all its negative connotations. When one bears in mind that both peasants and factory workers addressed their employers as *muthalali*, the ambiguity now introduced meant that deference would begin to carry an edge of mockery or defiance. In an article entitled 'Strikes', the anonymous writer stated, 'Some exploitative individuals who desire only profits are running the businesses. Since these individuals are the owners of capital they are called capitalists

---

[113] Ayyappan, *Iravas and culture change*, 34, 115.
[114] In the context of early unionisation in Bengal in the twenties, Chakrabarty makes a similar observation. Labour union tracts and manuals for unionisation emphasised the importance of study circles to discuss political matters. D. Chakrabarty, *Rethinking working class history: Bengal, 1890-1940* (Delhi, 1989), 129-30.
[115] Quoted in N.E. Balaram, *Keralathile kammyunistu prasthanam*, I, 50.
[116] *Mathrubhumi*, 9 September 1933.

(*muladhanam + muthalali*).' From 1932, articles on Lenin and Marxism had begun to appear in the *Mathrubhumi*, translated either from English or Hindi. The few articles on the Soviet Union referred to it as a Utopia where workers owned the industries and agriculture was organised for the needs and welfare of society.[117] The socialism delineated in newspaper articles was imprecise and in this precisely lay its appeal. The division into rich and poor, capitalist and labourer; meant that an appeal could be made transcending caste and religion.

It was only in 1939, when the socialists migrated to the Communist Party that there was a concerted attempt to create a cadre conversant in the theory of Marxism. Activists like A.K. Gopalan still were more comfortable organising unions than trying to understand the mysteries of dialectics. In his autobiography, he attributed his conversion to Marxism to a desire to rid himself of 'false pride, self conceit and desire for power', which he believed to be the traits of his class.[118] E.M.S. Nambudiripad and K. Damodaran were the only party theoreticians who attempted to clarify the principles of Marxism for a general public. In 1938, Nambudiripad published *Keralam malayalikalude mathrubhumi* (*Kerala,the motherland of the Malayalis*), the first Marxist history of Kerala from the earliest times. Throughout the forties, he attempted to explain the perplexing shifts in the party line to the cadre through articles in the party journals. Yet it was Damodaran who emerged as the consummate populariser of Marxism, initially through his plays *Raktapanam* (*Draught of blood*) and *Pattabakki* (*Rent arrears*) of 1939, and subsequently, through a series of pamphlets on the essentials of Marxist thought.

A special edition of the *Prabhatham* in 1939 had sought to convey the excitement and the explosive potential of Marxism to its readers; the authorities, however, would have none of it. In this proscribed edition, articles written by the party leaders spoke of how caste divisions, poverty, illiteracy and starvation could be ended and inequality transcended. Damodaran stated that 'with the aid of this science (Dialectical Materialism) we can forecast the future of man and society and thus control it'. Society would be reordered and every individual would get the 'opportunity to live, enjoy and progress'.[119] It was this vision that Damodaran sought to convey in his plays as well. He employed the simple but effective strategy of putting paraphrases of Marx into the mouths of his protagonists at climactic points. At the end of *Raktapanam*, the hero Sanku is shot dead by the police following the brutal suppression of a strike. Sanku addresses the grieving labourers thus: 'All the present-day laws and the

---

[117] *Mathrubhumi*, 9 December 1933.
[118] Gopalan, *In the cause of the people*, 84.
[119] Extracts from proscribed edition of *Prabhatham* special number 1939. K. Damodaran, 'Science of Marxism'. *Public (General) Dept. G.O.1351 (Confdl.) dated 17 August 1939* (KS).

Government we know are to perpetuate the injustices of the exploiting class; but we shall not flinch. If you are to lose, we lose only the rusty chains of slavery. If we succeed we get a whole world.'[120]

Pattabakki was the most influential play of its time, performed in all the villages of Malabar as part of party conferences or by peasant unions. It criticised the heartlessness of the landlords; the links between the propertied and the State; and more effectively the apathy of the poor who were deprived of faith. The play is built as a downward spiral of misery and poverty which is halted by the discovery of an ideology of hope by the protagonist. The play begins with a four-year-old crying piteously, 'Mother, I am hungry'. From here things take a turn for the worse. The mother is denied food by shopkeepers unwilling to advance any more loans; an overseer arrives to collect the arrears of rent, makes a pass at the adolescent daughter, is repulsed, and goes away swearing revenge; the family is evicted from their house; the eldest son, Kittunni, a factory worker, resorts to petty theft which lands him in jail; the child dies of hunger; the mother dies of tuberculosis; and the daughter turns to prostitution. While in prison, Kittunni meets a Muslim socialist who instructs him in the principles of political organisation. 'In order to fight against the tyranny of capitalists and landlords, trade unions and peasant unions must be organised everywhere ... Every nook and cranny in a village must become the centre of opposition to the landlord and capitalist.' There is no option for the poor but to appropriate the apparatus of the State through a struggle. Kittunni is released from jail, has a traumatic and tearful reunion with his sister, and realises that poverty was at the root of his resort to theft and that of his sister to prostitution. Together they resolve that 'we must demand restitution from society. We must destroy and rebuild the social system.'[121]

Behind all this melodrama is a simple fact; it was the first time that the wretched and the poor had entered the stage of Malayalam literature. In Travancore, novels provocatively titled *Thottiyude makan* (*Scavenger's son*) by Thakazhi Sivasankara Pillai and *Odayil ninnu* (*From the gutter*) by P. Kesava Dev were being published, marking the beginning of a movement towards what came to be called Progressive Literature. It was part of a whole-scale attack on both the structures and the values of traditional society, the story of which remains to be told.[122]

The reading rooms emerged as central to both formal attempts at organisation

---

[120] Translated excerpts from the proscribed play *Raktapanam*. *Public (General) Dept. G.O. 2232 (Confdl.) dated 14 December 1939* (KS). I have been unable to trace a complete edition of the play.

[121] K. Damodaran, *Pattabakki*.

[122] For brief accounts of the Progressive Writers movement see P.K. Gopalakrishnan, *Purogamana sahitya prasthanam: nizhalum velicchavum* (*The progressive literature movement: light and shadow*) (Trichur, 1987); E. Sardarkutty, *Purogamana sahitya nirupanam* (*A criticism of Progressive Literature*) (Trivandrum, 1985).

by the left wing within the Congress as well as local initiatives. In 1934, when the Beedi Workers' Union was formed in Cannanore, one of its first resolutions concerned the setting up of a reading room.[123] At the first anniversary of the Thozhilali Yuvajana (Working youths) reading room in 1935, the setting up of such institutions in villages was hailed as a vital step in the 'fight against injustice and oppression'.[124] By the end of the thirties, peasant unions were formed out of what began as groups of peasants reading together. When the All India Student's Federation sent a procession to Chirakkal, they discovered that informal peasant unions had set up reading rooms in the forest regions of the north east, where copies of the *Prabhatham* occupied pride of place.[125] The socialists recognised the extent of popular involvement with the paper and made it the organ of political mobilisation. By 1938, full-time activists of the KCSP functioned as newspaper agents in twenty-three major towns and villages all over Malabar.[126] The reading rooms became such a vital part of the new culture that, in June 1937, a Malabar Vayanashala (Malabar reading rooms) conference was held in Calicut to coordinate the activities of disparate organisations and people. A committee was set up with K. Damodaran as convenor and M. Sankaran, K.P.R. Gopalan and M.K. Kelu as members. This represented more an aspiration by the KCSP to establish some degree of control over a popular movement, than the setting up of a formal coordinating body.[127]

Thus, literacy became an essential part of the KCSP programme. In 1938, directives were issued to all town and primary Congress committees regarding the public services they were expected to maintain. These included the setting-up of reading rooms, night schools, study classes and the maintenance of blackboards outside the office for advertising the daily news. A library was to be organised by every committee and kept open daily between 5 pm and 8 pm so that labourers could read after work. Besides newspapers, there were to be political books and pamphlets which could be made the focus of study classes for the politically conscious.[128] A detailed syllabus which included several papers on revolutions – the French, Chinese and Russian – was outlined for volunteer classes. The Mappila rebellion was incorporated as an indigenous version of peasant revolt and given the neutral and more strategic title of the Malabar Rebellion.[129] Just as the *Prabhatham* portrayed a world of oppression and the reaction of workers and peasants, the syllabi of the volunteer classes constructed a history purely in instrumental terms of revolts against injustice. The reading rooms became central to socialist organisation in the villages,

[123] *Mathrubhumi*, 3 October 1934.
[124] *Mathrubhumi*, 24 October 1935.
[125] *Prabhatham*, 9 October 1938 and 9 January 1939.
[126] *Prabhatham*, 14 November 1938.
[127] *Mathrubhumi*, 12 June 1937.
[128] *AICC Files P-13 (part I and II)/1938* (NMML).
[129] *Ibid.*

managing to create space for camaraderie and intellectual discussion. However, the KCSP never managed to exercise more than a formal degree of control over these establishments. And, as with the *jathas*, collective experience, in this case of reading and discussing together, bred militancy. This became evident in the confrontations with the police in 1940.

Towards confrontation – Protest Day, 1940

The erosion of rural authority by the unions, along with the possibility of tenancy legislation proved to be the last straw for powerful tharavadus. They bristled at the general decline in 'respect'. Peasant union members were arrested on charges of criminal intimidation, dacoity and unlawful assembly. Punitive police stations were set up in the north of Chirakkal, the worst-affected region. The close link between the police and the dominant tharavadus was clear in the locations chosen to set up the bastions of order. The police station at Peringome in Payyanur was situated in part of the house of Vengayil Nayanar and in Ellarenhi, the Karakkatidathil Nayanar made available one of his houses. As David Arnold has rightly pointed out, rather than the State having to use police coercion because elites were unable to maintain control, the police in the Madras Presidency became an arm of the local elite.[130]

The Congress ministry, under the conservative premier Rajagopalachari, was equally alarmed by the agitation and anxious to contain what it saw as the challenge from the socialists. It adopted a tough line on 'political' offenders and left wing agitation.[131] As early as October 1937, E.M.S. Nambudiripad had written to the president of the Congress Working Committee that it was reprehensible that the representatives of the Congress had 'begun to speak the language of "Law and Order" of the old regime'.[132] The socialist sleight of hand which represented them as the radical wing of the Congress offered a partial solution to the repression by the ministry at Madras. Thus, when there were complaints from the village authorities of peasant unions subjecting landlords to social ostracism, Keraleeyan informed them that such activities were 'approved of' by the ministry.[133]

If the socialists were to continue to maintain an important role in rural politics, something more was needed than a mere rhetoric of equality or pleas of acting as the conscience of the Congress. Relations between landlords and

---

[130] Kurup, *Kunhambuvinte katha*, 154; Arnold, *Police power and colonial rule*, 108-10.
[131] A.R.H. Copley, *The political career of C. Rajagopalachari, 1937-54: a moralist in politics* (Madras, 1978), 49.
[132] E.M.S. Nambudiripad to President, CWC, 22 October 1937, *AICC Files PL-18* (NMML).
[133] *Prabhatham*, 5 December 1938.

cultivators had at most times been informed by violence, and it had become more so with the intervention of unions and armed police. With the growing backlash from landlords, the socialists had to show that they were capable of resisting the authority of the elites and the state. They needed to provide an alternative force themselves. At a meeting of peasants in Kottayam in 1935, Nambudiripad had stated that 'the habit of the peasant is to avoid confrontation in the face of injustice and oppression'.[134] This was no longer true but an organisation was urgently needed. In 1938, Chandroth Kunhiraman Nayar, a one-time member of the police force, was put in charge of organising volunteer squads to train them on military lines. By 1939, all the villages in north Malabar, particularly in Kottayam had volunteer organisations.

	Officers	Volunteers
Hosdrug	26	240
Chirakkal	33	473
Kottayam	34	426
Total	93	1139

At the end of 1939 another thousand volunteers had joined up.[135] The volunteer organisations intervened in disputes over land, prevented evictions and, by 1939, began to attack local courts where members of peasant unions were being tried.[136] Once a counter force to the police was built up, the socialists followed a deliberate strategy of attacking the police at every rally they addressed and 'exposing' the links between the big landowners and the police. They were caught in a bind of keeping up with the radicalism of the unions at the same time as trying not to seem oppositional to the Congress. Attacks on the credibility of the police were often justified as a means of winning people over to the Congress. As an article in the *Prabhatham* stated, 'that the people think of carrying on opposition to the police is because a Congress government is in power'.[137] Once the fear of the police had been subverted, peasant unions began going further in their attempts to change the rural order. By the beginning of 1940, alternative judicial structures were set up and union leaders launched enquiries into the misdemeanours of landlords.[138]

From 1939, the socialists adopted a more radical stand in rural politics, having by then gained control over the Congress organisation. Earlier, the Congress Right had managed to debar those suspected of being socialists from contesting elections by accusing them of not being 'habitual *khadi* wearers'.

[134] *Mathrubhumi*, 13 October 1935.
[135] *Public and Judicial Files 117-C-81, 1937 (IOL); AICC Files, part I/1939* (NMML).
[136] Fortnightly Report for the second half of February 1939, *L/P and J/5/199* (IOL).
[137] *Prabhatham*, 28 November 1938.
[138] *Home Political 7/9/41* (NAI).

They utilised to the utmost, Gandhi's suggestions at the Bombay session of the AICC in 1934, that the *'khadi* clause' and the spinning franchise be used to distinguish the true Congressman.[139] Meanwhile, complaints flowed into the AICC from Muslims and Tiyyas against the communal and casteist nature of the KPCC which, they alleged, had been taken over by the old 'Chalappuram Gang'.[140] In 1938, the deadlock between the Right and the socialists was resolved. The socialists swept the KPCC elections in alliance with a liberal section among the Mappilas led by Muhammad Abdur Rahman and Moithu Maulavi; the Right derisively dubbed them the 'Mecca–Moscow axis'.[141] Pragmatic elements within the Right, like Samuel Aaron, played an important part in assuring the success of the Mappila-socialist alliance. Worried by the possibility of the Muslim League presenting a point of unity for the Mappila mercantile community, Aaron, along with several Hindu *seths* of Calicut financed political conferences held by the socialists to woo the Mappilas.[142] However, a significant proportion of the Mappila elite remained suspicious of both the Congress as well as the socialists. A routine decision to hoist the Congress flag on municipal buildings in Cannanore led to a minute of dissent at a Municipal Council meeting. It stated in unequivocal terms that the 'Congress flag is at best the flag of a party. It has not secured the allegiance of the Mussalmans ... and other minorities.'[143]

In May 1939, the socialists annulled the *khadi* clause and in June, a new constitution was drafted with a crucial proviso that the working committee could enquire into election complaints. Using this power, eight out of nine primary committees with non-socialist majorities were dissolved by the end of the year. In some areas, elections were set aside even though no complaints had been made.[144] Towards the end of 1938, Abdur Rahman issued a circular to all taluk and district Congress committees. It asked the primary members to make allegations against the administration of the Malabar District Board, then controlled by the Right, and conduct 'secret enquiries' about the President, K. Kelappan. Particular caution was recommended so that 'no more unnecessary notoriety' would be created by the news of the enquiry becoming public.[145] In victory, the socialists did as they had been done by. The Right followed the path

[139] *AICC Files P-12/1937* (NMML).
[140] Letter from the Secretary, Kondotti Congress Committee to Nehru, 23 October 1937; Letter from V.P. Balakrishnan, Tiyya to the President, AICC, 1 October 1934. *AICC Files P-12/1939* (NMML).
[141] *AICC Files P-12, part I/1939* (NMML); *AICC Files P-38/1939-40* (NMML).
[142] Moithu Maulavi, *Maulaviyude katha*, 198-9.
[143] *Local Self Government Dept. G.O.2985 dated 4 August 1938* (KS).
[144] E.M.S. Nambudiripad to General Secretary AICC, 23 May 1939. *AICC Files G-31/1939* (NMML); E.M.S. Nambudiripad to General Secretary AICC, July 1939. *AICC Files P-12, part I/1939* (NMML); Proceedings of enquiry into Congress election disputes, Palghat, 4 November 1939. *AICC Files P-12, part I/1939* (NMML).
[145] *AICC Files P-12, part II/1939* (NMML).

of righteous indignation; Kelappan fulminated privately that the Congress 'had been prostituted for socialist propaganda'.[146]

Even as the socialists gained control over the KPCC, their leaders secretly formed the Communist Party of Kerala (KCP) in May 1939. Units of the Congress Socialist Party all over India had been infiltrated by members who had converted to communism. By September 1939, provincial branches of the CSP in Punjab, Bengal and Bihar had covertly renounced the policy of the all India leadership.[147] However, it made political sense to continue within the Congress organisation and, in the KPCC elections of 1940, two-thirds of those elected belonged to the 'unclassified left'.[148] Meanwhile, the increasing radicalism of the peasant unions threatened to leave the converted communist leadership behind. They were faced with the dilemma of stepping up their activity in the countryside, while trying to work within the Congress organisation. The coordination of anti-war propaganda provided a means of reconciling rhetoric with local needs. A resolution of the Kottyam taluk Congress committee criticised 'Gandhian control' over the Congress which 'obstructed ... the desire of ordinary Congressmen to generate a mass movement against Britain's war efforts'.[149] Most of the speeches, ostensibly directed against helping an imperialist power in waging its battle, were actually redolent with immediate, local concerns. The most important was the continued repression by the police. An 'anti-war' speech made by E.P. Gopalan in Walluvanad excoriated police persecution and, amidst much applause, he stated: 'After attaining independence would we not level these police stations to the ground and cultivate cucumbers and pumpkins in their place.'[150]

The authorities perceived these activities as the consequence of the 'socio-communist' nature of the KPCC. Rajagopalachari's vehement dislike of the communists continued. He wrote to Lord Erskine that they ought to be prosecuted immediately, adding that 'in the previous civil disobedience we did not hit hard enough'.[151] By the end of June 1940, the leadership of the Kerala Communist Party (KCP) – Nambudiripad, Krishna Pillai, A.K. Gopalan – were in jail.[152] The police stormed a meeting of the KPCC on 7 August 1940 and arrested thirty-three 'socialist' members including the Secretary, Manjunatha Rao and two prominent members of the working committee, K.P.R. Gopalan and T.C. Narayanan Nambiyar.[153] They were replaced by another committee

---

[146] K. Kelappan to A.C. Kannan Nayar. 5 April 1939. *Diaries of A.C. Kannan Nayar.*
[147] Tomlinson, *The Indian National Congress*, 145-6.
[148] *Home Political Files 4/4/40* (NAI).
[149] Nandkeolyar Report, part I. *AICC Files P-11/1942-6* (NMML).
[150] Speech of E.P. Gopalan, 4 June 1940, *Public (General) Dept. G.O.1509 (Confdl.) dated 1 August 1940* (KS).
[151] Copley, *The political career of C. Rajagopalachari*, 69-70.
[152] *FR* for the first and second half of June 1940, *L/P and J/5/200* (IOL).
[153] *Public (General) Dept. G.O. 2135 dated 29 October 1940* (KS); *FR* for the first half of August 1940, *L/P and J/5/200* (IOL).

of socialists almost immediately. The Congress right wing took advantage of the confusion and set up a rival committee in Palghat, far away from the ferment in the north Malabar countryside. On 18 August, the left attempted to resolve the deadlock by meeting at Cannanore and passing a resolution declaring the 'Gandhist' committee illegal.[154] In protest against the arrests, the Left KPCC called for demonstrations on 18 August to celebrate Civil Liberties Day. The working committee then resolved to observe 15 September as 'Protest Day' against the recent statements of the Viceroy and Secretary of State which expressed the repressive policy of the government. There was a call to all the members of the left to hold meetings in north Malabar. The choice of the date was not arbitrary as there was a meeting of the AICC in Bombay and the secretary and other office holders of the KPCC were expected to attend.[155] This allowed them to disavow all responsibility for the form that demonstrations could assume. At the same time, the blame could be laid squarely on individual initiatives, while the KPCC as a body could remain above reproach.

On 15 September, meetings were held all over north Malabar. The most vehement demonstrations were at Calicut, Tellicherry, Pappinisseri, Mattanur and Cannanore. In Calicut, seventeen people were arrested as they attempted to take a march up to the beach and the police dispersed a stone-throwing crowd. At Badagara and Payyanur too, large crowds assembled but they were contained by the massed police force.[156] In Tellicherry, on the coast, the police had to resort to firing to disperse a stone-throwing crowd of over a thousand, and two *beedi* workers were killed. Further north and in the interior, where peasant unions were strong, crowds proved more difficult to contain. At Mattanur, rifles and ammunition were snatched from the police. In the most significant engagement between crowds and the police, a sub-Inspector was killed at Morazha. In connection with 'Protest Day', a total of 108 arrests were made all over north Malabar.[157] A day after the events, a belated cautionary note arrived from the AICC; Kripalani wrote that 'in celebrating days it is always best to refer to the AICC office'.[158]

Nevertheless, a closer analysis of the events at Morazha and Mattanur demonstrates that calls for the observance of protest day and protest against the war were of less consequence than the presence of local rivalries and tensions. The subversion of rural authority had been initiated by political processions which led to the jettisoning of deference and the formation of unions. This

---

[154] *Mathrubhumi*, 11 and 20 August 1940.
[155] Nandkeolyar report, part I, *AICC Files P-11/1942-6* (NMML).
[156] Report of the D.M., Malabar to Chief Secretary, Madras, 17 September 1940. *Home Political Files 5/18/40* NAI).
[157] *Home Political F5/18/40* (NAI); *AICC Files 58/1940* (NMML).
[158] Report of D.M., Malabar to Chief Secretary, Madras, 17 September 1940. *Home Political 5/18/40* (NAI).

process reached its climax in 1940, with pitched battles between the police and the volunteer squads who represented the peasants. In a sense, the authorities too were more apprehensive about local conflicts than the nationalist implications of Protest Day. To prevent any trouble at Pappinisseri, where the workers at Aaron Mills were known to be militant, section 144 of the IPC was imposed to prevent the assembling of more than four people. Soon it was extended to Kalliasseri and Baliapatam from where the majority of the workers were recruited. As a result the demonstrators moved to Morazha where, to escape the ban, the meeting was held in Anchampeetika *bazaar*. It was a strategic choice: a narrow road with rows of shops on either side and a wide space in the middle where Congress and communist flags were flown. A crowd of 700 to 1,000 had gathered, and sixty volunteers in green shirts were lined up under the command of T.R. Nambiyar. Most of the volunteers had been workers at the Aaron Mills till their dismissal during a strike in 1939.

The sub-Inspector of Police, Kuttikrishna Menon, was known for his proclivity towards violence. During the strike at Aaron Mills in April 1939, Menon had been responsible for bodily removing prostrate picketers and on one occasion had charged at and dispersed a crowd of workers with only four constables to assist him.[159] At Morazha, when he ordered the crowds to disperse, Vishnu Bharateeyan lay on the ground in front of the police and refused to move. Meanwhile, T.R. Nambiyar, the captain of the volunteer squad, blew his whistle and the sixty volunteers faced the police. When Menon attempted to move Bharateeyan, there was a cry of 'all people should join together and resist the police'. A *lathi* charge was ordered and in the mêlée that followed Menon was struck on the head with an iron ladle and killed.[160]

At Mattanur, as in Morazha, the crowd departed from the Congress reading room holding aloft the tricolour and a red flag. They assembled on the local common and when the police attacked, their *lathis* were snatched from their hands. There were shouts of 'Kill the police' and one member of the crowd, Kupyatt Govindan, was overheard telling a policeman, 'You sent my elder brother to jail. You ought to be killed.' The police were attacked with sticks, umbrellas and stones but there were no casualties on either side. Eight members of the crowd were arrested and forty-six accused of rioting.[161] The change of mood was evident. Force was being met with force and a disciplined volunteer force acted as the backbone of the randomly expressed anger of marchers and bystanders. The other significant element was that confrontation was more

[159] Report of D.M., Malabar to Chief Secretary, Madras, 17 September 1940, *Home Political Files 5/18/40* (NAI). The District Magistrate described Kuttikrishna Menon as a 'determined man of fiery temper'.

[160] Court of Sessions, north Malabar division, Saturday, 16 August 1941. *Sessions Case no. 6 and 11 of 1942* (TCRR); *Home Political Files 7/9/41* (NAI).

[161] *Court of Sessions, north Malabar division, Tuesday, 16 September 1941. Sessions case no. 3 of 1941* (TCRR).

organised. The socialists had attempted to build an alternative culture of political discussions and camaraderie in reading rooms which dotted the interior. These however, had come to serve as a focal point in rural violence – a point from which the expressions of resentment could diverge on to the streets.

In 1940, the Madras Government suddenly woke up to the fact that something was rotten in the district of Malabar. The Intelligence Bureau expressed concern at the events of September 1940 and Richard Tottenham observed that it 'was a most surprising development as coming from Malabar'.[162] Notwithstanding the fact that north Malabar had been in a state of ferment for the last two years, Malabar had always been a neglected outpost of the Presidency and only the Mappila Rebellion of 1921 had wakened the authorities to the troubles brewing on the agrarian front. The event had been so overwhelming in its impact that the Bureau remained caught up in old concerns. It expressed great relief that all the events of September 1940 were 'well away from the scene of the Mappila Rebellion in 1921'.[163]

Conclusion

The confrontations at Morazha and Mattanur showed the dramatic transformation within rural attitudes of deference. Peasant unions had managed to undermine erstwhile structures of authority in a manner beyond the vision of Gandhian reformers. Caste subservience could no longer be expected; it had to be enforced, and could very often be challenged. The significant difference with the politics of the first half of the decade was the localised nature of rural politics. No longer were wider communities of caste, religion or nation being appealed to. Caste deference and caste subordination were tackled at the level of the relations between the tharavadu and its cultivators and dependents.

Initially, the KCSP activists had envisaged a limited renegotiation of rural relations, in the process of which only the excesses of tharavadus could be questioned. However, the experience of collective activity in *jathas* and the formation of volunteer squads increased both the independence as well as the militancy of the unions. There were soon a bewildering array of peasant organisations. Some of them provided muscle for resisting the actions of landowners and acted as a force on behalf of the poorer tenants and agricultural labourers. Others acted as extensions of erstwhile caste councils and tried to extend their own spheres of authority by the imposition of customary sanctions. The flurry of union activity in this period has been characterised as

[162] *Home Political 7/9/41* (NAI).
[163] *Ibid.*

'militant anti-imperialist and anti-feudal agitations'. This confuses, at one level, KCSP rhetoric with actual rural political activity. Moreover, it tends to subsume the differences between unions themselves.[164] An important point to bear in mind is that constructions of the allegiances of 'middle' and 'poor' peasants are not possible, since categories tended to be quite blurred.[165] As we saw in the first chapter, a single person could be landlord, tenant and cultivator in different contexts, which makes rigid divisions along the lines of class difficult.

In the next decade, the character of peasant union militancy would be transformed. Conflicts over the arbitrary exercise of authority by tharavadus would escalate into more militant and organised struggle for resources of cultivation – wastelands, commons and forests. Socialist attempts to renegotiate rural community had spawned political activity pulling in different directions. Attempts to conceive of rural community in the next decade were temporarily successful. A crisis of food necessitated the expansion of cultivation to wastelands, binding landowners and cultivators in a transient unity. This harmony was thwarted by the radicalism of unions, as well as the willingness of the State to intercede on the side of those with landed property, with violence if necessary.

[164] See K. Gopalankutty, 'The task of transforming the Congress'.
[165] For an effective critique of attempts to subsume the flexibility of agrarian categories in hard distinctions between rich, middle and poor peasants see Eric Stokes, 'The return of the peasant to south Asian history' in *The peasant and the Raj: studies in agrarian society and peasant rebellion in colonial India* (Cambridge, 1978), 265-89.

6   Community and conflict, 1940–1948

The outbreak of the Second World War in 1939 precipitated a crisis among the socialists, and those among them who advocated a campaign against the war moved towards the Communist Party. Gandhi had agreed to launch a limited, controlled programme of individual civil disobedience in 1940 but this initiative petered out by the middle of the next year. By 1942, both the Communist Party as well as the Congress had shifted their stances. The Quit India Resolution of 1942 called for a mass struggle by the Congress on non-violent lines. Communist strategy however, was conditioned by wider, international concerns particularly the German attack on the Soviet Union in 1941. For the communists this changed the character of the imperialist war, making it a struggle against Fascism, in which Britain had to be supported in the war effort. At the same time, the Communist Party, though ostensibly standing against the national mainstream, was able to extend its sway in the countryside.

In 1942, the Communist Party announced a policy of support to the British government in its fight against Fascism and promoted the idea of political harmony towards this end. Between 1942 and 1945, the party line was transformed in Malabar into a creative endeavour to regenerate rural community, albeit a conjunctural one. In a context of food shortage, and the need to expand cultivation, the communists in Malabar negotiated with landowners for wasteland, providing them with pragmatically compliant cultivators. Simultaneously, there was an attempt to revive the religious culture of the shrines. The shrines had suffered both from the efforts of caste movements as well as the Congress. In the aftermath of the Depression, tharavadus lacked the wherewithal to provide patronage to religious institutions. Now that the structures of authority and deference around the shrines had been dismantled to a certain extent, it appeared to be possible to reconceive them as a locus of community. However, the fragile unity built up between 1942 and 1945 collapsed as a result of increasing rural militancy, and the intervention of the government, now keen on crushing communism. From 1946, north Malabar became a turbulent zone, but there were limits to militancy. The power of landowning tharavadus was not questioned, only their excesses were – profiteering in grain and an intransigent control over wastelands and forests. Conflict reached a climax in 1948 but was effectively quelled by police action.

In a sense the limits of rural radicalism had been reached. Over two decades, the power enjoyed by landowning tharavadus had come to be questioned and arbitrary acts were challenged, if necessary with force. There was room for the negotiation of rural relations, in a manner different from that at the turn of the century, when conflict had often been expressed within ritual. However, the authority of the tharavadus continued, both in their control over resources as well as the willingness of the state to intercede on their behalf.

Economic pressures of the forties

In this decade, attempts to renegotiate rural relations were constrained by two major factors. One was the increasing shortage of foodgrains, which re-emphasised the control exercised by the dominant tharavadus over foodstocks and wetlands. The other was related to the buttressing of the rights of the larger landowners over wastelands and forests, born of the government's desire to contain rural conflict. Thus, at a time when subsistence cultivation was forced to expand to the poorer margins, landowners were vested with the power to set limits.

The decade began ominously, with food shortages and semi-famine conditions aggravated by the Second World War. During the Depression, the crash in the prices of coconut and pepper had upset the delicate balance of an economy in which imports of rice had been sustained by the profits of cash crops. There was an attempt to return to the cultivation of paddy and, by 1940, land available for wet cultivation was becoming scarce. Cropping began to eat into the upper slopes above paddy flats.[1] Even so, Malabar produced only 45 per cent of its rice requirements and was dependent on Burma for the major portion of its demand. Prices in the local markets faithfully registered the fluctuations in production in Burma, as well as the price of transportation from Rangoon.[2] With the onset of the war and the pressure put on Burmese ports from Japan, supplies of rice became unreliable. Imports of rice to Calicut declined rapidly, and by February 1941 they had fallen to 13,000 tons from the annual average of 32,000 tons over the past two years.[3] In 1941, a shortfall in the production of paddy in Malabar meant that there was just enough to meet the food requirements of the district for eight more months. With the anticipation of dearth in the market, stocks were withheld and speculation in grain

[1] *Revenue Dept. (Ms) G.O.1911 dated 17 June 1943* (KS).
[2] *Development Dept. G.O.1138 dated 23 June 1941* (KS).
[3] Collector, Malabar to Secretary, Development, 16 February 1941. *Revenue Dept. (Ms) G.O.1911 dated 17 June 1943* (KS).

was rife. Paddy was diverted to Trichur and Coimbatore where prices were higher.[4]

In May 1941, a cyclone hit Malabar; the rivers overflowed with startling suddenness, and over 1,000 acres of paddy land were silted up in Chirakkal. Following the cyclone, there were typhoid epidemics in Badagara, Tellicherry, and Cannanore. The incidence of deaths was marked between July and September 1941, the months of heavy monsoons and want; most of the casualties were caused by fever and nutritional disorder. The District Health Officer stated in no uncertain terms that the 'diseases [are] attributable to exposure and semi-famine conditions'.[5] In Calicut, the political conflict between the Congress Right, which controlled the Municipal Board, and the socialists gave rise to bizarre situations. An epidemic of cholera broke out among the beggars of the Municipality. Anxious not to be castigated for their ineptitude in maintaining standards of hygiene and sanitation, the Congress officials arranged for the beggars to be put on to trains and transported out of Calicut. Needless to say, the beggars left a train of disease in their wake.[6] For the distant government at Madras, the illusion of green palms and sparkling rivers prevailed over the reality. Even as the District Medical Officer was writing urgently that 'poverty and starvation' had pushed people to the 'verge of death', the Finance department had decided it was not going to cough up any finances for aid. The Assistant Secretary observed that between August and May, 'the Malayalis eat well and during the period Malabar is one of the best, if not the best, area in India as tourists have declared'. He went on to state emphatically that 'it is not possible for anyone to die of starvation in Malabar because of the gifts of nature and the charitable disposition of the people'.[7]

In 1942, the government finally intervened, allowing trade in rice and paddy only under permits issued by the Commissioner of Civil Supplies. By December 1942, all movement of grain by sea was brought under control. In February 1943 permits for consignment by rail were introduced and by May all controls were 'consolidated'.[8] Since a few merchants in the port towns of Malabar controlled the rice trade, such measures did not help to curtail speculation, and this was evident in the activities of the rice cartel at Calicut. Rice could have

---

[4] Note of Director of Agriculture and Collector, Malabar to Secretary, Development, 22 February 1941. *Development Dept. G.O.1138 dated 23 June 1941* (KS); Collector to Secretary, Development, 3 December 1940. *Development Dept. G.O.356 dated 25 February 1941* (KS).
[5] Note on epidemics by Isaac Joseph, DHO, 12 October 1941. *Revenue Dept. G.O.1875 dated 14 June 1943* (KS).
[6] K.J. Sivaswamy and V.R. Nayanar *et al.*, *Food control and nutrition surveys – Malabar and south Kanara* (Madras, 1946), 8-10.
[7] Report of DMO, Malabar to the Surgeon-General, Madras, 29 August 1941; Note by Assistant Secretary, Finance Department (Expenditure). *Revenue Dept. G.O.1875 dated 14 June 1943* (KS).
[8] *ARMP*, 1942, 50-1; Sivaswamy and Nayanar, *Food control and nutrition surveys*, 27.

been imported into Malabar from elsewhere in the Presidency – the Circars, Chingleput or Tanjore – but the cartel of Mappila and Cutchi Memon merchants preferred to import rice from Burma. For one, transportation costs were far cheaper; moreover they had an advantage over the other merchants, mainly Gujaratis, who formed the Rice Importer's Syndicate. The latter had agents only in Rangoon and with the outbreak of war with Japan, exports from Burma began to be restricted to the other ports.[9] Rice was amassed at the port towns of Calicut, Tellicherry and Cannanore and in the hands of Mappila importers. Just as the government had been unsuccessful in controlling the import trade in rice, it was equally at a loss in its attempt to intercede in the distribution of rice. By May 1944, the food situation became acute and rationing was informally introduced, providing a pound of rice per adult in the towns and a quota of six ounces per adult in the countryside.[10] The quota for the towns was gradually reduced and the rest diverted to the villages. Australian wheat had to be imported to cover up the disparity and it was used as a supplement to rice.[11] District wide rationing was finally introduced in October 1944.

Both before the introduction of rationing in October 1944, and after, dominant tharavadus in the interior were able to withhold large stocks under the flexible category of the needs of 'domestic consumption'. The Grain Purchase Officer was authorised to determine the quantity that could be retained for a landholder's family. Since dominant households, in conception, consisted not only of immediate members of the family but a wider ambit of dependents as well, there was not a little scope for corruption.[12] A dramatic example of this came up in 1946 when the Raja of Chirakkal applied to remove 10,000 seers from his granaries for the use of the 'Palace, temples, *pujas* and feasts'.[13] Apart from piling up stocks of grain, large tharavadus had begun to cash in on the high market prices for rice. Land was reclaimed from tenants and, till 1944, there was a dramatic increase in the number of redemption suits instituted by landowners on the plea that they needed the lands for their own cultivation.[14] That this was directly connected to a desire to produce rice for the market became clear in October 1944 when eviction suits declined dramatically after

---

[9] Director of Agriculture to Secretary, Development, 15 March 1941. *Development Dept. G.O.1138 dated 23 June 1941* (KS).

[10] This had been preceded by a chaotic stage of attempted control of food prices between May 1942 and May 1943 and a period of partial control between May 1943 and May 1944. Sivaswamy and Nayanar, *Food control and nutrition surveys*, 26.

[11] Governor's report, 1 May 1944 and FR for the second half of May 1944. *L/P and J/15/204* (IOL).

[12] *Development Dept. G.O.3380 dated 5 August 1944* (KS).

[13] Judgement, *Sessions Case no. 14 and 18 of 1947* (TCRR).

[14] The MTA, 1930 had provided that a landlord could evict a tenant for reasons of bona fide cultivation for the household. In 1942, the High Court at Madras had decreed that courts need examine only whether the landlord needed to cultivate and not whether he already had enough land. This inevitably resulted in a dramatic rise in the number of suits for eviction. *Revenue Dept. G.O.18 dated 4 January 1949* (KS).

rationing was introduced and excess stocks of paddy were purchased by the government at controlled rates.[15] In the course of the Depression the rural community had been stripped down to its bare essentials; the provision of sustenance by dominant *tharavadus* in times of dearth. However, they were not too keen to dispense their obligations in a period when their social superiority was being comprehensively questioned. Besides, the existence of dearth provided an opportunity to make quick profits. Thus, even as their position as the repositories of grain was strengthened, they became the foci of rural resentment.

All through 1944, the problem of shortage was compounded by people holding on to their stocks as a safeguard against rationing, and the September harvest took its time appearing in the market.[16] With the introduction of rationing in October 1944, 0.78 pounds of paddy was allotted per adult and wheat made up a sixth of the total ration, despite local disapproval. Rice was imported from Punjab to make up the shortfall, but increasingly, a rice-eating people were constrained to eat wheat.[17] Rice and rice gruel which had been the standard breakfast of generations of Malayali labourers was replaced by *cholam* and sugarless tea – each vying with the other as foods lacking in nutrition.[18] The enforced change in diet was no small matter and became one of the planks of rallying the peasantry by the KCP. While the immediate programme of the KCP was to ensure a steady supply of rice, the attack on wheat was linked to more transcendental complaints. A pamphlet of the KCP in 1948 insisted that *cholam* and wheat were being forced on the people to help American capitalism![19]

In this context of a shortage of foodgrains and the control exercised over existing stocks by merchants and large landholders, there seemed to be only one possible solution. Cultivators had begun pressing this alternative between 1938-39 in their demands for the lease of wasteland. The less-fertile areas had been brought under cultivation to grow subsistence crops like horsegram and *cumbum*. Faced with the insistent pressure from peasant unions for making more land available for cultivation, the Malabar Tenancy Committee was set up, and it published its report in 1940. There was an unequivocal recognition that 'the existence of a large body of landless proletariat [is] becoming a social and political menace in Malabar'.[20] Nevertheless, the proposals in the Report were addressed to the problems and debates of an earlier decade. All cultivating *verumpattakarans* were given fixity of tenure regardless of whether they held wetland or not. *Kanakkarans* and *kuzhikanakkarans* were granted fixity of

[15] *ARMP*, 1944, 11.
[16] *Ibid.*, *FR* for the first half of September 1944.
[17] *Ibid.*, Governor's report 12/44 dated 1 December 1944 and 3 November 1944.
[18] Madhavan, *Payaswiniyude teerattu*, 182-3.
[19] *Janangalka ethiraya Congressinte yuddham* (*The war waged against the people by the Congress*) (KCP, 1948), 11.
[20] *MTCR, 1940*, I, 50.

tenure which was both heritable and alienable. Eviction by a landlord, for personal cultivation of the land, was allowed only if the landlord and his family held less than five acres per head. Thus, one chapter of the tenancy struggle ended, satisfying those who already possessed some rights over land, but the next chapter foreboded deep trouble. The committee left landlords with absolute control over wastelands and forests, even though they departed from tradition in stating that 'there [was] no evidence to show that the *janmi* was the absolute owner of the soil'. Moreover, no security of tenure was provided for the *punam* and pepper cultivators.[21] Throughout this decade, the degree of ownership vested in landowners was contested fiercely, and the recommendations of the tenancy commission served more to exacerbate tensions than provide solutions.

Over the decade, the expansion of cultivation would be on terms set by the large landowners in a way it had not been before the Depression. Tharavadus with forests and wasteland began to reconsider the lease of their forests for the doubtful profits of shifting cultivation. Beginning in the late thirties, Syrian Christian planters had begun to move into Malabar to set up rubber, coffee and tea plantations. By 1941, there were 71,000 people born in Travancore – Cochin enumerated in Malabar of whom 52 per cent were in north Malabar.[22] Many of the larger tharavadus, beleaguered by militant peasant unions, began leasing out their land to these entrepreneurs who were willing to pay large rents as well as inflated prices for land.[23] A.C. Kannan Nayar recorded the sale of 175 acres of the Belur hills at the rate of Rs. 19 per acre to Joseph, a planter from Travancore. Joseph presented two silk umbrellas as *nazrana*, which, in the aftermath of the battle over feudal levies in the previous decade, must have been reassuring for Kannan Nayar.[24] There was a considerable migration of labourers from Travancore to work on the new plantations. Local labour therefore, did not benefit overly from the investment of capital by the Christian entrepreneurs. The growth of these new plantations marked the final assault on the forests of Malabar; a process including Tipu's depredations and the East India Company's attempts to create roads for military campaigns in the late eighteenth and early nineteenth century; the large-scale exploitation of the forests for teak till the mid nineteenth century; the thrust of pepper cultivation; and the leasing of forests for private felling at the onset of the Depression. Now,

[21] *Ibid.*, 12, 23-8.
[22] P.K.M. Tharakan, 'Intra-regional differences in agrarian systems and internal migration: a case study of the migration of farmers from Travancore to Malabar', *Centre for Development Studies: Working Paper 194* (Trivandrum, 1984), 2-7. Between 1941-51, the Christian population of the district went up by 97.69 per cent while the population rise was 21.09 per cent.
[23] *Ibid.*, 14. The average price per acre of land rose from Rs. 4 in 1925 to Rs. 35 in 1947.
[24] *Diaries of A.C. Kannan Nayar*, 19 June 1943.

it was the turn of the virgin forests: 'poisonous virgins', in Pottekkat's evocative phrase, that felled the pioneers with malaria.[25] Tharavadus hit by the Depression had resorted to curtailing customary rights over the use of forests, making them conditional on the payment of cash levies. The entry of planters further eroded the possibility of negotiation for the use of resources. An instance of this was in the Mattanur-Chavasseri region to the north east, where agricultural labourers and small cultivators used to collect green leaves for manure and firewood from the nearby forests. Three hundred acres of the forest had been leased to Christian planters who forbade such activities on the grounds of encroachment on their property.[26] From the mid forties a further element of conflict was introduced, with the renewed demand for pepper in the world market following the devastation of plantations in Indonesia, Malaya and Sarawak during the war. The world turned again to Malabar and there was a rush to cultivate pepper.[27] By then, the fertile tracts of the forests had been leased to the planters. Tharavadus wishing to reclaim their other lands from cultivators to plant pepper found them unwilling to relinquish it in a period of continuing shortage of food. It was a piquant reversal. In the twenties, cultivators had neglected subsistence crops for the more lucrative pepper.

The Madras Preservation of Private Forests Act of 1949, which laid down rules for *punam* cultivation in forests, strengthened the tharavadus' control over wastelands and forests. Only land with no trees, those which had been under cultivation for more than ten years, and those which had sparse growth could be cleared and cultivated. Steep slopes were to remain unplanted.[28] The amendment of the MTA in 1950 further eroded the position of shifting cultivators by not granting them fixity of tenure.[29] Thus, cultivation was condemned to a reworking of the same cleared patch without any access to the richer, virgin soil of the steep slopes. Moreover, cultivators themselves were tied to a particular patch of forest land and therefore to a landlord. By sealing off expansion, or at least making it conditional on the whims of the dominant landowners, the government had created the conditions for continued agitation.

---

[25] For a thinly disguised fictional account of the experiences of migrant labourers from Travancore see S.K. Pottekkat, *Vishakanyaka* (*The poisonous virgin*), trans. V. Abdulla (Trichur, 1980).

[26] *Deshabhimani*, 16 September 1945.

[27] By the end of the decade pepper growers were receiving up to 1,400 per cent of the pre-war prices. The pepper exported from Malabar was undecorticated and there were fears among the growers of a slump in demand once the south east Asian countries resumed production. See Miller, 'An analysis of the Hindu caste system', fn 1, 5.

[28] *Revenue Dept. G.O.3555 dated 31 December 1951* (KS).

[29] *Revenue Dept. G.O.433 dated 21 February 1951* (KS).

The communists and rural politics, 1940-42

In the previous decade, a conjunctural unity had been achieved between organisational imperatives and individual initiatives. The confrontations with the police in September 1940 had brought home to the peasant unions the necessity of having their own force. By the end of 1940, there were over 2,500 volunteers in north Malabar, trained in fighting with *lathis*, who added muscle to the unions.[30] As it became clear to the unions that they could force issues, they slowly moved out of the ambit of the KCP. There was another major factor allowing this. The Communist Party was banned in 1940, following the statement of policy which spoke of a 'Proletarian Path' for 'revolutionary use of the war crisis'.[31] Once the KCP was driven underground, the leaders had to face the major flaw in their organisation; basically, the lack of it. Through study classes, the KCP had tried to create a cadre sound in theory, but a few organisers could not be a substitute for an organisation which could incorporate agricultural labourers and small cultivators.

In 1941, a police report, in its own hyperbolic way observed that 'even in 1938, the framework of a communist government was in being, which now holds the countryside well under the OGPU – Gestapo type of control'.[32] How true was this picture? In theory the KCP had an organisational structure consisting of four levels of command. There was a provincial secretariat consisting of individuals whose duty it was to avoid arrest, and who were to be in constant touch with the headquarters at Bombay. Below the secretariat were the provincial committees, which had subordinate chains of 'regional' and 'district' committees, which in turn supervised local communist 'cells' among 'workers and peasants'.[33] While, at the top, the necessity of avoiding arrest cut off the secretariat from involvement in rural everyday affairs, at the bottom the KCP cells had become more in the nature of study classes incorporating the radical youth of the larger tharavadus. An underground publication of 1941 stressed that 'real agriculturists' ought to be enrolled into the KCP through peasant unions. 'It is a weakness of our organisation that only educated young men join our party units'.[34] It was clear that unions were being formed by initiatives taken in the *desams*, rather than by the scattered efforts of KCP activists. While party pamphlets urged the setting up of peasant unions in each revenue unit or *amsam*, by early 1941, it had been decided that they should

---

[30] *AICC Files G-28 part I/1940* (NMML).
[31] See Overstreet and Windmiller, *Communism in India*, 180-1.
[32] D.S.P., Malabar to I.G., Madras, 3 April 1941. *Public (General) Dept. G.O.811-12 (Confdl.) dated 24 April 1941* (KS).
[33] *Home Political Files 7/9/41* (NAI).
[34] 'Communist news and notes', leaflet of Calicut taluk committee of the KCP. *Home Political Files 7/9/41* (NAI).

rather 'attempt to gain control over the [existing] peasant unions'.[35] Local party units were asked to formulate the programme for the region under their control and try to have it adopted by the respective unions.

The attempt to use existing organisations rather than build new ones may have arisen from the rigours of underground life and the fear of arrest. In real terms, this hitchhiking strategy meant that the KCP could never exercise more than a formal control over the various unions. The policy adopted towards the unions reveals the conception behind the proposed reorganisation. Full-time workers were not considered essential for the local peasant union; the office was to be kept open daily and the local peasants were to come in twice a week and submit their grievances. What this meant, in effect, was that the KCP organiser, usually from a dominant tharavadu in the region, would be contacted by the local union when it wished to negotiate the lease of land for cultivation. Once again, these members of dominant tharavadus and their branches began to emerge as the bridges between prospective cultivators and landowners.

In 1939, the attempts of the KCSP organisers to limit opposition only to feudal exactions and irregular measures of rent had not been very successful. Peasant unions had gone further in challenging both the imposition of social deference and the use of the police to curtail political activity. By early 1941, it was clear that the situation called for negotiation rather than conflict. The worsening food crisis necessitated the opening up of more land for cultivation. However, the tenancy committee of 1940 had reiterated the absolute control of the larger landowners over wastelands and forests. This reflected a stiffening in the attitude of the Madras government, further manifested in their willingness to send in platoons of the Malabar Special Police to combat the 'communist menace'.[36] Moreover, the KCP itself stood in danger of losing ground if it could not unite the loose alliance of small cultivators, agricultural labourers and small landowners which was increasingly being pulled apart by the militancy of the landless.

On 12 March 1941, a batch of people belonging to the peasant unions in Hosdrug went in a procession clad in volunteer uniform, shouting anti-war slogans. Two members of the procession were arrested, and to bring the other four into custody, two police constables remained behind in Kayyur. One of them was stabbed on the night of 26 March as he lay asleep. On 28 March, three processions of peasant union members forced the other constable to carry the red flag and shout anti-government slogans. When he tried to escape by jumping into the river, he was stoned to death by the crowd.[37] Sixty members

---

[35] KCP circular no. 14. *Home Political Files 7/9/41* (NAI).
[36] By 1942, the Malabar Special Police (MSP) with a large complement of 'Nayar fighting men' had replaced the army garrisons in Malabar. There were seventeen companies of the MSP in Malabar by the end of 1945. See Arnold, *Police power and colonial rule*, 124–6.
[37] D.M., South Kanara to Chief Secretary, Madras, 31 March 1941, *Public (General) G.O.811–12 (Confdl.) dated 24 April 1941* (KS).

of the 200 strong crowd were arrested and charged with attempted murder. Eventually, four of them were sentenced to death by the High Court of Madras. This decision was significant in that K.P.R. Gopalan had been granted a reprieve in the case of the killing of the police inspector at Morazha on the grounds of the difficulty of determining who from the crowd had actually dealt the blow.[38] The events of March 1941, in the village of Kayyur, marked a watershed in agrarian political activity. Primarily, it showed how the local dread of the police had been replaced by a spirit of open defiance and confrontation. Of the sixty accused in the Kayyur incident, more than half were agricultural labourers.[39] Vishnu Bharateeyan had observed before the tenancy commission of 1940 that the peasant '[stood] a little erect' as a result of the growth of collective activity.[40] The other side to this was that party programmes and the strictures of peasant unions lost their way amidst the settling of scores with a police force which had so far held labourers in their thrall.[41]

From 1941 onwards there emerged a shift in the balance of power between the police and the people in the interior of north Malabar.[42] Operations were put on a war footing and the older conflicts of a few policemen struggling to contain a irate crowd were replaced by the systematic forays of the Malabar Special Police to 'flush out' communist activity. In April 1941, the DSP, Malabar spoke of a 'spring offensive' to bring the 'general run of people into right ways'. Punitive stations were set up all over north Malabar and platoons of the MSP were permanently stationed 'to make the people realise that the Government really rules and not Communism'.[43] On 25 April 1941 all peasant unions in Malabar and south Kanara were declared unlawful.[44] The lack of an organisation and the attempt to hitchhike on existing peasant unions meant that the KCP could not control union radicalism. Besides, the unions were in a more confrontational mood as they realised the potential of volunteer squads as a force against the police. However, the state was now willing to deploy force on a significant scale in favour of the tharavadus, making it an unequal contest.

---

[38] See Kurup, *The Kayyur riot.*
[39] *Public (General) Dept. G.O.811-12 (Confdl.) dated 24 April 1941* (KS).
[40] *MTCR, 1940,* II, 260.
[41] Kurup, *The Kayyur riot,* 79-80.
[42] *Home Political Files7/9/41* (NAI); Court of Sessions, north Malabar Division, Tuesday 16 September 1941. *Sessions Case no. 3/1942* (TCRR).
[43] *Public (General) Dept. G.O.811-12 (Confdl.) dated 24 April 1941* (KS).
[44] DSP, Malabar to I.G., Madras, 3 April 1941 and DSP, South Kanara to I.G., Madras, 14 April 1941. *Public (General) dept. G.O. no. 811-12 (Confdl.) dated 24 April 1941* (KS); *Fort St. George Gazette, 25 April 1941, Extraordinary, Home Political F 7/1/41* (NAI).

The 'People's War' line of 1942 – local transformations

In 1942, as the Indian National Congress raised more militant demands and called upon the British to Quit India, the Communist Party stood against the mainstream. The Congress in Malabar, now controlled by the Right, had retreated so far into the quietism of *khadi* that 'Quit India' passed without incident except for the random sabotage of fish curing yards, government girls' schools and the like.[45] Ostensibly moved by the considerations of international politics, the latter supported the British government in its fight against Fascism.[46] In Malabar, local politics evidenced a dynamic and flexible approach to the problems besetting the region. Calls for harmony between classes and slogans like 'Grow more Food' were translated into negotiations with rural elites for letting out wastelands for cultivation. A fragile sense of rural community was created between cultivators in need of land and landowners requiring compliant labourers. Secondly, the creation of a broad alliance with political groups and parties allowed the KCP to act as the intermediary between those holding stocks of grain and those in need of it.

The People's War line of 1942 came at an opportune juncture. The restoration of the legal status of the Communist Party nationally allowed the KCP to coordinate the disparate activities of unions and individuals under the programme of cultivating wasteland and growing more food. It could retain the support of a section of landless labourers by promoting the reclamation of wasteland. This allowed the KCP to limit conflict, thus assuaging the fears of the large landowning tharavadus. In Malabar, it permitted the creation of a conjunctural community in which landowners would dispense their obligations providing land in return for a compliant and less militant tenantry, at least for the moment. However, the KCP did not lose the opportunity to harness local militancy, which allowed for an occasional flexing of muscle by the volunteer squads. Implicit in this was the recognition that landowners were not going to accede to the demands of cultivators once the food crisis had passed. A particular kind of vocabulary borrowed from the directives of the CPI was creatively used to address local concerns. It was not so much the ostensible ideology which was important but its translation into political practice in innovative and flexible ways. An important example of this was the seemingly absurd exercise of anti-Japanese propaganda in the towns and villages of

[45] There were a few attempts to burn village courts, and in one instance, the railway station at Payyoli, near Badagara. *Court of Sessions, south Malabar Division, Calicut. Sessions Case no. 21 of 1944; High Court of Madras Criminal Appeal 422-3 of 1944. K.B. Menon Papers* (NMML).

[46] In 1942, the Politbureau of the CPI declared that with Hitler's attack on the Soviet Union, the 'imperialist war' had been transformed into a 'people's war'; 'a sacred and final war waged by the camp of the people'. *India in the war of liberation* (CPI Politbureau, February 1942), 3-4.

Malabar. Between 24 and 31 May 1942, an 'anti-Jap week' was held in Calicut and the Congress was berated for its destructive programme 'when the Jap barbarians are at our very gates'.[47]

At one level it was a continuance of the critique of the Congress, but at the other, this propagandising was paraphrased into more practical concerns. With the banning of peasant unions in May 1941, the collective strength of agricultural labourers had been weakened. The volunteer squads were reconstituted as 'anti-Jap' committees but, in the countryside at least, landowners were not deluded by this thin disguise. In Irikkur, a local landlord, Govindan Nambiar, warned his labourers that if they did not resign their membership of 'anti-Jap' organisations they would not be allowed to reap the crop. At the harvest, 200 'anti-Jap' volunteers arrived to guard the field, wielding sticks, while fifty of them reaped the crop.[48]

The problem of expanding local cultivation was tackled under the 'Grow more food' programme of the CPI. Since 1941, there had been a revival of fines and evictions with the new power granted to landlords after the Tenancy Committee report of 1940. Landlords increasingly denied cultivators even the customary rights to collect green leaves for manure. In Irikkur, where the Kalliattu tharavadu had large forest tracts, a plea was made 'in the name of patriotism' to allow cultivation on payment of rent. When the Kalliattu Nambiar did not agree, a *jatha* of 1,000 peasants put pressure on him to grant permission to cultivate as well as postpone the collection of rent arrears for another year.[49] This was a *jatha* with a difference. In 1938, processions had made demands on landlords, now they were placatory. As the party newspaper explained, the Kalliattu tharavadu was reluctant to give out land because they feared that cultivators would not pay rent. Therefore, '[we] must unite and remove the doubts from the minds of *janmis* if we are to save our country'.[50]

This proved to be impeccable strategy. Landowners wanted an income from their wastelands and the KCP promised them accommodating cultivators who were only too willing to make some compromise at a time of food shortage. Moreover, landowners were more forthcoming after the Madras government decreed that single crop cultivation on dry lands would be exempt from assessment for the duration of the war.[51] Nevertheless, there was one major step backward. Feudal levies which the peasant unions had opposed strongly in 1938-39 now found their way back. The Kalliattu Nambiar was paid an extra levy of Rs. 1 per acre in an acknowledgement of deference.[52] The pliancy of the KCP was exploited to the utmost by tharavadus which now found them-

[47] *People's War*, 26 July 1942.
[48] *People's War*, 4 October 1942.
[49] *Deshabhimani*, 12 February 1943.
[50] *Ibid.*
[51] *Revenue Dept. (Ms.) G.O.1911 dated 17 June 1943* (KS).
[52] *Deshabhimani*, 12 February 1943.

selves replaying their erstwhile roles as dispensers of benevolence. Peasant unions were granted six acres of land in Karivellur and over seventy acres in Kottayam, of which more than half was sown with paddy.[53] The acquiescence of the landlords would not outlast the war and the KCP was only too conscious of this. As an editorial in the *Deshabhimani* stated, 'to destroy landlordism is not the present aim of the peasant, but to ensure that even one cent of land does not remain uncultivated'.[54]

Throughout this period there was a process of renegotiation with the old order, now buttressed by the government and the police. The enemies of 1938, like the Kalliattu tharavadu and large landowners like Samuel Aaron, were rehabilitated along with figures like the rural moneylenders.[55] An article in the Party journal stated rather disingenuously that 'the opposition towards us from the ... janmis and the capitalist is diminishing; indeed some of them have actually begun to desire our growth'.[56] K.A. Keraleeyan, who wrote a regular column for *People's War*, applauded the actions of some peasants in Chirakkal who dutifully paid their dues to a moneylender in kind at a time of grain shortage. They reputedly did this because the moneylender had helped them in 'a time of need'.[57] Whatever the truth behind these programmatic stories, underlying them was sound pragmatism. The government had declared a moratorium on assessment for dry cultivation, landlords were willing to give out wastelands and cultivators needed loans for seeds, implements and the like. In villages like Ellarenhi, Kavumbayi and Kaitapram, over 95 per cent of the families were shifting cultivators who needed loans for clearing, planting and harvesting.[58] A temporary truce with moneylenders and landlords made eminent political sense.

Apart from bargaining for cultivable land, party workers were able to intercede skilfully between the government and those holding stocks of grain, in order to resolve the shortage of foodgrains. The success of the rationing policy introduced by the government was blunted by the reality of the monopoly of the rice cartel on the coast and the granaries in the interior. Here again the party built a conjunctural unity with hoarders and assumed the role of assurers if not the providers of subsistence. From 1941, the KCP had begun to organise around the issue of the rise in prices of foodgrains and several 'hunger marches' were organised to meet *tahsildars* and Revenue Divisional officers. In the countryside, the party enquired into prices obtained by cultivators for paddy after the harvest. After adding on 6 per cent to allow for profit to the merchant, a 'fair' price was proposed. People were encouraged to pay for

[53] *Deshabhimani*, 28 February 1943.
[54] *Ibid.*
[55] *Deshabhimani*, 13 June 1943.
[56] *Party Sanghadakan*, 2 (1944), 5.
[57] *People's War*, 24 October 1943.
[58] *Deshabhimani*, 4 March 1943.

grain at that rate to avoid any conflict at ration shops. Any urge to loot rice shops was to be controlled and '[this] mentality was to be converted into a planned effort and an organised fight'.[59]

The People's War thesis of the CPI had called for the broadest unity of all political parties and a programme in the rural areas of relieving the peasantry. In Malabar, the KCP transformed this into a far-reaching policy of uniting their activities in the towns and the countryside and of building bridges with other political groups. Ostensibly, this was a *volte face*. The KCSP had consistently distanced itself from 'communal' Hindu and Muslim groups in an effort to move out of the legacy of the Congress. Now, in the interests of national unity and to combat food shortage, they formed alliances with the Muslim League, the Hindu Mahasabha, the SNDP Yogam, the Nayar Service Society, even the YMCA and the Devadhar Malabar Reconstruction Trust.[60] Moreover, all the erstwhile bogies – capitalists, feudal elements, the petty bourgeoisie, landowners – were rehabilitated. As the party organ, the *Deshabhimani*, stated, 'Our main policy today is not the withholding of rent. It is to increase the production of food grains and solve the food problem.'[61]

The theme of unity with the Muslim League was translated very effectively at the local level. As we have seen, the rice trade had come to be controlled by a cartel of Mappila merchants. Food committees were used as a tool for negotiations, and at least one prominent Mappila merchant was included on each committee. The Muslim League leader, Kadirikoya Haji became a prominent speaker at meetings organised by the KCP on the food situation.[62] Using these contacts with the League as a springboard, the KCP was able to spread its organisation to places like Kattur and Palattunkara which had been strongholds of the Mappilas.[63] If the KCP was using the food committees to extend its sphere of control, the Mappila merchants too began to manipulate the committees to undermine ration regulations. In Mattanur, Janab Moosakutty, the leading rice merchant, set up a food committee of his own and cornered a major share of the rice market. In Cannanore, the Muslim League, the Jamait and ten other Muslim organisations met to discuss rationing procedures and the organisation of food distribution through their own networks. By 1946, the scene of the battle shifted to the Producer cum Consumer Cooperatives (PCC), in which the government had vested the entire responsibility for the procurement and distribution of foodgrains in Malabar. The KCP and the Congress squabbled

---

[59] KCP circular no. 37, *Home Political Files 7/9/41* (NAI).
[60] E.M.S. Nambudiripad, *Deshabhimani* (*Patriot*) (Calicut, 1943), 56-7.
[61] *Deshabhimani*, 28 February 1943.
[62] *Deshabhimani*, 7 March and 4 April 1943.
[63] *Deshabhimani*, 14 March 1943.

for control of the PCCs, creating resentment among the Mappila rice merchants edged out of the trade.[64]

Apart from negotiations with the cartel, the KCP reached into every home through the food programme. In Chirakkal taluk, it had eighty squads which undertook a census of needs for every home.[65] Popular price control committees were set up and *jathas* approached the Collector to 'open' the government stores and feed the poor. Volunteer patrols inspected ration shops and reported any irregularities to the district Munsif.[66] Food committees mediated between the authorities and merchants and, in Baliapatam, the committee arranged that each dealer would get one bag of sugar. In return only two dealers were allowed to sell in a day so that prices could be monitored.[67] The KCP exploited their association with the authorities to the utmost. Much to the annoyance of officials, negotiations were presented to the public in a manner that implied that the 'KCP had the power to force the hand of the authorities'.[68]

In the interior, food committees seem to have continued with the militancy of the late thirties, despite the KCP's attempt to smother rural conflict. In Kathirur, the entire machinery of food distribution was taken over by volunteers. In Taliparamba, a landlord was forced to release 15,000 seers of rice which were subsequently sold at prices lower than those prevailing in the market.[69] In the towns, the food committees remained the means for negotiation with recalcitrant traders and acted as an informal arm of the government. In rural areas however, the knitting of food committees with volunteer squads produced a potent local force for maintaining distribution. The party thus managed to create a temporary balance by mediating between rural elites and the militancy of the landless. Its appeal lay in its perceived ability to exercise a degree of control over the peasant unions on the one hand, and bargain with the dominant landowners on the other. Nevertheless, if the KCP was not to fall between two stools, it had to try and create a support base which was not dependent on economic and political circumstance alone.

An alternative order in the villages, 1942-45

Between 1942 and 1945 the KCP attempted to build a base for itself in the rural areas. Hitchhiking on the Congress organisation had become difficult. Following

[64] *Deshabhimani*, 18 April and 30 May 1943. *ARMP*, 1946, 63; Board of Revenue (Civil Supplies) dated 26 April 1949 (Confdl.), *Development Dept. G.O.3881 dated 20 July 1949* (KS).
[65] *People's War*, 3 January 1943.
[66] *People's War*, 2 August and 18 October 1942.
[67] *Ibid.*, 24 January 1943.
[68] *FR* for the second half of September 1942, *L/P and J/5/201* (IOL).
[69] *People's War*, 2 May 1943.

the events of 15 September 1940, R.K.K. Nandkeolyar was imported into Malabar by the Congress high command to 'resuscitate Congress orthodoxy',[70] and the subordinate committees, assiduously built up by the socialists were dissolved.[71] At the beginning of 1942, the Kerala Congress was in a sorry state, with no funds, several parallel committees and rampant factional fights.[72] Meanwhile, the KCP attempted to put its own house in order and tried to exercise some degree of control over the mushrooming groups informally allied with it. It proved difficult to reconcile the need for a formal party organisation with the presence of individual bodies pressing their own claims. By 1944 'a terrible fight of factions' had emerged within the loose hierarchy of units.[73] The rupture may have been partly a result of the attempts by the central leadership, under E.M.S. Nambudiripad, to exercise control in the name of 'democratic centralism', and partly a perception that the leaders, mainly from upper caste tharavadus were trying to exclude lower caste members from deciding matters of policy. C.H. Kanaran, the prominent organiser of *beedi* workers in Cannanore and Tellicherry, and Raju (?), both Tiyyas, were removed from the central committee. Nambudiripad argued with characteristic sophistry that the party should not become 'the display case of the religions and castes of India'.[74] In 1945, the uneasy and informal association that the KCP had managed to maintain with the Kerala Congress was formally ended. The KPCC decided to exclude communists from primary membership of the Congress.[75]

In the period between 1942 and 1945, the KCP gained a strong foothold in the villages of the interior of north Malabar, particularly those lying along the foothills. These were the areas where large tracts of forest and wasteland were available for cultivation. The KCP consolidated its hold over the eastern parts of Chirakkal and the north eastern region of Kottayam, by trying to create an alternative society of unions. By the beginning of 1943, there were 133 *balasanghams* (children's unions) in north Malabar with a membership of 3,909. Chirakkal taluk alone had 106 organisations with 3,031 children as members. Again in Chirakkal there were over 1,000 members in the women's organisations, Irikkur accounting for 372 and Madayi for 200.[76] In Malapattam,

---

[70] *Public (General) Dept. G.O.2351 dated 28 November 1940* (KS).

[71] *AICC Files 33/1940-41*; Report of Nandkeolyar, *AICC Files P.22 (part I)/1942* (NMML).

[72] *AICC Files G-28 part I/1940*; Letter from R.K.K. Nandkeolyar to General Secretary, AICC, 3 February 1942, *AICC Files P-11/1942-6* (NMML).

[73] *CPI Malabar zilla committee, Special conference resolutions, 28 September to 1 October 1945* (KCP, 1945), 22. It is not very clear from the party documents that survive from this period what this 'terrible fight' was all about, references to it being veiled in allusions to the presence of factions! C. Unniraja, a member of the central committee in this period, appeared not to remember the intra-party conflicts. Interview with C. Unniraja, Calicut, March 1989.

[74] *Party Sanghadakan*, 6 (1944), 3-6.

[75] Resolution of KPCC working committee, 21 August 1945, *AICC Files P-111/1942-6* (NMML). Overstreet and Windmiller, *Communism in India*, 221-2.

[76] *People's War*, 21 February 1943, 8 September 1944; *Deshabhimani*, 28 February 1943.

members of every family belonged to one or the other organisations of the KCP. The success of the KCP can be gauged by the fact that in September 1942, the membership of the All Kerala Kisan Sangham, which had replaced the All Malabar Peasant Union, had been only 7,000 members.[77]

With the organisation of the population of the *desams* of eastern Chirakkal and Kottayam into separate unions of men, women and children, the KCP at last managed to build up a base in the interior. A parallel party organisation was set up for settling social disputes and small thefts in the countryside.[78] Ellaranhi and Irikkur, the two strongholds came to be known in local parlance as Stalingrad and Moscow respectively.[79] These references to the Soviet Union had less to do with any conscious attempt to recreate socialist society than with an idealised notion of Utopia. One of the most famous communist poems of the forties, 'Naniyude chinta' (The thoughts of Nani), highlighted more the concerns of Malabar than any idea of Soviet society.

> I have heard of a land called Soviet
> I would like to go there some day ...
> Over there one does not suffer the pangs of hunger
> Nor the shame of oppression day after day
> That I wasn't born there, I rue most sorely
> In Soviet land so pure and holy.[80]

Irikkur and Ellarenhi were the centres of KCP power, primarily because they had a population which was entirely dependent on shifting cultivation.[81] Moreover, the two powerful tharavadus of Kalliattu and Karakkatitathil held the majority of the wasteland available for cultivation. Figures of landholdings are not available for the forties but in 1901, the Karakkatitathil Nambiar owned nearly all the land in Ellarenhi, including 215 acres of the total of 232 acres of wasteland available for cultivation.[82] The Kalliattu and Karakkatitathil tharavadus between them held 3,105 of the 4,490 acres of wasteland (69 per

[77] *People's War*, 28 February 1943.
[78] *Deshabhimani*, 21 March 1943.
[79] Report of DSP, Malabar to IG, Madras, 21 December 1946 and Report of DM, Malabar to Chief Secretary, Madras, 28 December 1946. *Public (General) Dept. G.O.3003 (Confdl.) dated 2 December 1948* (KS).
[80] *Deshabhimani*, 29 August 1943.
[81] *Deshabhimani*, 4 March 1945. Over 95 per cent of the families in this region were shifting cultivators in 1945.
[82] The Karakkatitathil tharavadu was related to the powerful Kalliattu tharavadu by marriage. In 1901, K. Unnaman Nambiar held 33 of the 36 acres of wetland and 35 of the 41 acres of garden land in Ellarenhi *desam*. *Settlement Register of Ellarenhi desam*, Kanhileri *amsam* (Calicut, 1904). The resettlement registers of 1934 are not available in the Kozhikode Regional archives.

cent) in Kanhileri *amsam*.[83] Of the 1,260 acres of wasteland in Irikkur *amsam*, the two tharavadus held 806 acres (63 per cent).[84] In the Irikkur and Kanhileri *desams*, the KCP could focus their agitation against these two landowners who possessed a near monopoly of wastelands and forests. In both these *desams*, the KCP knitted the more material concern of the fight for wasteland with a recreation of the culture of the reading room. In Karivellur, the party collected Rs. 20,000 from the population, itself a remarkable feat, and constructed a reading room which, in the words of the D.S.P. of Malabar, was 'the size of an average Roman Catholic church'.[85]

The reading rooms, which soon became the centre of village life for the labourers, were a sphere in which the KCP became involved with what the conference of 1945 called the 'everyday life of the people'. They made another, and more significant intervention by resuscitating the shrine culture. The decades of the twenties had witnessed a withdrawal from the shared culture of worship of significant numbers from the upper and lower castes. With the temple entry campaigns, the attack on the shrines had become more profound. The theme of caste mobility had meshed with the rhetoric of cleanliness purveyed by the Congress in its attempt to create a purged and revivified Hinduism. The KCSP, like the Congress, had distanced itself from the shrines when in the wake of the failure of temple entry, more and more of the lower castes were returning to them. In the attempt to transcend associations of religion and caste, it had set itself above involvement with a vital aspect of rural life. However, rural political activity initiated by the KCSP had attacked the caste privileges of the dominant tharavadus and landowners which, to an extent, dismantled the structures of social deference seen as intrinsic to worship at the shrines.

As part of the general renegotiation of the rural order, the communists returned to the theme of the shared religious culture, albeit in an instrumental way. Folk arts were harnessed in the cause of anti-Japanese and anti-hoarding propaganda and the *ottan thullal, poorakkali, kolkkali, teyyattam*, all of these found patronage.[86] In the aftermath of the Depression, many of the less prosperous tharavadus had stopped sponsoring the *teyyattam* and other shrine performances. The leadership of the KCP, coming as they did from branches of the larger tharavadus, were in their element as patrons of the rural arts. Later in this decade, victims of police action would be lauded as heroes and martyrs,

---

[83] *Settlement registers* for the *desams* of Kavumbayi, Ellarenhi, Kanhileri, Nitungott, Cherukkot, Kanhileri and Kattapuram (Calicut, 1904).

[84] In Irikkur *desam* itself, Kalliattu Chathu Nambiyar and Karakkatitathil Unnaman Nambiyar held 308 of the 376 (81 per cent) acres of wasteland. *Settlement registers* of the *desams* of Pattuvam, Kolat, Nituvalur, Irikkur, Kuzhinna and Kuttavu (Calicut, 1904).

[85] Report of DSP, Malabar for the period 14 January 1947. *Public (General-A) Dept. G.O.3003 (Confdl.) dated 2 December 1948* (KS).

[86] *People's War*, 26 July 1942, 22 November 1942, 11 April 1943, 26 December 1943.

and many individuals incorporated within the *teyyattam* tradition of victims of injustice. Among the persons arrested in the fighting at Karivellur in 1946 was a *teyyattam* performer who 'used to dance communism'.[87] In December 1942, the slogan 'make every temple festival into an all night street corner meeting', was launched.[88] Participation in shrine festivals was combined with judicious propaganda. For the festival at Andalur shrine, near Tellicherry, the KCP activists managed to get twenty sacks of rice at controlled rates from the *tahsildar*. Communist Party members were active in organising the temple festivals at Jagannatha temple and Payyavur shrine in Chirakkal.[89] Here again, what began as an intervention in the interests of the party was transformed into something far richer.

The community around the shrine was a new one within which the arbitrariness of power had been mitigated somewhat. In one sense there was a return to the former idea of the community of household, shrine and cultivators. At a time of food shortage, the shrines and temples with their lands and granaries had become oases of relative plenitude. They continued to collect rents in grain from those who held their wetlands. In a period of scarcity many of the dominant tharavadus found a lifeline in this resuscitation of the shrine festival as centres of collective worship. A.C. Kannan Nayar recorded in his diary the holding of a *teyyattam* in his family shrine which brought in a 'profit' of Rs. 475.[90] K. Madhavan records another incident more revealing of the ambiguities of the relation between tharavadus and shrines as well as the persistence of the aura of the dominant tharavadus in the countryside. In 1944, when a tenant was evicted in Madikkai, Madhavan assisted him to harvest the crop and collect his share. This was in defiance of local authority as well as the party line which pressed for harmonious relations with landowners. Madhavan was arrested and released on bail, paid for with borrowed money. In order to hire a lawyer and repay the loan, he visited the shrine at Erikkulam, a *desam* populated by potters dependent on his tharavadu. In his role as manager of the shrine he demanded grain from the potters, sold it and used the money to hire a lawyer![91]

Therefore, the KCP managed to negotiate a conjunctural community of landowners and cultivators. Since the KCP activists came from prominent tharavadus themselves, they were back in the role they had played between 1938-40, i.e. intermediaries between large landowners and cultivators. At a time of economic distress, they managed to exercise a degree of control over unions and individuals, but this conjuncture would soon pass. What continued

---

[87] *Judgement, Sessions Case no. 14 and 18 of 1947 (TCRR)*; *Home Political 5/8/46 Poll I* (NAI).
[88] *People's War*, 27 December 1942.
[89] *People's War*, 7 March 1943.
[90] *Diaries of A.C. Kannan Nayar*, 28 March 1947.
[91] Madhavan, *Payaswiniyude teerattu*, 164.

however was the power of the dominant tharavadus. The party line between 1942-45 had emphasised negotiation rather than conflict with the tharavadus and by 1946, they were back in control. However, the moderate line had also allowed several cultivators to gain a foothold for themselves, creating a large number with interests to protect.

Towards a militant stance, 1946-48

From 1946 to 1948, rural politics took an increasingly violent turn, and exposed the fragility of the balance achieved in rural relations by the KCP. The willingness of the provincial government to quell rural militancy with a heavy hand provoked landowners to break the truce and reassert their control over agricultural resources. Moreover, the return of demobilised soldiers after the war added an element of organisation to the activities of unions and cultivators who were willing to meet force with force. Nevertheless, combativeness remained within limits; there were no demands for non-payment of rent, redistribution of land, or the overthrow of landlords as in Bengal or Telengana. This was in part the consequence of the check on rural militancy in the period 1942-45, which had allowed several cultivators to gain a foothold on plots of land. Only profiteering in grain at a time of shortage and the intransigence of landowners in prohibiting the use of resources like wastelands and forests were opposed. There was again an inchoate recognition of obligations, offset by the willingness to challenge the excesses of authority.

This recreation of community was necessarily transient since it was premised on the possession by tharavadus and shrines of stocks of grain, as well as the temporary recognition by landowners of the need to lease out their wasteland. Landowners were only too aware of the inherent dangers of transferring lands on lease to cultivators who were backed by a strong organisation. At Blathur and Urathur, the Kalliattu tharavadu refused to give lands except on very high rents. At Dharmadam, landlords began sending notices to cultivators to clear rent arrears and surrender their renewal rights.[92] With the introduction of rationing in Malabar in October 1944, the supply department sent directives to all revenue officers that cultivators should pay rent to landlords in grain. The remaining grain had to be sold to the supply department at a low price and daily requirements bought from the market where a higher price prevailed.[93]

With the end of the war, the moratorium on the collection of assessment from dry cultivation ceased. In 1945, an amendment was made to the MTA of

[92] *Deshabhimani*, 4 March 1945, 11 April 1945.
[93] *Deshabhimani*, 15 July 1945.
[94] *Revenue Dept. (Ms.) G.O.2007 dated 16 September 1946* (KS).

1930, giving fixity of tenure to the cultivator unless the landlord could prove bona fide need for cultivation to support his family.[94] As a result, tenants and cultivators were in possession of land, were empowered, at least in law, to continue there and they were unwilling or unable to pay rents in kind. The temporary truce in the countryside was about to be broken as landlords attempted to forcibly collect rent in kind from their tenants at a time of food scarcity. If the latter refused to accede, they were evicted on dubious protestations of personal need from landlords. In the period between 1940 and 1946 over 20,000 evictions were ordered under the provisions of the MTA, 1930.[95] In 1946, the Madras Tenants and Ryots Protection Act had to be passed to provide security for tenants from eviction and sale of their holdings. Landowners became increasingly belligerent and in March 1946, when a deputation went to solicit the Kalliattu landlord to give land for *punam* cultivation, the police were called in and sec. 144 of the IPC was imposed.[96]

A brief foray into electoral politics in the 1946 provincial Legislative Assembly elections proved disastrous. The big guns of the KCP – E.M.S. Nambudiripad, K.P. Gopalan, A.K. Gopalan, C.H. Kanaran and E. Kannan lost to relative unknowns fielded by the Congress.[97] The policy of the communists had been to support the Congress in general constituencies; the League in Muslim constituencies; and put up their own candidates where they were strong. It was a piquant situation. Kannan Nayar wrote in his diary on 27 November 1945; 'A few communists have gone by in a *jatha* shouting "Vote for the Congress!", "Vote for the League!" Quite amusing!' The rapprochement with the Muslim League had considerably strengthened its base in Malabar. In 1944, Liaquat Ali Khan and other north Indian Muslims toured Malabar to encourage League organisations. In the 1946 elections, they swept all the Muslim seats.[98]

The Party would have to return to a militant line; landlords who had been regarded as friends under the People's War line became enemies again. In a bid to invent a revolutionary past for itself, the CPI launched a campaign for tracing its ancestry to the revolutionary terrorist movements which had followed the Swadeshi upsurge between 1905-08. P.C. Joshi, the Party Secretary observed of the Chittagong Armoury Raid that 'terrorism was the infant as communism is the mature stage of their revolutionary life'.[99] This theme was taken up in Malabar and Nambudiripad wrote that the seeds of the growth of the Left were sown in Cannanore jail where the Malayali internees for civil disobedience had

[95] *Revenue (Ms). Dept. G.O.1935 dated 12 August 1947.* (KS).
[96] *Deshabhimani*, 4 March 1946.
[97] It must be borne in mind, however, that only 14 per cent of the adult population were enfranchised, the primary qualifications being property and income. *AICC Files E-D-1/1946 KW I and II* (NMML); Overstreet and Windmiller, *Communism in India*, 237.
[98] Miller, *The Mappila Muslims of Kerala*, 161-2.
[99] Overstreet and Windmiller, *Communism in India*, 233-5.

encountered the incarcerated Bengal terrorists.[100] At one stroke this gave the communists both an indigenous genealogy and incorporated them in the tale of the struggle for independence, wiping out their embarrassment about the stance of 1942. Now the KCP could envisage direct confrontation both because of the demise of the conjuncture of the People's War line and also because it had the backing of the little Moscows and Stalingrads in Chirakkal. In May 1946, a peasants conference was held at Eranjoli and it was clear from the very first resolution that the party was willing to go further than it had in 1942. 'The aim of the present movement is to end the feudal lord-*janmi* system and establish the ownership of the cultivator over the land'.[101] Land to the cultivator was the new slogan and it was presented as the panacea for 'material, social and cultural progress'. For the first time the KCP explicitly linked its programme of social reform with the fight for economic equality. It promised to work 'to remove untouchability, caste and other vestiges of feudalism'.[102] Once again a consideration of caste was fuzzed by characterising it as a specific phenomenon of the traditional order which would vanish with the demise of the power of the landlords.

With the KCP ostensibly willing to espouse a more radical programme, an edge was added to the situation by the return of demobilised soldiers with the end of the war. By 1945, Malabar had the highest number of recruits in the Madras Presidency, having contributed over 60,000 men. Chirakkal alone sent 13 per cent of the total.[103] The government's half-hearted efforts at resettling them foundered in the face of the intransigence of landlords, and these ex servicemen became willing converts to the fight for wasteland.[104] They trained the volunteer squads to take advantage of the natural cover provided by the forests, to make use of the hilly terrain, establish outposts on vantage points and above all to use rifles. In the event of any confrontation with the police, these squads would be more than able to hold their own. To the north of the town of Payyanur, the jurisdiction of police stations consisted of a heavily forested and inaccessible area. There was only one road to Irikkur which went on to Srikandapuram; the rest was hilly, scrub region. From Irikkur and Ellarenhi, the KCP had an almost impregnable base from which to operate.

Yet again, it was individual initiative which forced the issue. Towards the end of 1946, leaders began to spring up locally, and demand that the landlord's

[100] E.M.S. Nambudiripad, *Atmakatha (Autobiography)* (Trivandrum, 1976), 157. See also his official history of the Communist Party of Kerala, *Kammyunistu party keralathil (The Communist Party in Kerala)*.

[101] *Aikya kisan sangham kettipedukkuka (Build up a united peasants organisation)* (Calicut, 1946), proceedings of Eranjoli Malabar Kisan sammelan, 14-5 May 1946, 1.

[102] *Ibid.*, 4. Overstreet and Windmiller, *Communism in India*, 245.

[103] *ARMP*, 1945; *Public (Resettlement) Dept. G.O.1937 dated 19 August 1945* (KS).

[104] In Bengal too, the districts of Mymensingh, Malda and Dinajpur, where the *tebhaga* agitation developed, were the areas where the government had unsuccessfully attempted to resettle ex-servicemen. See D.N. Dhanagare, *Peasant movements in India, 1920-50* (Delhi, 1983), 174.

share of the crop should not be paid. They also prevented the collection of rent. Throughout the month of November, there were attacks on consignments of paddy.[105] In December 1946, two confrontations took place between the MSP and armed villagers which showed the nature of the transformation of rural politics.

The first was in Karivellur, where the overseer of the raja of Chirakkal had made several unsuccessful attempts to collect rent from tenants. Local 'communist' groups were led by A.V. Kunhambu, the foremost KCP activist in the region, who also came from a prominent Nayar tharavadu. These groups obstructed the removal of the harvest and its transport out of the area. Since Karivellur was accessible only on foot or by using the river, the grain had to be transported by boat. On 20 December 1946, the overseer backed by police strength attempted to transport grain by river. They were opposed by a 300-strong crowd armed with tapper's knives, sticks and clubs who approached the police in an orderly manner led by C. Kunhambu, an ex-military man. They launched an attack with *coir* slings and then closed in for hand to hand combat with shouts of 'Kill the police' and 'Kill the MSP'. The leaders of the crowd were heard shouting that the police bullets would only go into the air and would not hurt them. In the mêlée, a local communist leader, Kannan Nayar was shot dead.[106] Subsequent enquiries by a member of the Legislative Assembly revealed a further element of organisation and logic behind the actions of the crowd. The raja of Chirakkal had been trying to transport 6,000 *seers* of rice from his granaries for sale on the open market. The villagers had attacked only after the raja turned down their requests to hand over the grain to cooperative stores, to be sold at the fair price fixed by the government.[107] Labourers at Karivellur had refused to help transport the grain and the overseer had been forced to hire coolies from nearby Azhikkal.[108]

Ten days later another confrontation took place on Kayambayam hill near Irikkur. Here, as in Karivellur, the removal of grain from the area for sale in the open market had been resisted fiercely throughout 1946. In October, the MSP had received information that some 'communists' were training volunteers in Irikkur, but they had been unable to trace the camp or round up the participants because the area was inaccessible. In early December, a local leader, M.C. Rayarappan had been arrested but a crowd surrounded the police station and released him. Subsequently, a volunteer training camp at Kuzhilur was raided by the police and seven men arrested. The police station at Irikkur was attacked

[105] Report of DSP, Malabar to IG, Madras, 21 December 1946. *Public (General) Dept. G.O. 3003 (Confdl.) dated 2 December 1948* (KS).
[106] Report of DM, Malabar to Chief Secretary, Madras, 21 December 1946. *Public (General) Dept. G.O.3003 dated 2 December 1948* (KS).
[107] *Ibid.*, Letter of P. Venkateswarulu, MLA to PM, Madras, 27 December 1946.
[108] Judgement, *Sessions Case no. 14 and 18 of 1947* (TCRR).

by an armed crowd but with no success. On 30 December, the MSP got news of a camp on Kayambayam hill with about 500 volunteers. As the platoon approached the hill there were two shrill blasts on a whistle and under covering fire, the volunteers charged down the hill. Five men died in the encounter, three of whom had served in the army during the war.[109]

These incidents reveal the degree to which the KCP had managed to harness what had been individual initiatives towards occupation and cultivation of wasteland. The volunteer squads, now reorganised as a disciplined rural militia, coordinated what had been the random actions of opposition to the police and landowners. There was another element of coherence, partly the result of the conjuncture of 1942 when the KCP had endeavoured to renegotiate the rural order. Both at Karivellur and Irikkur, there had been overt acts of violence and confrontation only when there had been a transgression of the obligation to provide subsistence at a time of death. It was the attempt to sell grain for profit which had acted as the flashpoint. In the concerted attempts to bring wasteland under cultivation, provide grain at a time of need and, lastly, to make the dominant tharavadus aware of their obligation to sustain their dependents, the KCP had created yet another conjunctural sense of community.

In north Malabar, there was none of the militancy evidenced in the *tebhaga* agitations of 1946 in Bengal. One of the chief slogans of *tebhaga* had urged sharecroppers to take grain to their own yards instead of to the landowner.[110] In Malabar, food shortage had not reached the levels of Bengal in 1943-44; a controlled movement had managed to keep the community of subsistence alive. Landholders had pragmatically provided wasteland for cultivation in cases where they had not provided food. Bengal during the great famine had witnessed a breakdown of rural relations: the famine had assured the survival of those with resources of grain; women, children, and marginal groups had perished.[111] The failure of the rural elites to provide in 1943-44 probably explains the militancy of 1946. In Telengana, far more radical ventures were inaugurated, with the Communist Party establishing 'soviets' which provided parallel administration in well over 4,000 villages. Land was seized and given to agricultural labourers.[112]

---

[109] *Home Political F 7/3/47* (IOL); Proceedings of enquiry by Jt. Magistrate, Tellicherry, 2 January 1947. *Public (General) Dept. G.O.3003 dated 2 December 1948* (KS).

[110] Bose, *Agrarian Bengal*, 264-9.

[111] P.R. Greenough, 'Indian famines and peasant victims: the case of Bengal in 1943-44', *Modern Asian Studies*, 14, 2 (1980), 205-35; A. Sen, *Poverty and famines: an essay on entitlement and deprivation* (Oxford, 1981).

[112] Dhanagare, *Peasant movements in India*, 165-9, 194-5. In Travancore, the coir workers of Alleppey embarked upon a short-lived rebellion in 1946; the complex outcome of post-war economic depression, food shortages, state politics, and princely intransigence. In a tendentious article, Jeffrey argues that this rebellion was the outcome of a directive from Moscow. R. Jeffrey, "India's working class revolt: Punnapra-Vayalar and the communist "conspiracy" of 1946', *Indian Economic and Social History Review*, 18, 2 (1981), 97-122.

All through 1947, militant activity continued in north Malabar and even cultivation had to be carried on with the help of the police.[113] Many large landowners had already decamped from the areas which had become communist strongholds and the Karakkatitathil Nayanar took up residence twenty miles away from Ellarenhi for fear of reprisals.[114] The Congress ministry in Madras headed by T. Prakasam began working in close alliance with the Special Branch to intensify the deployment of police forces in the 'battle against communism'.[115] In 1947, the Madras Maintenance of Public Order Act was passed empowering the government with wider powers of preventive detention, requisitioning of property and censorship, in order to deal with 'subversive activities'.[116]

The KCP followed a policy of undermining the morale of the police force. They subjected them to ridicule and questioned their legitimacy by propagating tales of atrocities. At one public meeting, the MSP was described as the 'special army ... against the Congress, trade unions, *kisans*, and even against temple entry and Harijans'.[117] The *Deshabhimani* was the organ of propaganda and since it was read aloud in reading rooms and factories all over Malabar, the government was not far wrong in characterising it as the 'mainspring of the communist machine'. Every edition of the *Deshabhimani* carried stories of rape and torture committed by the MSP. A typical extract read, 'The local blackmarketeers are getting [*sic*] elated; the landlords – the social pests – are dancing in ecstasy; the capitalists who indulge in atrocious profiteering are overjoyed; corrupt, autocratic and imperious officialdom are extremely delighted ...'[118] The second strategy adopted was to petition the Prakasam ministry to negotiate a *quid pro quo*. As a part of this, if wastelands were made free for cultivation and landlords collected their rents only in cash, the KCP would cultivate the land at rates recommended by the *MTCR, 1940*. Moreover, surplus grain would be handed over to the government.[119] The Prakasam ministry proved to be intractable in its policy towards wasteland and in 1947, the Madras Estates Communal Forest and Private Lands (Prohibition of Alienation) Act made void, with retrospective effect, all alienation of private

[113] *ARMP*, 1947, 9.
[114] *Diaries of A.C. Kannan Nayar*, 17 December 1946.
[115] Arnold, *Police power and colonial rule*, 220. The Prakasam ministry was seen by landowners as representing the bulwark against communism. Kannan Nayar observed, 'I have faith in the Prakasam ministry ... they are of a propertied temperament'. *Diaries of A.C. Kannan Nayar*, 1 March 1947.
[116] *ARMP*, 1947, 3.
[117] Speech of E.M.S. Nambudiripad at Madras committee of CPI, Triplicane beach, 5 January 1947. *Public (General) Dept. G.O.3003 (Confdl.) dated 2 December 1948* (KS).
[118] *Deshabhimani*, 26 February 1947; Report of the DM, Malabar. *D. Dis. 2624 M47 (Confdl.) dated 5 September 1947* (KRA).
[119] E.M.S. Nambudiripad to T. Prakasam, 31 December 1946 and 14 January 1947; Memorandum to the Secretary of the Board of Revenue reproduced in *Malabarile karshika kuzhappam (Agrarian strife in Malabar)* (KCP, 1947), 1–2.

lands since 1 November 1945.[120] Vesting greater powers of ownership of wasteland with the larger landowners proved, in the event, to be the surest way of exacerbating conflict.

Coupled with its intransigence in not allowing any concessions in the matter of wasteland, the Prakasam ministry continued with its policy of severe repression through the MSP. By the end of January 1947, the communist stronghold in Karivellur had been broken and 176 'known' communists arrested. It was a hollow victory, for many of the inhabitants had decamped and the older people who were left behind refused to divulge information to the police. Village revenue officers participated in attacks on the police and once an area had been brought under control by force, there was no infrastructure of official administration to keep the peace. Malapattam and Kandakkayi, *desams* in which communist organisation was strong, held out against the MSP since they were adjacent to forests. Every time the *desams* were raided, the population fled into the jungles. Once the police had moved on, fields were attacked by union activists and standing crops harvested. Ten platoons of the MSP were active around the *desams* of Irikkur, Kandakkayi, Payyavur and Ellarenhi, yet the unions had the upper hand.[121]

In an attempt at a placatory gesture, the government decided that all communist under-trial prisoners were to be treated as a special class.[122] This measure backfired, and communist activists used it as part of their propaganda to show the rightness of their cause. In the *desams* of the east, the activity of the Party became bolder and more innovative. Plays were staged extolling the achievements of the peasant unions, and leaflets distributed calling for violent agitation to cultivate wastelands. Released communist prisoners returned to their villages and spoke of the ineffectiveness of the law and order agencies. Party cadres were sustained by house-to-house collections of rice and families were advised to keep back sufficient paddy for themselves and party activists. At Mangat, in a bold move, the village common was taken over by the unions of Morazha and Kalliasseri and tapioca and chillies planted.[123]

On 15 August 1947, India gained independence. Congress branches began to be established in the interior. A police report of 1947 noted hopefully the presence of ninety-seven Congress members in the communist heartland of Ellarenhi whereas there had been none in 1946-47.[124] In the eastern villages, support for Congress was limited and its policy was restricted to the formation

[120] *ARMP*, 1947, 5-6.
[121] Report of the DSP, Western Range between 14 January 1947 and 4 February 1947. *Public (General) Dept. G.O.3003 (Confdl.) dated 2 December 1948* (KS).
[122] *Home Dept. (Ms.) G.O.822 dated 1 March 1947* (KS).
[123] Report of DSP, Western Range, 16 March to 13 September 1947. *Public (General) Dept. G.O.3003 (Confdl.) dated 2 December 1948* (KS).
[124] Report of DSP, Western Range, September to December 1947. *Public (General) Dept. G.O.3003 (Confdl.) dated 2 December 1948* (KS).

of Desh Raksha Samajams. These were volunteer committees ostensibly created to patrol the countryside but more often they engaged in pitched street battles with groups thought to be communists. In Kottayam taluk, a model Congress village was made at Pullot *desam* in an attempt to parallel the 'red' *desams* of Karivellur, Ellarenhi and Irikkur, but its major activity of spinning did not appeal to many.[125] Eventually, Congress organisation in north Malabar could not subsume the other affiliations of its members, even temporarily, as the KCP had managed to do. In Hosdrug taluk, the same person acted as the secretary of the Congress committee, the Socialist Party as well as the SNDP Yogam. From different platforms, people were organised under tricoloured, red and yellow flags![126]

What sealed the fate of the Congress was its hesitant approach towards land reform, even as the situation in north Malabar pointed the direction in which political strategy lay. There was a strong lobby within the KPCC led by G. Sankaran Nayar, the doyen of tenancy reform in Malabar, which argued against giving land to the cultivator. Sankaran Nayar felt that distributing land among the cultivators would 'have the disastrous effect of wiping out the middle classes of the district'.[127] A tenancy sub committee appointed by the KPCC stated firmly that the 'aim of land reform should not ... be the mere distribution of land among the landless' and suggested that smaller holdings should be 'gradually consolidated into large scale cooperative farms'.[128] Once again, the Congress showed itself completely out of touch with the political mood of the tenants and agricultural labourers and provided no suggestion other than collectivising the lands of the small cultivators!

The revolutionary line of 1948

By January 1948, the increasing reluctance of landowners to give out their wastelands for *punam* cultivation prompted the Collector to take matters into his own hands. A temporary truce was achieved by the signing of the *punam* charter between landowners and tenants, which assured land for cultivation at low rents.[129] In April 1948, the central committee of the CPI met at Calcutta and called for a revolution in the countryside. 'Agrarian movements uniting the

---

[125] *AICC Files G-41/1948* (NMML).
[126] Report of Sadiq Ali's tour of Kerala. *AICC Files P 24 (II) and P 24 (III)/1947* (NMML).
[127] Letter from G. Sankaran Nayar, Secretary, Malabar Tenancy Association to President, AICC, 13 June 1947. *AICC Files G-10 (part IV)/1946* (NMML).
[128] Report of the tenancy sub-committee of the KPCC (E. Moithu Maulavi, K. Bhaskara Menon, A. Ramachandra Nedungadi, K. Raghavan). *Development Dept. G.O.311 dated 22 January 1951* (KS).
[129] *Public (General) Dept. G.O.630 (Confdl.) dated 12 March 1948* (KS).

entire mass of the poor peasants, middle peasants and the agrarian proletarians' were to be launched.[130] Landlordism was to be liquidated without compensation to landlords, all forms of feudal and semi-feudal exactions were to be ended and the rallying slogan was to be 'land to the tiller'. For the first time, vague, yet emotive categories of 'cultivator' and 'tiller' were defined and distinctions made within the broad mass of the peasantry. A pamphlet inaugurating the new programme stated that it was:

against the tradition we have followed so far in peasant organisation. That the peasant movement is a united movement of everyone other than the *janmi* in the countryside is a false notion. Peasants do not form a single class; among them there are the better off, the middling and the poor. Below them are the labourers even without land.[131]

The KCP would throw its weight behind 'agricultural labourers, other rural labourers and poor peasants' who were 'the backbone of the movement'. Nevertheless, amidst all this talk of class alignments in the forthcoming struggle, there was a streak of pragmatism. An arrangement would have to be arrived at with caste organisations but as a part of 'class organisation and class struggle'![132]

The necessity of differentiating within the broad support base of the KCP precipitated a crisis. A heterogenous front of forces had been built up behind the slogan of land to the cultivator, integrating the desire for land of the labourer and small cultivator. K.A. Keraleeyan was despatched by the party to explain to units all over north Malabar that agricultural labourers, and not the tenant cultivators, were now to be considered the bulwark of the party. In Hosdrug taluk there was immediate discord. Those tenant cultivators who had gone to prison in 1946-48 as part of the KCP campaign for land returned to find themselves out in the cold. An organisation was set up to work against the agricultural labourers and the KCP unit split three ways. The small landlords and a section among the tenant cultivators joined the Congress while a few of the latter enlisted in the newly formed Socialist Party.[133]

The other conflict arose over whether grain should be grabbed or be paid for and then redistributed. Many of the veteran leaders of the KCP preferred the latter and believed that landlords should be made to give up their grain through peaceful persuasion. In Kasergode taluk, T. Subramaniam Thirumumpu received a card from Keraleeyan asking him to go ahead with 'a violent programme on

[130] *Calcutta Conference of the CPI, 1948* (CPI, 1948), Resolution, 99.
[131] *Vadakke malabarile samaravum athilninnulla pathangalum (The struggle in north Malabar and its lessons)* (KCP, January 1949), 34-5.
[132] *Ibid.*, 35, 39-40.
[133] Madhavan, *Payaswiniyude teerattu*, 212-13, 219; Interview with K.A. Keraleeyan, Calicut, March 1987.

the Telengana model'. Thirumumpu temporised, asking the district council of the KCP for advice while leading *jathas* in Madikkai, Klayikode, Kodakkat and Kayyur for purchasing grain at a fair price from landlords. He received a message from the council criticising him for continuing to have 'illusions of the Nehru government'. Moreover, the tenuous control of the KCP over local initiative finally gave way and in Karivellur people raided a granary and carried away the stocks. Thirumumpu decided to resign from the Communist Party in protest against what he saw as illegal acts.[134] Chandroth Kunhiraman Nayar, who had organised and trained the first volunteer squads, resigned from the KCP a few months later.[135]

The crisis within the leadership had repercussions for the extent of KCP control over rural militancy. The situation fast became a confrontation between the police and maverick 'unions'. North Malabar was turned into a semi-war zone. Four companies of the MSP were active in the interior, and the police administration report for 1948 expressed relief that the 'boredom which had hitherto been the bane of the force had been alleviated'.[136] 'Peasant unions' sprang up all over north Malabar asking cultivators to retaliate if they were asked to give up their wetlands, and offering to fight on their behalf. Many of the volunteer squads seemed to have taken up freelance political activity particularly in the areas less accessible to the police.[137] April and May 1948 were the cruellest months and groups of armed agricultural labourers clashed with the MSP at Kodom, Thillenkeri, Peralam and Onjiyam. Revolutionary strategy was planned at meetings disguised as study classes prompting the government to issue memos to all police officers to raid 'study classes' wherever they were being held.[138]

By June 1948, there was a lull in hostilities, but the authorities looked forward with trepidation to September when the harvests were likely to bring on a fresh spate of attacks. Depending on how much control the KCP managed to retain over their units, political activity was more or less systematic. In the 'red' *desams* of Chirakkal – Irikkur, Ellarenhi and Malapattam – volunteer camps were organised with training in unarmed combat and methods of snatching rifles. Letters intercepted by the police showed that activists had been advised to attack the police only when they were in small groups. Ex militiamen organised *jathas*, looting of granaries and ration shops, raiding of the houses of landlords and even attempts to demolish public bridges to impede

[134] Statement of T.S. Thirumumpu to sub-inspector, Cheruvathur on arrest, 21 May 1948, *Madras Govt. Secret USS no. 71 dated 29 November 1948* (TNA); Madhavan, *Payaswiniyude teerattu*, 203.
[135] *Diaries of A.C. Kannan Nayar*, 29 March 1949.
[136] *RAPMP*, 1947-48, 5-6.
[137] *Public (General-A) Dept. G.O.729 (Ms.) dated 17 March 1949* (KS).
[138] Special Branch CID to the Chief Secretary, Madras, 11 May 1948. *Madras Govt. Secret USS no. 71 dated 29 November 1948* (TNA).

police movements.[139] In other *desams*, people took the law into their own hands. A.C. Kannan Nayar came upon a crowd of old women and children armed with sticks who had managed to get grain from a landlord at Kundlaya and were proceeding to get more from a neighbouring one.[140] There was considerable alarm among the district authorities who saw a replication of activities in Hyderabad and requested the banning of the KCP. The Government of India, however, was not keen to drive the party underground which would have made it more difficult to contend with.[141]

While the Congress and the MSP worked hand in glove to root out the communists, the KCP managed to extend the struggle even further into the foothills of Karivellur, Ellarenhi and Kodakkat. Cultivators were led into the forests to collect manure and firewood, rights which had been progressively denied them throughout the forties. In September 1949, the KCP was banned and, by October, the entire leadership of the Malabar committee, the Chirakkal committee and the firka committees was jailed. Even though the political programme of the KCP had ended in disarray, an important principle had been established. Agricultural labourers and cultivators had shown themselves willing to fight for negotiation of resources and against the excesses of large landlowners, like the curtailment of customary rights and profiteering in grain. On the other hand, the Indian state like its predecessor, the colonial state, had shown itself able, and willing, to suppress rural militancy effectively.

Conclusion

Throughout the forties, the state gave tharavadus greater control over waste-lands and forests, beginning with the recommendations of the tenancy committee of 1940 and culminating in the Preservation of Private Forests Act of 1949. Moreover, it was willing to bolster the power of these dominant households by coming down severely on rural militancy. Throughout this decade, Malabar was brought more firmly under the framework of law and order imposed from Madras. Malabar, and particularly its northern regions had been neglected outposts of the Madras Presidency till the events of 1940. In September 1940, the Intelligence Bureau had expressed its concern at being caught unawares,

---

[139] *Ibid.*, Secret letter DSP to DM, Malabar, 15 August 1948; DM, Malabar to Chief Secretary, Madras, 26 December 1948, *Public (General) Dept. G.O.3003 (Confdl.) dated 2 December 1948* (KS); Court of Special Addl. Magistrate, Cannanore CC/7/48, *Public (General-B) Dept. G.O.1806 dated 9 July 1953* (KS).

[140] *Diaries of A.C. Kannan Nayar,* 16 March 1948.

[141] Most Immediate Top Secret Telegram no. 2818 dated 29 March 1948 from Government of India, Home Affairs to all provincial governments. *Madras Govt. Secret USS no. 71 dated 29 November 1948* (TNA).

observing that it was 'a most surprising development as coming from Malabar'. By 1948, however, any militant activity was rendered increasingly difficult by the presence of an armed constabulary willing to defend order and property.

The limits of rural radicalism had been reached in a period of economic crisis, allowing the KCP to exercise a degree of control over peasant radicalism. Between 1942 and 1945, the KCP translated the national Party doctrine of class harmony and cooperation with the state into a programme of renegotiating rural relations. This was done at two levels. First, the tharavadus reemerged in their roles as dispensers of benevolence, granting wastelands to desperate, therefore compliant cultivators. In this period, the pragmatism of cultivators, the caution of the KCP, and the violence employed by the state ensured that political activity would go thus far and no further. The second aspect of KCP mediation in rural relations was the revival of the shrine culture. Paradoxically, if viewed only through the eyes of theory, the communists were responsible for restoring the shrines as the site of rural worship and community. The old structures remained but the relations which sustained them were altered. By 1948, it was clear that rural community could no longer be negotiated as before. The willingness of the government to deploy force to suppress militancy and maintain the control exercised by landowners meant that KCP politics would now have to look outward from the villages of north Malabar. The politics of Malabar would henceforth consist of an engagement with the state in an effort to recreate rural relations. In 1951, the KCP would make the transition towards respectability and the politics of engaging with the state, in a move from 'ultra leftism' to, what one of their leading theoreticians called, 'parliamentary cretinism'.[142] In the 1951 general elections, the first with universal suffrage, the KCP won a resounding victory in north Malabar, securing over 70 per cent of the votes in Taliparamba and Mattanur.

---

[142] K. Damodaran, 'The tragedy of Indian communism', in Tariq Ali ed., *The Stalinist legacy* (Harmondsworth, Middlesex, 1984), 355.

Conclusion

From 1900 to 1948, different conceptions of community were projected, created and negotiated, but, inevitably, they were inflected by the antagonisms within society. Both social reform and political ideologies offered intimations of equality to a society where caste inequality was the central issue of politics. Each notion of community failed; either because it could not be inclusive enough, or it was too all embracing to allow for the recognition of disparity. The efforts of the socialists and communists were relatively more successful compared to other movements, because they started from the premise of social differences and tried to mediate between these. Paradoxically, the threat of conflict helped to sustain the negotiation of community between its constituent elements. The actions of peasant unions reminded tharavadus forcefully of their obligations. However, it was precisely this factor which undermined a temporary mediation. Peasant unions had a proclivity to pull in different directions, and to fragment into the actions of diverse individuals. Moreover, the state increasingly intervened to restore 'order'. This meant, initially, that the volume of conflict over rural resources increased and that eventually, disparities remained.

Each redefinition of community by political ideologies was presented by its authors as an advance over the previous ones. The Tiyyas had projected a community only of equal Tiyyas; nationalism envisaged a wider community of Hindus devoid of differences; socialism and communism sidestepped the issue of caste altogether, but envisaged a community of workers and peasants. Each created a metaphor for the inequality prevailing within society. The Congress attacked untouchability, and this was reflected in its politics both in the campaigns for cleanliness as well as the venture to gain temple entry for all castes. Socialist discourse had posited capitalism as lying at the root of all evils in society. As Krishna Pillai, co-founder of the Socialist Party wrote in 1934, 'Capitalism will be destroyed and the ruling of the country will pass into the hands of the *daridranarayan* [the poor]'.[1]

---

[1] Krishna Pillai, *'Fascisavum kammyunisavum' (Fascism and Communism), Mathrubhumi*, 18 April 1934.

Many groups fell outside the broad categories of 'worker' and 'peasant' that political movements attempted to project. The artisanal groups (Kammalar) were a case in point. They had been bypassed by caste movements, nationalism and socialism since they could not be categorised as untouchables, workers or peasants. Right through our period, they remained petitioners of the Madras government and were unaffected, on the whole, by the changes in political colouring and idiom. As late as 1937, artisanal groups in Malabar were lobbying the government to allow them to attach honorifics like Brahmasri and Avargal to their names.[2] They aspired to a higher secular status through such strategies. This was true of ritual performers like the Peruvannans (washermen given a title by the locally powerful tharavadus) as well, who were affected by the decline of patronage for shrines. In Nilambur, the senior raja himself intervened on behalf of his ritual performers, so that their status could be lowered from backward caste to depressed caste, entitling them to more concessions![3] Castes caught in the backwash of political movements had already begun to turn to distant Madras for a resolution of inequality. At the end of the forties, the communists too had come to realise the necessity of engaging with the state, as their political actions were increasingly curbed by the use of force by the state.

It was not only that definitions of community did not include certain groups within their purview. Very often, the consequences of such projections were quite at variance with the initial objectives. Tiyya elites had conceived of a community of equal Tiyyas standing apart from Hinduism and, therefore, a caste society. Their growing strength in the towns had repercussions in similar attempts to build bonds both among the Mappilas on the coast and between tharavadus in the interior. Meanwhile projections of nationalist unity had worked out in practice as assertions of authority by tharavadus, and finally, the conception of a Hindu identity around the issue of temple entry. By 1936, all these themes had come together and been transformed into communal conflict in the towns. This was the result of a younger generation of Tiyyas allying with the Congress, as Hindus, to engage in 'communal' clashes against the Mappilas. Thus, in the end, nationalist politics in Malabar engendered particular identities, like a sense of 'Nayarhood' amongst the many sub-castes of Nayars and, even 'communal' affiliations. The process of creating a wider national unity was blunted by local issues.

In contrast to nationalist politics, socialist and communist political activity attempted to build 'class-based' unities. Nevertheless, the peasant unions

[2] *Development Dept. G.O. 1800 dated 13 October 1936* (KS); *Development Dept. G.O. 1094 dated 15 May 1937* (KS).
[3] *Mathrubhumi*, 9 October 1935, 2 January 1936, 2 January 1936. In 1952, A.C. Kannan Nayar presided over a meeting of Malayanmar (*teyyattam* performers and ritual musicians) and made them 'swear that they would not use the customary words of deference' while speaking to him. *Diaries of A.C. Kannan Nayar*, 21 May 1952.

reflected less a consciousness of 'class' interests, than temporary associations towards specific ends. Some of them were *desam*-based units which included both landless labourers as well as landowners. Others drew upon caste affiliations and imposed caste sanctions on those who would not join. Yet others were thoroughly utilitarian and were formed for submitting representations to the Malabar Tenancy Committee between 1939 and 1940. A striking example of the conjunctural nature of 'class' identities is offered by the Chirakkal taluk Harijan League. It had been founded in 1940 as a 'peasant union' in order to acquire wasteland for cultivation, and included only untouchable castes in its membership. Though allied to the socialists, and later the communists, it maintained close links with the Congress as well. In 1945, the Congress disavowed all connections with the Harijan League denouncing it as a 'communist' body. The League promptly took up the cause of temple entry, and its new leaders formed a committee headed by the raja of Chirakkal.[4] In another instance in 1945, C.H. Kanaran, the stalwart of the Communist Party in Cannanore, spoke vehemently in favour of caste associations, stating that 'caste was a reality in contemporary society'.[5] Thus, the boundaries of communities, and identities themselves, were constantly fluctuating, conditioned by necessity, pragmatism and opportunism.

Though notions of community remained unrealised, and at the level of an aspiration alone, some of the consequences were concretely manifested. There had been some change in attitudes in the countryside; lower castes no longer stepped off the roads at the sight of Nayars, and overt marks and demonstrations of deference and subordination decreased. To an extent, this represented the limited, but significant, achievement of political activity over the thirties and the forties. The power of the tharavadus and more generally, of the upper castes, had been checked considerably. However, they still continued to exercise authority in their control over resources and in the ready access they had to the law enforcing machinery of the state. Communist activity, particularly between 1942 and 1945, attempted a renegotiation of rural relations after the fervid political demonstrations at the end of the previous decade. In the context of food shortages and land hunger, the tharavadus had reemerged in their role as dispensers of benevolence, granting land and subsistence, and, on occasion, receiving feudal levies as well. Much more significant was the restoration of the shrines at the centre of a reconstituted rural community. Here it was not so much the reproduction of certain social roles that was stressed, but the element of worship alone. In a simple view, the origins of communism have been situated in the context of the collapse of 'social and religious structures' and the rise of a situation in which communism provided the answers that gods and

---

[4] *Deshabhimani*, 10 September 1945.
[5] *Ibid.*, 23 September 1945.

ceremonies did not.[6] However, it was the ability of communism to shore up existing relations, and at the same time, attack the excesses, which helped to ensure its success.

Several arguments have been advanced to explain the success of the communists. One set deals with their ability to identify themselves with 'the chauvinism of region and caste' and their rootedness in the 'communal fabric of society'.[7] However, the career of the party, as much in the period we have studied as later, has been characterised by political pragmatism rather than permanent affiliations of any kind. There have been conjunctural and tactical partnership with parties and groups of all hues, justified by theoretical legerdemain. The 1967 elections are a case in point. Out of power for eight years, the communists came to power through an alliance with the Muslim League, a few socialist parties and an agrarian party led by a Christian priest. In subsequent years, relations with the Muslim League were to undergo swings from revulsion towards its 'communal' nature to attraction towards its potential as a vote bank. Nor has the party managed to create 'class consciousness' and mount this steed past the post to victory. Arguments which work on the premise that the party relied on the 'class identity and solidarity of the peasantry' do not take into account the vicissitudes of the relation between the communists and agrarian classes.[8] The events of 1948 were a lesson in practical politics: the party clarified its theoretical position regarding its 'actual' base of support, i.e. the agricultural labourer, and gained only the alienation of those agrarian groups which had been loosely aligned with it. On the question of land reform too, pragmatism has prevailed. The emotive slogan of 'land to the tiller' has been translated not to the benefit of the small peasants who actually contribute physical labour to the production process. As Herring points out, 'tiller' has been defined generously to signify the small-scale capitalist farmer who bears the financial and managerial risks of cultivation. It is ironical that by following through land reform to its logical conclusion, i.e. the abolition of landlordism, the party seems to have lost its *raison d'être* for the beneficiary groups. The tenants of yesterday became the landlords of today; their adherence to the party is by no means clear. This is unlike Bengal where a policy of controlled mobilisation and the creation of an institutional base of support in the *panchayats* has ensured a reasonably stable base for the Communist Party.[9]

---

[6] Jeffrey, 'Peasant movements and the Communist Party', 132; and 'Matriliny, Marxism and the birth of the Communist Party in Kerala, 1930-1940'.

[7] Selig Harrison, *India: the most dangerous decades* (Princeton, NJ, 1965), 137; Fic, *Yenan of India*, 17.

[8] Radhakrishnan, *Peasant struggles, land reforms and social change*, 271; R.J. Herring and H.C. Hart, 'Political conditions of land reform' in R.E. Frykenberg ed., *Land tenure and peasant in south Asia* (Delhi, 1984); Herring, *Land to the tiller*; Kannan, *Of rural proletarian struggles*, 90.

[9] A. Kohli, *The state and poverty in India: the politics of reform* (Cambridge, 1987), ch. 3; Nossiter, *Communism in Kerala*; *Land to the tiller*, 153-216.

Some scholars have contended that the communists were seen as carrying on the good work of nationalism; in fact they may have been more nationalist than the Congress.[10] However, if we look at the two regions of India where parliamentary communism is well entrenched, i.e. West Bengal and Kerala, the alienation from the Congress of important sections within society was the predominant reason for the success of the communists. In Malabar, lower castes and a group within a fractured elite were estranged from a Congress unwilling and unable to tackle the question of caste inequality. Communism represented as much a reaction against nationalism as a satisfactory conclusion of incomplete business. In Bengal, the *bhadralok* defection to communism reflected their alarm and revulsion towards the consequences of Congress mass politics which undercut their influence.[11] Moreover, the fortunes of the Congress and communism seem to have an inverse and probably perverse relation. Whether in the *tebhaga* agitation and Telengana, or the Naxalite and Jharkhand movements in independent India, the communists seem to have been most successful in organising on the fringes of society – tribals and landless labourers; groups the Congress was reluctant to mobilise.[12] This leads us to a further irony. Even though revolutionary communist activity – whether Malabar in 1946-48 or the Naxalite agitations of 1967-70 – has been directed against the state, it has been indirectly responsible for the extension of the control of the Indian state to regions which it had not controlled earlier. Malabar, a neglected outpost of the Madras Presidency, was firmly brought within the purview of Law and Order following 1948, as were the tribal belts of Andhra and Orissa following the suppression of the Naxalites in 1970.[13]

The history of the Communist Party has been characterised by occasional splits between pragmatic parliamentarians and radical secessionists: the Communist Party of India (CPI) till 1964; the CPI (Marxist) following the split; the CPI (Marxist-Leninist) in 1969 which spearheaded the Naxalite schism; and the minuscule factions of the CPI(ML) thereafter. But on the whole pragmatism and accommodation have prevailed over strict adherence to ideology. In Malabar, the achievements of socialism and communism at the conjuncture of 1948 were conservative. They had helped to refashion an earlier

[10] Damodaran, 'The tragedy of Indian communism', 346; R. Ramakrishnan Nair, *How communists came to power in Kerala* (Trivandrum, 1965), 58-60. In a recent study Joshi argues that the communists were not nationalist enough. S. Joshi, *Struggle for hegemony in India, 1920-47: the colonial state, the Left and the national movement* (New Delhi, 1992).

[11] J. Gallagher, 'Congress in decline: Bengal, 1930 to 1939' in Gallagher *et al.*, eds., *Locality, province and nation: essays in Indian politics, 1870-1940 (Cambridge, 1973)*; M. Franda, *Radical politics in West Bengal (Cambridge, MA, 1973)*, 12.

[12] Dhanagare, *Peasant movements in India*; S. Bannerjee, *In the wake of Naxalbari: a history of the Naxalite movement in India* (Calcutta, 1980); E. Duyker, *Tribal guerillas: the Santals of West Bengal and the Naxalite movement (Delhi, 1987)*; Ajita, *Ormakurippukal (Notes on a life) (Kottayam, 1982).*

sense of negotiated community; one in which the tharavadus were at the centre of social relations. Tharavadus commanded agricultural resources, were buttressed by the state, provided subsistence in times of dearth and dispensed patronage to the shrines. But there was a radical outcome as well. The two decades of political activity initiated by socialism and communism had comprehensively challenged subservience, and caste authority could no longer be exercised with impunity. As the communists moved towards an involvement with parliamentary politics, they remained deeply rooted in the villages. North Malabar would be the bastion of parliamentary communism in Kerala, and a reconstituted tradition of community underpinned their radicalism in matters of legislation. And, though things fell apart, the centre did hold.

Bibliography

MANUSCRIPT SOURCES

PRIVATE PAPERS

(a) New Delhi, Nehru Memorial Museum and Library
   Diaries of G. Sankaran Nair, 1930-31
   Diaries of A.C. Kannan Nair, 1920-57
   M.C. Rajah Papers
   All-India Congress Committee Papers, 1930-47
(b) Manuscript of Murkkoth Kumaran's autobiography, dated 7 June 1937 (In author's possession)
(c) Trivandrum, A.K. Gopalan Centre
   File on the oral history of Kasergode taluk

GOVERNMENT RECORDS

(a) London, India Office Library and Records
   Files of the Public and Judicial Department (L/P and J)
      Fortnightly Reports of Governors, Chief Commissioners and Chief Secretaries, 1937-48 (L/P and J/5/197-210).
      Local Government Fortnightly Reports on the Political Situation, 1929-34 (L/P and J/12/8,19,31,42,53,64)
      Weekly and Fortnightly Reports from British High Commissioners and Deputy High Commissioners, 1947-50 (L/P and J/5/310-314)
   Files of the Economic and Overseas Department
   Files of the Government of Madras
      Local and Municipal
      Home Political
      Public Works and Labour
      Revenue Department
(b) New Delhi, National Archives of India
   Files of the Home Political Department, Government of India
(c) Trivandrum, Kerala Secretariat, Cellar Records
   Files of the Government of Madras

Development Department
Education Department
Home Department
Judicial Department
Law (Education) Department
Law (General) Department
Law (Legislative) Department
Local and Municipal Department
Local Self Government Department
Public Department
Public Works Department
Revenue Department
(d) Kozhikode Regional Archives, Calicut
  DR Files
    Magisterial Department
    Public Department
  Files of the Malabar Collectorate
  R. Dis. Files
    Public Department
    Revenue Department
(e) Madras, Tamil Nadu Archives
  Proceedings of the Government of Madras
    Development Department
    Public (General) Department
    Public Works and Labour Department
    Revenue Department
    Madras Government Secret Files (Under-Secretary's Safe)
(f) Tellicherry Court Record Room, Tellicherry
  Court of the Joint Magistrate, Tellicherry (CC 106/38, CC 93/38, CC 5/39)
  Court of Sessions, North Malabar Division (Sessions case no. 3 and 6/11 of 1941 no. 14 and 18 of 1947)

INTERVIEWS

Between February and March 1987
  K.P.R. Gopalan, Kalliasseri
  P. Govinda Pillai, Trivandrum
  Chenkodi Kannan, Dharmadam
  T.V. Krishnan, Cherukunnu
  C. Kuttikrishnan, Calicut
  K. Madhavan, Kanhangad
  T.C. Narayanan Nambiar, Narath
April 1988
  P.T. Bhaskara Panikkar, Trivandrum
  Murkkoth Kunhappa
  S. Sarma, Trivandrum
  C. Unniraja, Calicut

Tapes of interviews made by Dr K.K.N. Kurup, University of Calicut
  K.P.R. Gopalan
  Kanthalot Kunhambu
  N.C. Sekhar

PRINTED SOURCES

NEWSPAPERS

Malayalam
(a) Nehru Memorial Museum and Library, New Delhi (Microfilm)
    Mathrubhumi (1923-40)
    Mithavadi (1913-19)
(b) Communist Party of India, State Council, Trivandrum
    Deshabhimani (1943-46)
    Party Sanghadakan (1944)
    Prabhatham (1938-39)
English
(a) Nehru Memorial Museum and Library, New Delhi (Microfilm)
    People's Age (1944)
    People's War (1942-46)
(b) Centre for South Asian Studies, Cambridge (Microfilm)
    Hindu (1920-36)

PARLIAMENTARY PAPERS

PP 1828, XXIV (125) – Slavery in India: Correspondence and Abstracts of Regulations and Proceedings.

GOVERNMENT PUBLICATIONS

Rickards, Bentinck *et al.* (1804). *Papers on the Administration of the Malabar District.*
P. Clementson (Calicut, 1916). *A Report on Revenue and other matters connected with Malabar*
H.S. Graeme (Calicut, 1898). *Report on the Revenue Administration of Malabar*
Major MacLeod (Calicut, 1911). *The Jamabundy Report of the Division of Coimbatore and the Province of Malabar* dated 18 June 1801
Sullivan (Calicut, 1911). *Report on the Provinces of Malabar and Canara, 1841*
William Thackeray (Calicut, 1911). *A Report on the Revenue Affairs of Malabar and Canara* dated 7 September 1807
Thomas Warden (Calicut, 1910). *Report on the Land Tenures in Malabar, 1815*
Censuses of India 1881-1951
Census of India 1961
Malabar Gazetteer, 1908

Malabar Manual, 1887, 3 volumes
Malabar Special Commission, Malabar Land Tenures Report, 1881-82, 2 volumes (Madras, 1882)
Papers relating to the Industrial Conference, Ootacamund, September 1908
Report of the Indian Industrial Commission, 1916-18, vol. III, *Evidence* (London, 1919)
Report of the Indian Police Commission, 1905
Report of the Madras Provincial Banking Enquiry Committee, 1930 (Madras, 1930)
Report of the Malabar Marriage Commission, 1890-91
Report of the Malabar Tenancy Committee, 1927, 2 volumes (Madras, 1928)
Report of the Malabar Tenancy Committee, 1940, 2 volumes (Madras, 1940)
Report on Public Instruction in the Madras Presidency, 1937
Report of the Royal Commission on Labour in India, vol. VII (London, 1931)
Report of the Special Officer for the Investigation of Land Tenures, on the recommendation of the Malabar Tenancy Committee, May 1947 (Madras, 1950)
Report on the Survey of Cottage Industries in the Madras Presidency (D. Narayana Rao), 1929 (Madras, 1929)
Statistical Appendix to the Malabar Gazetteer, 1905, vol. II
Statistical Appendix to the Malabar Gazetteer, 1933

ANNUAL REPORTS

Administration Report of the Agriculture Department of the Madras Presidency
Annual Statement of the Sea-Borne Trade of the Madras Presidency
Report on the Administration of the Abkari Department of the Madras Presidency
Report on the Administration of the Police Department of the Madras Presidency
Report on the Administration of the Registration Department of the Madras Presidency
Report on the Settlement of the Land Revenue in the Madras Presidency
Report on the Working of the Department of Industry in the Madras Presidency
Season and Crop Report of the Madras Presidency
Statistical Atlas for Malabar for the year 1904-05 (Calicut, 1907)
Statistical Atlas for Malabar for the quinquennium ending 1913
Statistical Atlases for Malabar for the decennium ending 1931 and 1941

BOOKS

Achutha Menon, C., *Kali worship in Kerala*. Madras University, Malayalam Series, 8. Madras, 1943
Adas, M., *The Burma delta: economic development and social change on an Asian frontier, 1852-1941*. Madison, WI, 1974
Aiyappan, A., *Iravas and culture change*. Bulletin of the Madras Government, new series, V i. Madras, 1944
Ali, Hamid, *Custom and law in Anglo-Muslim jurisprudence*. Calcutta, 1938
Andalat ed., *Sakhakkale munnottu. (The collected works of P. Krishna Pillai)*. Trivandrum, 1978
Appadurai, A., *Worship and conflict under colonial rule: a South Indian case*. Cambridge, 1981

Arnold, D., *Police power and colonial rule: Madras, 1859-1947*. Delhi, 1986
Ayrookuzhiel, A.M.A., *The sacred in popular Hinduism*. Madras, 1983.
Baker, C.J., *The Politics of south India, 1920-37*. Cambridge, 1976
    An Indian rural economy, 1880-1955: the Tamilnad countryside. Delhi, 1984.
Baker, C.J. and D.A. Washbrook, *South India: political institutions and political change, 1880-1940*. Delhi, 1975
Balaram, N.E., *Keralathile kammyunistu prasthanam (The communist movement in Kerala)*, volume I. Trivandrum, 1973.
Bannerjee, S., *In the wake of Naxalbari: a history of the Naxalite movement in India*. Calcutta, 1980
Barnett, M.R., *The politics of cultural nationalism in south India*. Princeton, NJ, 1976
Barrier, N.G. ed., *The Census in British India: new perspectives*, Delhi, 1981
Bose, S., *Agrarian Bengal: economy, social structure and politics, 1919-49*. Cambridge, 1986
Brass, P. and M.F. Franda eds., *Radical politics in south Asia*, Cambridge, MA, 1973
Brown, J.M., *Gandhi and civil disobedience: the Mahatma in Indian politics, 1928-34*. Cambridge, 1977
Buchanan, Francis M.D., *A journey from Madras through the countries of Mysore, Canara and Malabar*, volume II. London, 1807.
Chakrabarty, D., *Rethinking working class history: Bengal, 1890-1940*. Delhi, 1989
Chandra, B., *The rise and growth of economic nationalism*. Delhi, 1966
Chanthera, C.M.S., *Kaliyattam*. Kottayam, 1978
Chathan, C., *Pulapattu (Songs of the Pulayas)*. Calicut, 1917
Cohn, B.S., *An anthropologist among the historians and other essays*. Delhi, 1987
Copley, A.R.H., *The political career of C. Rajagopalachari, 1937-54: a moralist in politics*. Madras, 1978
Dale, S.F., *Islamic society on the south Asian frontier: the Mappilas of Malabar, 1498-1922*. Oxford, 1980
Damodaran, K., *Pattabakki (Rent arrears)*. Trivandrum, 1987
Das, T.V., *Kodungallur bharani (The Kodungallur festival)*. Calicut, nd
Dhanagare, D.N., *Peasant movements in India, 1920-50*. Delhi, 1983
Dirks, N.B., *The hollow crown: the ethnohistory of an Indian kingdom*. Cambridge, 1987
Dumont, L., *Homo Hierarchicus: the caste system and its implications*, trans. Mark Sainsbury *et al*. Chicago, IL, 1980
Duyker, E., *Tribal guerillas: the Santals of West Bengal and the Naxalite movement*. Delhi, 1987
Edona, E.J., *The economic conditions of the Protestant Christians of Malabar with special reference to the Basel Mission Church*. Calicut, 1940
Fawcett, F., *The Nayars of Malabar*. Madras Government Museum Bulletin, III, 3. Madras, 1901
Fic, V.M., *Kerala: the Yenan of India*. Bombay, 1970
Franda, M., *Radical politics in West Bengal*. Cambridge, MA, 1973
Freitag, S.B., *Collective action and community: public arenas and the emergence of communalism in north India*. Berkeley, CA, 1989
Gandhi, M.K., *The collected works of Mahatma Gandhi*, volumes XXIII, LI-LIII. Ahmedabad, 1972
Gopalakrishnan, P.K., *Purogamana sahitya prasthanam: nizhalum velicchavum (The Progressive Literature Movement: light and shadow)*. Trichur, 1987

Gough, E.K., *Rural society in south east India*. Cambridge, 1981

Gough, E.K. and D.M. Schneider, *Matrilineal kinship*. Berkeley, CA, 1961

Govindan, P., *Keraliya karmmala samaja vijnapanam (An advertisement for the artisans of Kerala)*. Calicut, 1912

Adidravidarude ambalapravesanam (The entry of Adi Dravidas into temples). Calicut, 1915

Greenough, P., *Prosperity and misery in modern Bengal: the famine of 1943-1944*. New York, 1982

Guha, R., *Elementary aspects of peasant insurgency in colonial India*. Delhi, 1983

Gundert, H., *Malayalam nighandu (Malayalam dictionary)*. Kottayam, 1962

Hardgrave, R., *The Nadars of Tamilnad: the political culture of a community in change*. Berkeley, CA, 1969

Hardiman, D., *Peasant nationalists of Gujarat: Kheda district, 1917-34*. Delhi, 1981

Harrison, S., *India: the most dangerous decades*. Princeton, NJ, 1965

Henningham, S.J., *Peasant movements in colonial India: north Bihar, 1917-42*. Canberra, Australia, 1982

Herring, R.J., *Land to the tiller: the political economy of agrarian reform in south Asia*. New Haven, CT, 1983

Irschick, E.F., *Politics and social conflict in south India: the non-Brahman movement and Tamil separatism, 1916-29*. Berkeley, CA, 1969

Jeffrey, R., *The decline of Nayar dominance: society and politics in Travancore, 1847-1908*. New York, 1976

Politics, women and well-being: how Kerala became a model. Basingstoke, 1992

Jones, K.W., *Arya Dharma: Hindu consciousness in nineteenth century Punjab*. Berkeley, CA, 1976

Josh, B., *The communist movement in Punjab, 1926-1947*. Delhi, 1979

Joshi, S., *Struggle for hegemony in India, 1920-1947: the colonial state, the Left and the national movement*, vol. 1. New Delhi, 1992

Struggle for hegemony in India, 1920-1947: the colonial state, the Left and the national movement, vol. 2. New Delhi, 1993

Juergensmeyer, M., *Religion as social vision: the movement against untouchability in twentieth century Punjab*. Berkeley, CA, 1982

Kannan, K.P., *Of rural proletarian struggles: mobilisation and organisation of rural workers in south-west India*. Delhi, 1988

Karunakara Menon, K.P., *History of the freedom movement in Kerala*, volume II. Trivandrum, 1972

Kautsky, J.H., *Moscow and the CPI: a study in the post war evolution of international communist strategy*. New York, 1956

Kohli, A., *The state and poverty in India: the politics of reform*. Cambridge, 1987

Kumaran, M., *Ambu Nayar*. Calicut, 1965 edn

Kurup, K.K.N., *The Kayyur riot: a terrorist episode in the nationalist movement in Kerala*. Calicut, 1978

Aryan and Dravidian elements in Malabar folklore: a case study of Ramavilliam kazhakam. Trivandrum, 1979

Pazhassi samarangal (Pazhassi revolts). Trivandrum, 1980

Lemercinier, G., *Religion and ideology in Kerala*, trans. Y. Rendel. Delhi, 1984

Lewandowski, S., *Migration and ethnicity in urban India: Kerala migrants in the city of Madras, 1870-1940*. Delhi, 1980

Lieten, G.K., *The first communist ministry in Kerala, 1957-59.* Calcutta, 1982
Low, D.A. ed., *Congress and the Raj: facets of the Indian struggle, 1917-47.* Delhi, 1977
Ludden, D., *Peasant history in south India.* New Jersey, 1985
Madhavan Nayar, K., *Malabar kalapam (The ferment in Malabar).* Calicut, 1987 edn
Mayer, A.C., *Land and society in Malabar.* Bombay, 1952
Miller, R.E., *The Mappila Muslims of Kerala: a study in Islamic trends.* Madras, 1976
Minault, G., *The Khilafat movement: religious symbolism and political mobilisation in India.* New York, 1982
Moffatt, M., *An untouchable community in south India.* Princeton, NJ, 1979
Moore, L., *Malabar law and custom,* second edn. Madras, 1900
Nambiar, C.K., *Svatantryayuddham (The war of liberation).* Tellicherry, 1924
Nambudiri, M.V.V., *Uttara Keralathile thottampattukal (The thottams of north Kerala).* Trichur, 1981
Nambudiripad, E.M.S., *Deshabhimani (Patriot),* Calicut, 1943
    Kammyunistu party keralathil (The Communist Party in Kerala), 3 volumes. Trivandrum, 1984-88
Narayanan, K.S., *Teendalvairi (Against untouchability).* Calicut, 1927
Narayanaswamy Naidu, B.V. and P. Vaidyanathan, *The Madras agricultural debt relief act: a study.* Annamalai, 1939
Nayanar, V.K., *Kesari Nayanarude krithikal (The collected works of Kesari Nayanar).* Calicut, 1987
Nayar, Chirakkal T.B., *Kerala bhashaganangal (Folk songs of Kerala),* 2 volumes. Trichur, 1979
Nightingale, P., *Trade and empire in western India. 1784-1806.* Cambridge, 1970
Nossiter, T.J., *Communism in Kerala: a study in political adaptation.* London, 1982
Overstreet, G.D. and M. Windmiller, *Communism in India.* Berkeley, CA, 1959
Padmavathi Amma, C., *Chakramahima (The saga of the charkha).* Calicut, 1920
Pandey, G., *The ascendancy of the Congress in Uttar Pradesh, 1926-34: a study in imperfect mobilisation.* Delhi, 1978
Panikkar, K.N., *Against lord and state: religion and peasant uprisings in Malabar, 1836-1921.* Delhi, 1989
Panikkar, T.K.G., *Malabar and its folk: a systematic description of the social customs and institutions of Malabar,* second edn. Madras, 1900
Payyanadu, Raghavan, *Teyyavum thottampattum (The Teyyam and its literature).* Kottayam, 1979
Pottekkat, S.K., *Vishakanyaka (The poisonous virgin),* trans. V. Abdulla. Trichur, 1980
Presler, F., *Religion under bureaucracy: policy and administration for Hindu temples in south India.* Cambridge, 1987
Radhakrishnan, P., *Peasant struggles, land reforms and social change, Malabar, 1936-1982.* New Delhi, 1989
Raheja, G.G., *The poison in the gift: ritual, prestation and the dominant caste in a north Indian village.* Chicago, Il 1988
Ramakrishnan Nair, R., *How communists came to power in Kerala.* Trivandrum, 1965
Rao, M.S.A., *Social change in Malabar.* Bombay, 1957
    Social movements and social transformation: a study of two backward classes movements in Malabar. Delhi, 1979
Rudolph, L.K. and S.H. Rudolph, *The modernity of tradition: political development in India.* Chicago, Il, 1967

Sangren, P.S., *History and magical power in a Chinese community*. California, 1987
Sardarkutty, E., *Purogamana sahitya nirupanam (A criticism of Progressive Literature)*. Trivandrum, 1985
Sarkar, T., *Bengal, 1928-34: the politics of protest*. Delhi, 1987
Scott, J., *The moral economy of the peasant: rebellion and subsistence in south east Asia*. New Haven, CT, 1976
Sen, A., *Poverty and Famines: an essay on entitlement and deprivation*. Oxford, 1981
Sengupta. B., *Communism in Indian politics*. New York, 1972
Singh, K., *A history of the Sikhs, 1839-1964*, volume II. Princeton, NJ, 1966
Sivaswamy, K.J., V.R. Nayanar *et al, Food control and nutrition surveys – Malabar and south Kanara*. Madras, 1946
Stein, B. ed., *South Indian temples: an analytical introduction*. Delhi, 1978
Stokes, Eric, *The peasant and the Raj: studies in agrarian society and peasant rebellion in colonial India*. Cambridge, 1978
Thomas, P.J. and N.S. Sastry, *Commodity prices in south India*. Madras, 1940
Thurston, E., *Omens and superstitions of southern India*. London, 1912
Thurston, E. and K. Rangachari, *Castes and tribes of southern India*, 7 volumes Madras, 1909
Tomilinson, B.R., *The Indian National Congress and the Raj, 1929-42: the penultimate phase*. London, 1976
Turner, V., *The ritual process: structure and anti-structure*. Harmondsworth, Middlesex, 1974
     Dramas, fields, and metaphors: symbolic action in human society. Ithaca, NY, 1974
Unni Nair, M., *My Malabar*. Bombay, 1952
Varghese, T.C., *Agrarian change and economic consequences: land tenures in Kerala, 1850-1960*. Calcutta, 1970
Veluthat, K., *Brahmin settlements in Kerala*. Calicut, 1978
Vishnu Nambudiri, V.M., *Uttara keralathile thottampattukal (The thottam songs of north Kerala)*. Kottayam, 1982
Washbrook, D.A., *The emergence of provincial politics: the Madras Presidency, 1870-1920*. Cambridge, 1976
Werbner, R.P., *Regional cults*. London, 1977
Wood, C., *The Moplah rebellion and its genesis*. Delhi, 1987

ARTICLES

Appadurai, A., 'Is homo hierarchicus?', *American Ethnologist*, 13, 4 (1986), 745-61
Appadurai, A. and C.A. Breckenbridge, 'The south Indian temple: authority, honour and redistribution', *Contributions to Indian Sociology* (NS), 10, 2 (1976), 187-212
Arnold, D., 'Looting, grain riots and government policy in south India, 1918', *Past and Present*, 84 (1979), 111-45
Baker, C.J., 'Debt and the Depression in Madras' in C.J. Dewey and A.G. Hopkins eds, *The imperial impact: studies in the economic history of Africa and India*. London 1978
Barnett, S.A., A. Ostor, L. Fruzzetti, 'Hierarchy purified: notes on Dumont and his critics', *Journal of Asian Studies*, 35, 4 (1976), 633-7

Blackburn, S.H., 'Death and deification: folk cults in Hinduism', *History of Religions*, 24, 3 (1985), 255-74

Carroll, L.M., 'Caste, social change and the social scientist: a note on the ahistorical approach to Indian social history', *Journal of Asian Studies*, 35, 1 (1975), 63-84

'Colonial perceptions of Indian society and the emergence of caste(s) associations', *Journal of Asian Studies*, 37, 2 (1978), 233-50

'The temperance movement in India: politics and social reform', *Modern Asian Studies*, 10, 3 (1976), 417-47

Chandavarkar, R.S., 'Worker's politics in Bombay between the wars,' *Modern Asian Studies*, 15, 3 (1981), 603-47

Chatterjee, P., 'Caste and subaltern consciousness' in R. Guha ed., *Subaltern studies VI: writings on south Asian history and society*. Delhi, 1989, 169-209

Commander, S., 'The Jajmani system in north India: an examination of its logic and status across two centuries', *Modern Asian Studies*, 17, 2 (1983), 263-311

Damodaran, K., 'The tragedy of Indian communism' in Tariq Ali ed., *The Stalinist legacy*. Harmondsworth, Middlesex, 1984

Fuller, C.J., 'Misconceiving the grain heap: a critique of the concept of the Indian Jajmani system' in M. Bloch and J.P. Parry eds, *Money and the morality of exchange*. Cambridge, 1989

Gallagher, J., 'Congress in decline: Bengal, 1930 to 1939' in J. Gallagher, G. Johnson, A. Seal eds, *Locality, province and nation: essays in Indian politics, 1870-1940*. Cambridge, 1973

Gopalankutty, K., 'The task of transforming the Congress; Malabar, 1934-40', *Studies in History*, 5, 2 n.s. (1989), 177-94

'Mobilisation against the state and not against the landlords: the civil disobedience movement in Malabar'. *The Indian Economic and Social History Review*. 26, 4 (1989), 459-80

Gough, E.K., 'Changing kinship usages in the setting of political and economic change among the Nayars of Malabar', *Journal of the Royal Anthropological Institute*, 82, 1 (1952), 71-88

'Cults of the dead among the Nayars', *Journal of American Folklare*, 71 (1958), 446-78

Greenough, P.R., 'Indian famines and peasant victims: the famine of Bengal in 1943-44', *Modern Asian Studies*, 14, 2 (1980), 205-35

Hardiman, D., 'From custom to crime: the politics of drinking in colonial south Gujarat' in R. Guha ed., *Subaltern studies*, IV. Delhi, 1985

Hart III, G.L., 'Theory of reincarnation among the Tamils' in W.D. O'Flaherty ed., *Karma and rebirth in classical Indian tradition*. Berkeley, CA, 1980

Herring, R. and H.C. Hart, 'Political conditions of land reform' in R.E. Frykenberg ed., *Land tenure and peasant in south Asia*. Delhi, 1984

Jeffrey, R., 'The social origins of a caste association, 1875-1905: the founding of the SNDP Yogam', *South Asia*, 4 (1974), 59-78

'Matriliny, Marxism and the birth of the Communist Party in Kerala, 1930-1940', *Journal of Asian Studies*, 38, 1 (1978), 77-98

'Travancore: status, class and the growth of radical politics, 1860-1940, the temple entry movement' in R. Jeffrey ed., *People, princes and paramount power: society and politics in the Indian princely states*. Delhi, 1978

'Peasant movement and the Communist Party in Kerala, 1937-60' in D.B. Miller ed.,

Peasants and politics: grass roots reaction to change in India. London, 1979
'India's working class revolt: Punnapra-Vayalar and the communist "conspiracy" of 1946', *Indian Economic and Social History Review*, 18, 2 (1981), 97-122

Karat, P., 'Organised struggles of the Malabar peasantry, 1934-40', *Social Scientist*, 56 (1977), 3-17
'The peasant movement in Malabar 1934-40', *Social Scientist*, 50 (1976), 30-44

Kurup, K.K.N., 'Inglish vidyabhyasavum samuhya puragatiyum malabarile tiyyaril' (English education and social progress among the Tiyyas of Malabar) in *Adhunika Keralam: Charitra gaveshana prabandhangal* (*Modern Kerala: essays in historical research*). Trivandrum, 1982

Ludden, D., 'Productive power in agriculture: a survey of work on the local history of British India' in M. Desai, S.H. Rudolph and A. Rudra eds, *Agrarian power and agricultural productivity in south Asia.* Delhi, 1984

Marriott, McKim, R.B. Inden, 'Towards an ethnosociology of south Asian caste systems' in K. David ed., *The new wind: changing identities in south Asia.* Hague, 1977

Mencher, J.P.,'Possession, dance and religion in North Malabar, Kerala, India', *Collected papers of the seventh congress of anthropology and ethnographic sciences*, Moscow. (1964), 340-5
'Kerala and Madras: a comparative study of ecology and social structure', *Ethnology*, 52 (1966), 135-71

Menon, K.V.R., 'Ancestor worship among the Nayars', *Man*, 25 19230, 42-3

Miller, E.J., 'Caste and territory in Malabar', *American Anthropologist*, 56 (1954), 410-20
'Village structure in north Kerala' in M.N. Srinivas ed., *India's villages.* Bombay, 1960

Narayana Rao, V., 'Epics and ideologies: six Telugu folk epics' in S.H. Blackburn and A.K. Ramanujam eds., *Another harmony: new essays on the folklore of India.* Berkeley, CA, 1986

Panikkar, K.M., 'Some aspects of Nayar life', *Journal of the Royal Anthropological Institute*, 48 (1918), 254-93
'Religion and magic among the Nayars', *Man*, 62 (1918), 104-10

Panikkar, K.N., 'Land control, ideology and reform: a study of the changes in family organisation and marriage system in Kerala', *Indian Historical Review* 4, 1 (1977), 30-47

Pisharoti, K.R., 'Notes on ancestor worship current in Kerala' *Man*, 60 (1923), 99-102

Prakash, G., 'Reproducing inequality: spirit cults and labour relations in colonial eastern India', *Modern Asian Studies*, 20, 2 (1986), 209-30

Pullapilly, C.K., 'The Ishavas of Kerala and their historic struggle for acceptance in the Hindu society', *Journal of Asian and African Studies*, 11 (1976), 24-46

Robert, B., 'Economic change and agrarian reorganisation in "dry" south India, 1890-1940: a reinterpretation', *Modern Asian Studies*, 17, 1 (1983), 59-78

Sallnow, M., '*Communitas* reconsidered: the sociology of Andean pilgrimages', *Man* (ns) 16, 2 (1981), 163-82

Sen, A., 'Subaltern studies: capital, class and community' in R. Guha ed., *Subaltern studies V.* Delhi, 1987, 203-55

Shea Jr, T.W., 'Barriers to economic development in traditional societies: Malabar, a case study', *Journal of Economic History*, 1959-22
'Economic study of a Malabar village', *Economic Weekly*, 7 (1955), 997-1003, 1030-33

Stein, B., 'The integration of the agrarian system of south India' in R.E. Frykenberg ed., *Land control and social structure in Indian history.* California, 1968

Stokes, E., 'The return of the peasant to south Asian history' in *The peasant and the Raj: studies in agrarian society and peasant rebellion in colonial India.* Cambridge, 1987

Taylor, Rev. William, 'Fifth Report of Progress made in the Examination of the Mackenzie Manuscripts, with an Abstract Account of the Works examined', *The Madras Journal of Literature and Science* 9, 23 (1839), 353-4

Tharakan, P.K.M., 'Intra-regional differences in agrarian systems and internal migration: a case study of the migration of farmers from Travancore to Malabar', *Centre for Development Studies: Working Paper 194.* Trivandrum, 1984

Washbrook, D.A., 'Country politics: Madras, 1880-1930', *Modern Asian Studies,* 7, 3 (1973), 475-531

'Law, state and agrarian society in colonial India' in G. Johnson *et al,* eds *Power, profit and politics.* Cambridge, 1981

'Caste, class and dominance in modern Tamil Nadu: non Brahmanism, Dravidianism and Tamil nationalism' in F. Frankel and M.S.A. Rao eds, *Dominance and state power in modern India: decline of a social order,* volume I. Delhi, 1989

Wood, C., 'The first Moplah rebellion against British rule in Malabar', *Modern Asian Studies* 10, 4 (1970), 543-56

Zelliott, E., 'Congress and the untouchables, 1915-50' in R. Sisson and S. Wolpert eds, *Congress and Indian nationalism: the pre-independence phase.* Berkeley, CA, 1988

AUTOBIOGRAPHIES AND BIOGRAPHIES

Aaron, C. Samuel, *Jeevithasmaranakal (Memoirs).* Cannanore, 1974

Achuthan, K.R., *C. Krishnan.* Kottayam, 1971

Ajita, *Ormakurippukal (Notes on a life).* Kottayam, 1982

Ayrookuzhiel, A.M.A., *Swami Anandateertha: Untouchability, Gandhian solution on trial.* Delhi, 1987

Gopalan, A.K., *In the cause of the people.* Delhi, 1973

Kesava Menon, K.P., *Kazhinja kalam (Times Past).* Calicut, 1962

Krishnan, T.V., *Kerala's first communist: the life of P. Krishna Pillai.* Delhi, 1971

Krishnan Nair, Kalamandalam, *Ente jivitham: arangilum aniyarayilum (My life: between the greenroom and the stage).* Trivandrum, 1991

Kunhappa, C.H., *Smaranakal matram (Memoirs).* Calicut, 1981

Kurup, M.N., *Kunhambuvinte katha (The life of A.V. Kunhambu).* Kottayam, 1982

madhavan, K., *Payaswiniyude teerattu (On the banks of the river Payaswini).* Trivandrum, 1987

Moithu Maulavi, E., *Maulaviyude katha (The Maulavi's story).* Kottayam, 1981

Nambudiripad, E.M.S., *Atmakatha (Autobiography)* second edn. Trivandrum, 1976

Nayanar, E.K., *My struggles: an autobiography.* Delhi, 1982

Sankaran, M., *Ente jivithakatha (An autobiography)* Calicut, 1965

Vishnu Bharateeyan, V.M., *Admakal engane udamakalayi* (How the slaves became masters). Trivandrum, 1980

COMMUNIST PARTY PAMPHLETS

India in the war of liberation. 1942
Deshabhimani. (Patriot). February, 1943
Keralattile kammyunistu pravartanam rajyadrohamo rajyasevanamo? (*Are the activities of the communists in Kerala Patriotic or treasonous?*) August, 1943
Aikyattinulla tadasthangal. (Hindrances to unity). October, 1943
Gramaseva sanghavum kammyunistukarum. (The Grama Seva Sangh and the communists). 1943
Resolutions of the special conference of the Communist Party of India, Malabar zilla (September 28 to October 1, 1945). 1945
Aikya kisan sanghatana kettipadukkuka. (Build a united peasants organisation). July, 1946
Malabarile karshika kuzhappam tadayan kammyunistu parishramangalude charitram. (The efforts of the communists in preventing agrarian strige). February, 1947
Vadakke Malabarile karshakasamaram. (The peasants' struggle in north Malabar). May, 1947
Political thesis of the Communist Party of India, adopted at the second Congress, Calcutta, February 28 to March 6, 1948
Janangalkethiraya Congressinte yuddham. (The war waged by the Congress against the people). May, 1948
Fascisatinte arangettam. (Fascism on the stage). 1948
Vadakke Malabarile samaravum atilninnulla pathangalum. (The struggle in North Malabar and its lessons). January, 1949

UNPUBLISHED DISSERTATIONS

Arunima G., 'Colonialism and the transformation of matriliny in Malabar, 1850-1940', Cambridge, 1992
Masani, Z.M., 'Radical nationalism in India, 1930-42: the role of the all-India Congress Socialist Party', Oxford, 1976
Miller, E.J., 'An analysis of the Hinducaste system in its interactions with the total social structure in north Kerala', Cambridge, 1950
Samuel, V.T., '"One caste, one religion and one God for man": a study of Sree Narayana Guru (1854-1928) of Kerala, India', Hartford Seminary Foundation, 1973
Shea Jr., T.W., 'The land tenure structure of Malabar and its influence upon capital formation in agriculture', Pennsylvania, 1959
Swai, B.S.W., 'The British in Malabar, 1792-1806', Sussex, 1975

Index

Aaron Samuel 65, 94, 153
Abdur Rahman, Mohammad 104, 153
Acts, Compensation for Tenants Improvements, 28-30, 63; Malabar Tenancy 127-8, 141-3
All Malabar Peasant Union 143
ancestor worship 45-6

Basel Mission 64, 65
bhagavathi shrines 54, 56

Caste, and cleanliness 83-7, 110, 120; and Hinduism 116; literacy 144; lower caste religion 47; and nationalism 2; restrictions 19, 134, 139; and ritual 41, 49, 51, 55, 61; and temple entry 107
Chaliyas 100
cherikallu 11-12
coconut 9, 10, 26-8; exports 26-7, 122
Civil disobedience, salt manufacture 94-7; liquor picketing 97-101; *khadi* propagation 101-3; and Muslims 103-5
Communications 23
Communal Award 113
'communal' conflict 73, 126, 191
'communal' identity 80, 82, 104, 126
community, conjunctural 4, 7, 169, 177; moral community 57; notion of 2, 3-7, 190, 191; of subsistence 31-2, 49; of worship 49
Communism, success of 193-4
Communist Party of India 159, 166, 185-6
Congress, and untouchability 80, 82, 84, 92; and Nayars 92, 104, 105-6; organisation in Malabar 91-3; right wing 133, 152-3, 154, 155, 161, 174; communal nature 92, 153; and tenancy 185
Congress Socialism 119-20
credit 35-6, 65-6, 123–4

Damodaran, K. 148, 150; plays of 148-9
death pollution 12, 13, 42-3
deference 20-1, 137-41, 192
demobilisation 180

Depression 4, 6, 38, 120, 121-4; and civil disobedience 90

economy 21-2, 121-4, 160-5
education 16-17, 64; literacy 143-5; schools 96
excise administration 64, 74-8, 99-100

feudal levies 124, 135, 170
food shortages 161-2, 182
forests, conservancy 12, 136; encroachment on 23-4, 121-3, 164-5; for manure 33, 136, 170

Gandhi, M.K., fasts 113-14; Guruvayur *satyagraha* 114-15; and temple entry 81-2, 110, 115-16; untouchability 83-6; Vaikkam *satyagraha* 81-2
Gopalan, A.K. 96, 103, 111, 131 *fns* 132, 142, 148, 154, 179
Gopalan, K.P.R. 131 *fns* 150, 168

Hindu identity 108, 110

janmis 12, 14, 37, 138
Jagannatha temple 67, 68, 71, 72, 73, 76, 107, 108, 125
jathas 82, 109, 121, 138-9, 170

Karivellur 181
Kayambayam 181-2
Kayyur riot 167-8
Kelappan, K. 81, 94, 104, 107, 109, 111, 113, 115, 133, 153
Kerala Communist Party 154, 163; and peasant unions 166-8; internal organisation 166; anti-Jap propaganda 169-70; 'Grow more food' 170-1; grain redistribution 171-3; factional struggle 174; village bases 174, 175-6, 187; popular religion 176-7, 189; electoral politics 179; controlled militancy 179-82; criticism of police 183; rural revolution 185-8

Cambridge South Asian Studies

These monographs are published by the Syndics of Cambridge University Press in association with the Cambridge University Centre for South Asian Studies. The following books have been published in this series:

1 S. Gopal: *British Policy in India. 1858-1905*
2 J.A.B. Palmer: *The Mutiny Outbreak at Meerut in 1857*
3 A. Das Gupta: *Malabar in Asian Trade, 1740-1800*
4 G. Obesyesekere: *Land Tenure in Village Ceylon*
5 H.L. Erdman: *The Swatantra Party and Indian Conservatism*
6 S.N. Mukherjee: *Sir William Jones: A Study in Eighteenth-Century British Attitudes to India*
7 Abdul Majed Khan: *The Transition of Bengal. 1756-1775: A Study of Saiyid Muhammad Reza Khan*
8 Radhe Shyam Rungta: *The Rise of Business Corporations in India. 1851-1900*
9 Pamela Nightingale: *Trade and Empire in Western India, 1784-1806*
10 Amiya Kumar Bagchi: *Private Investment in India, 1900-1939*
11 Judith M. Brown: *Gandhi's Rise to Power: Indian Politics, 1915-1922*
12 Mary C. Carras: *The Dynamics of Indian Political Factions*
13 P. Hardy: *The Muslims of British India*
14 Gordon Johnson: *Provincial Politics and Indian Nationalism*
15 Marguerite S. Robinson: *Political Structure in a Changing Sinhalese Village*
16 Francis Robinson: *Separation among Indian Muslims: The Politics of the United Provinces' Muslims, 1860-1923*
17 Christopher John Baker. *The Politics of South India, 1920-1936*
18 David Washbrook: *The Emergence of Provincial Politics: The Madras Presidency, 1870-1920*
19 Deepak Nayyar: *India's Exports and Export Policies in the 1960s*
20 Mark Holmstrom: *South Indian Factory Workers: Their Life and Their World*
21 S. Ambirajan: *Classical Political Economy and British Policy in India*

For EU product safety concerns, contact us at Calle de José Abascal, 56–1°,
28003 Madrid, Spain or eugpsr@cambridge.org.

www.ingramcontent.com/pod-product-compliance
Ingram Content Group UK Ltd.
Pitfield, Milton Keynes, MK11 3LW, UK
UKHW010043140625
459647UK00012BA/1585